Old English Glass Houses

by Francis Buckley

Old English Glass Houses
by Francis Buckley

The objects of the Society of Glass Technology are to encourage and advance the study of the history, art, science, design, manufacture, after treatment, distribution and end use of glass of any and every kind. These aims are furthered by meetings, publications, the maintenance of a library and the promotion of association with other interested persons and organisations.

This publication was instigated by members of the SGT's History and Heritage Special Interest Group.

Society of Glass Technology
Unit 9, Twelve O'clock Court
21 Attercliffe Road
Sheffield S4 7WW, UK
Tel   +44(0)114 263 4455
Fax   +44(0)114 263 4411
Email   info@sgt.org
Web   http://www.sgt.org

The Society of Glass Technology is a registered charity no. 237438.

ISBN 0-900682-46-9

© Society of Glass Technology, 2006 [POD]

Cover: Interior of a glass blowing hall, from *Encyclopédie Chimique, Tome 5, 5ᵉ Fascicule – Le Verre et le Cristal*, edited by M. J. Henrivaux, 1883. Paris, France.

Contents

Introduction	v
List of Glass Houses in England and Wales 1696	vii
Note on the Glasshouses of the Leeds District in the Seventeenth, Eighteenth, and Early Nineteenth Centuries	1
Glasshouses on the Wear in the Eighteenth Century	14
Glasshouses on the Tyne in the Eighteenth Century	24
The Early Glasshouses of Bristol	67
Old Nottingham Glasshouses	107
Cumberland Glasshouses	113
Notes on the Glasshouses of Stourbridge	117
The Glasshouses of Dudley and Worcester	145
The Birmingham Glass Trade: 1740–1833	155
Old London Glasshouses. I. Southwark	174
Notes on Various Glasshouses	194
West Country Glasshouses	204
Old Lancashire Glasshouses	213

Introduction

Between 1681 and 1703 John Houghton, an eminent member of the Royal Society, wrote a series of Letters to Parliament which were collected and published later under the general title of "Husbandry and Trade Improvement". One of the subtitles in the book being "Full and Exact History of Trades – with the manner of their improvement". By 1696 it was the turn of the glass industry and in Letter Number 198, dated 15th May 1696 Houghton listed all the glass works in England and Wales which were working at that time, around 90 in total, but some double counting may have occurred. Even though the list is quite exhaustive there may have been some omissions as in this era glass furnaces had very short lives and had to be rebuilt about every six to twelve months. So as most factories had only one furnace Houghton may have not counted the ones that were not working because the furnace was being rebuilt.

It is quite possible that Francis Buckley used Houghton's listing for his research, it is an obvious starting point, most of the glassworks in Houghton's list are mentioned along with many more. The additional ones are glassworks that were built after 1696, in fact in some of his papers Buckley continues into the early part of the 19th Century. There are also glassworks listed for areas not covered by Houghton for example Cumberland and many parts of Yorkshire, there is also some mentioned in Scotland.

Francis Buckley published at least three books on glass as well as the series of papers in the Journal of the Society of Glass Technology that this volume reproduces.

The reader may find that one of the fascinations of Buckley's papers is that he not only lists his references, he actually states what they are, giving additional information to that in the main text.

Buckley himself states:
"It is well to insist once again that the object of these articles on the Glasshouses of England is to stimulate further local research, and that they are limited in scope by the newspaper record. Thus famous firms may not appear in this record, just because they prospered from the start and made no partnership change."

An account of Francis Buckley's life can be found on: http://www.fairmile.fsbusiness.co.uk/buckleyfrancis.htm

This volume comprises reprints of the following papers:
Note on the Glasshouses of the Leeds District in the Seventeenth, Eighteenth, and Early Nineteenth Centuries, *JSGT*, 1924, **8**, T. 268–277.
The Early Glasshouses of Bristol, *JSGT*, 1925, **9**, T. 36–61.
Glasshouses on the Wear in the Eighteenth Century, *JSGT*, 1925, **9**, T. 105–111.
Glasshouses on the Tyne in the Eighteenth Century, *JSGT*, 1926, **10**, T. 26–52.
Old Nottingham Glasshouses, *JSGT*, 1926, **10**, T. 270–273.
Cumberland Glasshouses, *JSGT*, 1926, **10**, T. 384–386.
Notes on the Glasshouses of Stourbridge, *JSGT*, 1927, **11**, T. 106–123.
The Glasshouses of Dudley and Worcester, *JSGT*, 1927, **11**, T. 287–293.
The Birmingham Glass Trade: 1740–1833, *JSGT*, 1927, **11**, T. 374–386.
West Country Glasshouses, *JSGT*, 1929, **13**, T. 124–129.
Old Lancashire Glasshouses, *JSGT*, 1929, **13**, T. 229–242.
Notes on Various Glasshouses, *JSGT*, 1930, **14**, T. 30–37.
Old London Glasshouses. I. Southwark, *JSGT*, 1930, **14**, T. 137–149.

Houghton's List of Glass Houses in England and Wales, 15th May 1696

An account of all the Glass Houses In England and Wales	The several Counties they are in	The Number of houses	And the sorts of glass each house makes
In and about London and Southwalk		9	For bottles
		2	Looking glass plates
		4	Crown glass and plates
		9	Flint, green and ordinary
Woolwich	Kent	1	Crown glass and plates
		1	Flint, green and ordinary
Isle of Wight	Hampshire	1	Flint glass and ordinary
Topsham, Nr Exon	Devonshire	1	Bottles
Old Down, Nr Bath	Somersetshire	1	Bottles
Chellwood		2	Bottles and window glass
In and about Bristol		5	Bottles
		1	Bottles and window glass
		3	Flint glass and ordinary
Gloucester	Gloucestershire	3	Bottles
Newham		2	Bottle Houses
Swansey in Wales	Glamorgan	1	Bottles
Oaken-Yate	Shropshire	1	Bottles and window glass
Worcester	Worcestershire	1	Flint green and ordinary
Coventry	Warwickshire	1	Flint green and ordinary
Stowerbridge	Worcestershire	7	Window glass
		5	Bottles
		5	Flint green and ordinary
Nr. Liverpool	Lancashire	1	Flint green and ordinary
Warrington		1	Window glass
Nottingham	Nottinghamshire	1	Bottles
Awsworth		1	Flint green and ordinary
Custom Moor, Nr Awsworth		1	Bottles
		1	Flint, green and ordinary
Nr. Silkstone	Yorkshire	1	Bottle
Nr. Ferrybridge		1	Flint green and ordinary
		1	Bottles, flint green and ordinary
King's Lynn	Norfolk	1	Bottles
Yarmouth		1	Flint, green and ordinary
		1	Bottles
Newcastle-upon-Tyne	Northumberland	6	Window glass
		4	Bottle
		1	Flint, green and ordinary
		90	

Note on the Glasshouses of the Leeds District in the Seventeenth, Eighteenth, and Early Nineteenth Centuries
By Francis BUCKLEY
(Read at the Leeds Meeting, November 19th, 1924.)

The object of this paper is to set out as briefly as possible facts that have been discovered about the making of glass in the Leeds area, from the end of the seventeenth century to the middle of last century.

Local and private records of glass-making are either non-existent or not open to research; and the sources drawn upon are therefore confined to Parliamentary records, the old newspapers and directories, and, in one district, the registers published by the Yorkshire Parish Register Society. But it should be explained that early directories are not necessarily exhaustive, and public collections of old newspapers are far from complete; so that large gaps in our information may be due to these unfortunate circumstances. In addition, the search of the Leeds newspapers has been carried, as yet, only down to the year 1797; and further information may yet be found from this source.

It is well to remind ourselves that the glass-makers of Leeds, who were flourishing and famous in the middle of the nineteenth century, had predecessors whose very existence had been entirely forgotten, for example, when the Victoria County History came to be written. The facts relating to these early glass-makers are set out in the Appendices to this article; but some comment is first needed to show the significance and relation of some of the records. The numbers quoted refer to the extracts set out in Appendix 1.

The Glasshouse at Glass Houghton

John Houghton, writing in 1696, states that there were then three glasshouses in Yorkshire, one "near Ferrybridge" and two "near Silkstone." We can now identify these as the glasshouses at Ferrybridge, Bolsterstone, and Silkstone. The only one, however, in the Leeds area was the Ferrybridge glasshouse. Glass Houghton, an adjoining place name, suggests an early glass-making establishment; but its authenticated history starts in the year 1696. John Houghton tells us that the glasshouse was making flint glass and bottles; and we learn from another source (No. 1) that the owner was William Clifton. The business went on here, but we find no mention of it in old documents till 1740, when Henry Fenny was in possession (No. 5). The reason of an advertisement inserted by him in the *Leeds Mercury* was to announce that "all sorts of window glass" had been added to the list of articles manufactured.

Not only the Leeds district, but Yorkshire generally, owes a good deal to the enterprise of the Fennys at this time. They appear to have come from Stourbridge way, and to have practised glass-making at Rothwell, Bolsterstone, and Catcliffe, as well as at Eccleston in Lancashire. Unfortunately, we know little more about the later history of the Ferrybridge glasshouse.* Mr. Carter of Huddersfield, who was brought up at Ferrybridge, states that the old glasshouse was still used for making bottles by Breffit and Company between 1870 and 1880, but that it was shortly afterwards abandoned and has now become a ruin.

---

* It may be referred to in a notice in the Universal British Directory of 1790, which says: "A glass manufactory of black bottles is also carried on near this town [Barnsley] superior to any of the kind elsewhere."

The Glasshouse at Rothwell Haigh

About the glasshouse at Rothwell Haigh, between Leeds and Wakefield, we learn rather more. It was erected rather before 1726, a large glasshouse for those days, and was designed for making flint glass and bottles. A good description of it appears in a London newspaper (No. 2), and although it is not actually named therein, it is sufficiently identified. The making of glass at Rothwell Haigh is corroborated by the appearance in 1728 of "glass-makers" in the Rothwell Registers (see Appendix II). We may fairly assume from the advertisement in 1726 (No. 2) that the man who started this glass-works either died or was unable to carry it on successfully himself; for when it was offered on lease, it was only "lately erected," and yet it was offered as a going concern, with all materials ready on the place and workmen under articles "to work up the materials." We may assume, too, that it was first taken for a term of fourteen years, for the next offer on lease occurs in 1740 (No. 4).

From the Rothwell Registers it is fairly evident that the firm who took the glasshouse in 1726 included Stourbridge glass-makers, for example, Joshua Fenny and John Grazebrook; but with these were associated Marsden and Booth, typical West Yorkshire names, and also William Morton, whom we may connect with the Mortons of the Silkstone glasshouse. The difficulty in the Registers is to distinguish between the glass-owners and the glass-workers, all of whom may have been described as "glass-makers."

The advertisement of 1740 names William Sykes, Esq., of Swillington Hall, as a party interested, and he may have been the freeholder of the glasshouse property. Joshua Fenny continued to reside at Rothwell Haigh as "glass-maker," and died in 1754; whilst between 1750 and 1770 the most prominent glass-maker in the Registers is John Pimperton, although several others occur. The last actual mention of the glasshouse is April 13th, 1773, when Mr. Thomas Walker, "of the Glasshouse Rothwell," appears in conjunction with Thomas Fenton, of Rothwell Haigh (No. 14); but in 1777 Michael Clark "glass-maker" appears in the Registers. After this point, the trade of the persons entered in the Registers is no longer added. There was, so far as is known, no glasshouse here in the nineteenth century.

There was apparently a glasshouse also at Birstall in 1756, for the Rothwell Registers contain two references to it in that year. Nothing further is known of it.

Glass-making in Leeds

The only glasshouse actually in or near the town of Leeds in the eighteenth century was known as the Engine Glasshouse, and this was probably the factory that supplied all the ordinary needs of the town for the greater part of the eighteenth century. We know of it only in the hands of the Fentons, and it can be traced between 1738 and 1790 (Nos. 3, 9, and 12).

In 1738, James Fenton announced a new departure in his glass business. He had just procured the services of William Tyzack, a crown glass-maker of Bristol, and consequently he was able to supply the town with as good crown glass as they could get from any other part of the kingdom. But he was not without competitors; the London and Newcastle crown glass-makers had an agent in the town who took care to puff their wares (Nos. 6 and 7), and for this reason it may be concluded, either that Mr. Fenton's crown glass was not successful, or else it was so successful that it disturbed a previous monopoly.

The later owners of this glasshouse were William and Thomas Fenton (Nos. 9 and 12). The name "Fenton and Co. glass manufacturers, Glasshouses" appears in the British Universal Directory of 1790, but not in the Leeds Directory of 1798.

We do not yet know the exact situation of the Engine Glasshouse, but a very reasonable guess can be made. In Sayer's Plan of Leeds dated 1767 there is marked near the bridge at the south end of Briggate an erection called "the Water Engine"; this is thought to have given the name to the Leeds glasshouse, which probably therefore stood near the old Town Warehouses on the north bank of the River Aire.

It would seem that for some years Leeds was without a glasshouse of its own; but between 1814 and 1861, at any rate, the Bower family had several glasshouses at Hunslet, which became famous as the Hunslet Glass Works. The glasshouses are marked in a map of Hunslet dated 1824.

The people of Leeds must have owed as much to this family in the nineteenth century as they did to the Fentons in the previous century. In the directories (Appendix III) we can trace the gradual rise and extension of the Bower's glass works at Hunslet. They made flint glass, bottles, retorts, and fine window glass; and at one time even attempted the stained or painted windows for churches. In 1833 they had four glasshouses at work, and no competitors in the town itself.

Rather before 1850, however, we notice a sudden increase in the glass concerns in Leeds, and the surrounding district, especially in the neighbourhood of Castleford. If the Bowers had not been so successful – they had warehouses in Leeds, London, Manchester, and Liverpool – we can scarcely think the trade would have been so widely and rapidly extended round the city of Leeds. It is known, for instance, that a group of men, John Kilner, David and William Jephson, William Ezart, and James Winterbottom, left the Hunslet Glass Works in 1829 and founded, in 1830, a large bottle works at Whitwood Mere adjoining Castleford. In 1839 the firm name was Jephson and Co.; and later on Kilner and Winterbottom had glassworks of their own (see *West Riding Directory* for 1839).

Wibsey Moor, Thornhill, and Worsborough

Another interesting glasshouse stood near Wibsey Moor, between Halifax and Bradford. It is only mentioned once, in the year 1751, but it may have then been built some time (No. 8). It is stated that the stone of the place could be ground into sand suitable for making flint and crown glass. And we know that rather later, in 1794, they were selling fireproof clay from Ovenden near Halifax for use in glasshouses, etc. (No. 15). Local inquiry should surely yield further information about this isolated glasshouse.

An early nineteenth century glasshouse at Thornhill Lees, near Wakefield, can be traced back to 1830. Here Noah Turner made flint glass, until the glasshouse was taken over by the Kilners in 1844 and converted into a bottle works. Kilner's bottle works have only recently been discontinued; and a good deal of the fancy glass (consisting of walking sticks, door-stoppers and the like) made at these works has been found in the cottages round Wakefield. There was a glasshouse also at Worsborough Dale in 1833, worked by William Usherwood, Barron, Cartwright, and Perkes; but in the following year Messrs. Wood and Perkes are found in possession, making cut glass.

The author owes most of his information about the Bolsterstone glasshouse (which is incidentally mentioned) to the work of Mr. Joseph Kenworthy. It is only to be hoped that others will undertake in the Leeds district that local research, which Mr. Kenworthy has used to such advantage in the Sheffield glass-making area.

Prof. W. E. S. Turner, who has been kind enough to invite the author to present these notes to the Society, has also assisted materially with the later history of the Leeds glassworks.

TUNSTEAD, GREENFIELD,
    YORKSHIRE.

Appendix I. Newspapers

1. *Journals of House of Commons*, December 5th, 1696 (XI, 614).

"A petition of William Clifton of Houghton and Abigail Pilmy of Silkstone in Yorkshire, Glassmakers, in behalf of themselves and Servants, was presented to the House and read. This was presented against the War Tax on Glass &c. (6 & 7 Will. & Mary, c. 18) 1695. The Act laid an excise of 1s. per dozen on bottles, an excise of 20% on fine glass and looking-glass plates, of 10% on window glass, and of 15% on other sorts of glass."

2. *The Daily Post*, March 10th, 1726

"There is a round Glasshouse lately built which is 15 yards diameter within; the ovens to harden the bottles in, the pot-rooms, the lair, warehouses and other convenient rooms for so large a Glasshouse, built adjoining to it; to be let by the whole or in partnership; it is in Yorkshire, being within 3 miles of Leeds and Wakefield, and 5 miles of Pontefract, within a mile of a navigable river to send bottles and flint glass to London or any other port; coals to be laid at the store-house door at 5s. per chaldron; all the materials ready upon the place to make bottles and flint glass, also workmen to work up the materials."

3. *Leeds Mercury*, March 21st, 1738

"William Tyzack, Crown Glass-Maker from Bristol, being lately settled, and now at work at the Engine Glass-house near Leeds, Gentlemen and Tradesmen may there be furnished with it as well as from any other part of the kingdom; and also with Bottles, Vials and flint glasses by James Fenton."

4. *Leeds Mercury*, January 22nd, 1740

"To be let, to enter to at Candlemas next The Glasshouse in Rothwel, 3 miles from Wakefield, 3 from Leeds and 2 from the Navigable River Aire, with Gloass Yards and other necessary outhouses. Enquire of William Sykes at Swillington Hall. Note, the said Glass-House will be supply'd with Coals at reasonable rates from a Colliery within a quarter of a mile of it."

5. *Leeds Mercury*, April 8th, 1740

"At the Glass-house at Houghton near Pontefract is made after the best manner all sorts of Window Glass, where all Gentlemen, Glaziers &c. may be constantly supply'd at the most reasonable rates. N.B. Flint Glasses, Vials and all sorts of Bottles are sold at the aforesaid glasshouse by Henry Fenny."

6. *Leeds Mercury*, May 5th, 1741

"To be sold, the best Crown Glass from Mr. Bold's [*error* for Mr. Bowles's] Glasshouse in London or the best Crown Glass from Mr. Cookson's Glasshouse in Newcastle and Company; any day in the week at the house of Richard Butler, Glazier, nigh Woodhouse Bar, Leeds. Sash Glass is 6d. to 8d. a foot; clock faces and pictures from 8d. to 10d. a foot; cut glass for setting in lead from 2 3/4d. to 4d. a foot. Which far exceeds any glass made in this country, for fine and straight; cut out of the sheet by Richard Butler aforesaid; two of the best window glasshouses in England."

7. *Leeds Mercury*, January 9th, 1751

"Thomas Wiley, Glazier and Plumber, having taken the house and purchased the Stock belonging to Richard Butler of Leeds, lately deceased, gives this notice to all Glaziers that they may be supplied with table and square Glass as usual."

8. *Leeds Mercury*, June 11th, 1751

"To be lett a very good Glass-House adjoining to Wibsey-Moor, 3 miles from Halifax and 2 from Bradford. There is plenty of very good stone upon the place that grinds to as good sand and is as proper as any that can be brought to make Flint and Crown Glass with. Also very good coal within 300 yards of the said Glasshouse at 2d. a horse-load."

9. *Leeds Mercury*, November 21st, 1769

In the list of benefactions to the General Infirmary at Leeds for the year 1768–1769. Annual subscribers * * * * * *

"Messrs. W. and Thomas Fenton, Glasshouse, 5 guineas."

10. *Leeds Mercury*, January 30th, 1770

"Henry Reynolds, Briggate, Leeds, grinds polishes and silvers looking glasses in the best manner and on the same terms as in London."

11. *Leeds Mercury*, May 1st, 1770

"Henry Reynolds has just received from London a large assortment of the best Vauxhall Plates for looking glasses, coaches, etc."

12. *Leeds Mercury*, November 27th, 1770

"William Fenton, Esq., at the Glasshouse near this Town" is mentioned.

13. *Leeds Mercury*, March 2nd, 1773

"Nathan Greenwood of Halifax continues to make and repair all sorts of Barometers and Thermometers."

14. *Leeds Mercury*, April 13th, 1773

"The Rothwell Pottery was assigned to assignees for creditors. The assignees included Mr. Thomas Walker of the Glasshouse Rothwell and Thomas Fenton, Esq., of Rothwell Haigh."

15. *Leeds Mercury*, September 27th, 1794

"John Mitchell, Jun., Ovenden near Halifax, supplies pipe manufacturers, Iron forges, Glass Houses &c. with white clay perfectly fire proof at 10s. per ton."

Appendix II. Rothwell Registers

(Published by the Yorkshire Parish Register Society.)
Oct. 13th, 1728–Oct. 29th, 1754 (buried). Joshua Fenny, glass-maker.
Sept. 20th, 1729 (buried). John Marsden, glass-maker.
1731. William Morton, glass-maker.
1733–1737. William Booth, glass-maker.

1736–1738. John Rowlinson, glass-maker.
1737. John Grazsbrook,* glass-maker.
1742–1748 (buried). John Purchin, glass-maker.
1743 (buried). Thomas Clark, glass-maker.
1751–1760 (buried). George Bramley, glass-founder.
1752–1773. John Pimperton, glass-maker.
1756. Joshua Wilson, glass-maker.
1759–1764. William Alton, glass-maker.
1759. John Walton, glass-maker.
1761–1767. Richard Pimperton, glass-maker.
1767–1770. John Purchin, glass-maker.
1768. Thomas Pimperton, glass-maker.
1768. Richard Alton, glass-maker.
1771. John Alton, glass-maker.
1777. Michael Clark, glass-maker.

Also

1756. John Walton, glass-maker "from the Burstall Glass-house."
1756. Thomas Hathersley, glass-maker "from the Birstall Glass-house."

Appendix III.

Extracted from Directories, etc.

Leeds.

1798.	No glass-makers.
1800.	No glass-makers.
1809.	No glass-makers.
1814.	Bower, Smith and Co., glass-makers, Hunslet.

---

* Presumably a misspelling. Compare page 3 (EDITOR).

1816. Bower, Smith and Co., glass-makers, Hunslet.
1818. Joshua Bower and Co. (crown glass), Hunslet.
John Bower, manufacturer of soda, spirits of salt and glass bottle-maker, Hunslet.
1826. John Bower, Junr., flint glass and bottle manufacturer, Moorside, Hunslet.
Joshua Bower and Co. (crown window glass), Hunslet).
1830. John Bower, Junr. (flint, bottles, retorts), Hunslet.
Joshua Bower and Co. (crown window glass), Hunslet, with warehouses in Leeds, Liverpool, Manchester, and London.
1833. (Parliamentary Report.) Bower – 4 glasshouses at Hunslet.
1834. John Bower (flint, bottles, church windows), Hunslet.
Joshua Bower and Co. (crown glass), Hunslet.
1839. Joshua Bower and Co. (crown glass), Hunslet.
1845. Joshua Bower and Co. (crown glass), Hunslet.
1847. John Bower and Sons, Jack Lane, Hunslet.
Joshua Bower and Co. (crown glass), Jack Lane, Hunslet.
Scott, Roberts and Co., Hunslet Carr. ,
1849. John Bower and Sons, Hunslet.
Joshua Bower and Sons, Hunslet.
William France and Co. (bottles), Holbeck Lane End.
Roberts and Co. (flint and bottles), Balm Lane.
Mrs. Sarah Taylor (flint and bottles), Low Road, Hunslet.
1853. Joshua Bower and Co. (crown, flint, bottles, etc.), Jack Lane, Hunslet.
John Naylor, Hunslet Road.
Nicholson Booth and Co., Pepper Road, Hunslet.
Scott and Co. (bottles), Arch Bridge, Hunslet.

Thornhill Lees.

1830.	No mention of glass-works.
1830.	Another directory. Noah Turner, flint glass works.
1833.	Parliamentary Papers. Noah Turner.
1834.	Noah Turner, flint glass works.
1847.	John Kilner, Glass Bottle Works.
1848.	John Kilner, Glass Bottle Works.

Worsborough Dale.

1833. Parliamentary Papers. William Usherwood, Glass-house.
1834. Directory. Wood and Perkes, Cut glass manufacturers.

Castleford and Pontefract.

1836. Aire and Calder Glass Bottle Co. (Breffit and Co.).
1839. Jephson and Co.
1848. Pontefract Glass Bottle Works.
Aire and Calder Glass Bottle Co., Castleford.
Jepsons and Co. (Castleford Glass Bottle Works), Castleford.
John Lumb and Co, Castleford. James Winterbottom, Castleford.

DISCUSSION

MR. T. W. F. ROBERTSON asked if Mr. Buckley could say whether or not any of the coloured glass made by the firm of Bower in Leeds was actually in any church windows, and could be seen.

MR. BUCKLEY, in reply, said that he regretted he could not say where samples of the glass could be seen.

PROFESSOR W. E. S. TURNER said that the paper, being

read at Leeds, was of special interest. He himself had during recent years been endeavouring to collect information about the history of Yorkshire glass-making. It had been a surprise, however, to find how very few records had been kept and handed down by the glass manufacturers, and no factory appeared to have made any collection of its own products to illustrate the type of glass produced at different periods. This was much to be regretted. He would like to ask if any of the members present possessed items of interest in regard to the history of glass-making in the district, they would be good enough to send it to Mr. Buckley, either direct or through himself, and thus assist Mr. Buckley in his endeavour to make a complete record, for their instruction and encouragement, of the vicissitudes of the industry in the district.

MR. BUCKLEY showed samples of domestic ware made of green glass. The samples made in Lancashire he believed had a bluish green, and those in Yorkshire a yellowish-green colour. He would be glad of any comments from members of the audience which would give him information as to where similar articles had been made.

Glasshouses on the Wear in the Eighteenth Century
By Francis BUCKLEY

There is no record of glass-making at Sunderland in the 17th century, but between 1696 and 1737 at least 'three glasshouses were built on the Wear; and all of these are marked on a plan of the river, published by Burleigh and Thompson in 1737. They are called, respectively, "The Glasshouse" (near Salt Pans), the "Ayres Quay Glasshouse," and the "Suddick Glasshouse"; the latter, presumably the Southwick glasshouse, was a little to the west of the other two and on the north side of the river. It is not unlikely that all these glasshouses were built by a syndicate of owners, ten in number, who called themselves the "Company of Glass-Owners at Sunderland." [5]* It would seem that it was their practice at first either to let the glasshouses or failing that to work them themselves.

The Ayres Quay Glasshouses

The bottle, house at Ayres Quay is said to have been the oldest on the river. † In 1741, there were two glasshouses at Ayres Quay, one making bottles, the other broad glass. It is probable that the latter was set up between 1737 and 1741. In 1741, the Sunderland Glass Syndicate offered these two glasshouses and another at Salt Pans on lease. They were advertised both in London[2] and in Newcastle,[1,3] and it is interesting to note that some of the glass-makers on the Tyne, probably the Henzells and Tyzacks, considered the advisability of acquiring the Sunderland glasshouses.[4] This project, however, fell through. The two glass-houses

---

* The superior figures refer to the Appendix.
† *Victoria County History of Durham.*

at Ayres Quay were let for 14 years from February 1743 to Thomas Dennison,6 and soon after this the Syndicate of glassowners; was reconstituted, probably with a view to work the other glasshouses in the neighbourhood.[5,11] The new Syndicate was called the "Company of Ayres Key Glasshouses"[11]; there were now ten partners, and in 1751 one of the shares was offered for sale.[6]

On February 13th, 1756, the lease to Dennison came to an end; and a lease, for the next 13 years seems to have been granted to Thomas Wilson & Co.,[7,8] who were probably members of the Syndicate. At the end of the lease, disputes occurred between the members of the Syndicate, who were still ten in, number,[9,10] and the lease seems to have: been renewed to Thomas Wilson (who died in 1776*) and Russell. At any rate, the firm was Wilson & Russell in 1772.[13] The Ayres Quay glasshouses were offered on lease for 14 years from February 14th, 1783,[15] and taken over by "certain persons under the firm of The Proprietors of, Ayres Quay Glass Works."[17,20] One of these, William Barras, died in 1790.[19] The lease again ran its course, and on August 13th, 1795, was again offered to the highest bidder for a term not stated.[20]

A little further information, at a later date, can be obtained from Directories, etc. In 1819 only two bottle houses at Ayres Quay are mentioned by Garbutt†; and the broad glass business must therefore have been abandoned. In 1821, T. Bonner & Co. had the "bottle work" at Ayres Quay,‡ and it is stated that Messrs. Pemberton had bottle-works "at Ayres Quay,"§ called in 1819 "Hope Quay"|| and in 1821 " Now Quay."¶ One of the Pembertons was connected with the Ayres Quay Glassworks in

---

* See *Victoria County History of Durham.*
† "Sunderland" (1819), p. 408.   ‡ Directory.
§ Victoria County History, of Durham.
|| "Sunderland" (1819), p. 408.   ¶ *Directory.*

1768.[9]

The Salt Pans Glasshouse

We have already seen that this bottle house existed in 1737, and was offered on lease in 1741.[1,3] For the next 28 years nothing is heard of the glasshouse; but, as it was not offered on lease between 1741 and 1768, we may assume that it was worked meanwhile by the Company of Ayres Key Glasshouses, in whose possession it is found at the latter date.[11] Nothing further is known of its later history in the 18th century. There were, however, two bottle-houses and one crown glasshouse at "Panns" in 1819**; all of which were being worked in 1821 by the Sunderland Glass Company.††

The Deptford Flint Glassworks

"New Glasshouses" were set up in Sunderland rather before 1769, for the purpose of making flint glass and fine table-ware. John Hopton appears to have been the founder of the works, x2 which were probably situated at Deptford. This John Hopton may have come from the Whitefriars Glasshouse in London; for the types of glass, "double flint glass, white enamel, fine blue and green glass," were being made in London at this time, and in 1763 the firm at the Whitefriars Glasshouse was Hopton & Stafford, but in 1765 Corey Stafford alone.*

In 1819 there were at Deptford a flint glasshouse and a bottle-house. In 1821, the former was worked by White, 'Young &

** *Garbutt, loc. cit.*
†† *Directory.*
* *Directories.*

Tuer; the latter by the Wear Glass Bottle Company.*

The Suddick Glasshouse

Nothing has been learnt of this glasshouse in the 18th century, except that it was in existence in 1737 (see above) ; but we may infer that until 1741 it had been in the hands of the Company of Glass-Owners at Sunderland.[5] In 1819 it was worked as a crown glasshouse; in 1821 by the Southwick Crown Glass Company.*

General Information

It may be noted that the Sunderland glass-makers exported cargoes of glass, chiefly bottles, to the Continent from 1770 onwards. That they brought sand for the glassworks from Lynn,[18] most probably in the good Brigantine or vessel called the Ayres Key,"[17] and later on in The Margaret and Jane."[18]

The author is glad to acknowledge the excellent help of Mr. James McGarrigle, who searched a large proportion of the old Newcastle newspapers on his behalf.

TUNSTEAD, GREENFIELD,
    YORKSHIRE.

APPENDIX 1

Extracts from Contemporary Newspapers

1. July 11th, 1741. *Newcastle Courant*.

"Three current going Glass-houses, one of them now used for making common window-glass, the other two for Glass-bot-

---

* *Directories.*

tles; and with the said works will be assigned over to an Undertaker, two complete sets of workmen, the one for making such common Window-Glass, the other for making Glass-Bottles as aforesaid. They are commodiously situated upon the River Wear, Bishop-Wearmouth, near Sunderland, and have thereby the benefit of coals on very easy terms, and have also adjoining, and belonging to them, Wharfs, Warehouses and sufficient number of dwelling houses for Workmen, Utensils and all manner of conveniences. For further particulars enquire of Mr. Tho. Allen, steward to the said Works."

2. August 8th, 1741. *London Evening Post.*

"To be let at present for any reasonable term of years, so as to be entered on at Candlemas 1742–3, at Bishop Wearmouth, Salt Pans and Aires Quay, both very near Sunderland in the County of Durham. Three Current going Glasshouses, &c." (continued as in [1] above).

3. September 5th, *1741. Newcastle Courant/Newcastle Journal.*

"To be lett by inch of candle to the right bidder at the house of Mrs. Robson in Sunderland on 2nd October next. Three current going glass-houses at Aires Key and Pans upon the River Wear. For further particulars enquire at Mrs. Robson's aforesaid or to Mr. Allen at the said Glass-houses."

4. September 19th, 1741. *Newcastle Journal.*

"Whereas three current going glass-houses on the River Wear are, in this paper, advertised to be lett on Oct. 2nd next, the several proprietors of the Broad Glasshouses and Bottle Houses on the River Tyne, are desired to meet at the Crown Tavern on the Key on Wed: next to consider of the same; at which time, if any of the said owners be prepared with proposals for putting the glass and bottle trade on a better footing than at present, he is 'desired to communicate them'."

5. March 12th, 1743. *Newcastle Journal.*

"All persons indebted to the late Company of Glass-Owners at Sunderland are hereby desired to pay their respective debts (especially such as have been duo for months) to Mr. Thomas Allon, at the glass-houses on or before May-day next, or they will be prosecuted without further notice."

6. March 2nd, 1751. *Newcastle Journal.*

"To be sold a tenth part or share of the Glass-Houses with the appurtenances at Aires-Key, near Sunderland, now in the possession of Mr. Thomas Dennison as Tenant thereof. Enquire of Mr. Thomas Todd at Great Usworth or of Mr. Henry Wilkinson of Gateshead."

7. November 16th, 1754. *Newcastle Journal.*

"To be lett to the best Bidder and entered upon the 13th Feb. 1756. The Broad and Bottle Glass-Houses at Ayre's Key, upon the River Wear in the Township of Bishop-Wearmouth in the County of Durham, with all the Buildings and Conveniences thereto belonging.

"For further particulars apply to Mr. Matthew Noble or Mr. George Harrison both of Sunderland, who will treat about the same. N.B. There is and will be a compleat set of Workmen for each house."

8. April 5th, 1766. *Newcastle Journal.*

"William Shaw, Bottle Blower, apprentice to Messrs. Thomas Wilson & Co. Glass Owners near Sunderland, absented his Master's Service, &c." [Born near Warrington in Lancashire.]

9. January 2nd, 1768, *Newcastle Journal,* and January 23rd, 1768, *Newcastle Chronicle.*

"Ayres Key. To be let immediately and entered upon the 13th February 1769. The Broad and Bottle Glass-houses at Ayres Key, upon the River Wear in the township of Bishop Wearmouth, in the County of Durham, with all the buildings and conveniences thereto belonging.

"N.B. There is and will be a complete set of workmen for each house upon the premises; and whosoever chooses to apply for those works, are desired to be speedy in their application, otherwise the owners will agree to carry them on themselves; for particulars enquire of Mr. John Pemberton, in Sunderland, who is fully empowered by the Company to treat about and let the same."

10. January 23rd, 1768, *Newcastle Chronicle,* and February 13th, 1768, *Newcastle Journal.*

"Whereas an advertisement was inserted in the Newcastle newspapers for several weeks past: That the Broad and Bottle glass-houses at Ayres Key were to be let immediately. Notice is hereby given that on the 29th December last an agreement for a lease of the said glass-houses was entered into by one of the Proprietors of the said Glasshouse and in order to confirm the said agreement, 7 out of 10 of the proprietors of the said Glasshouse executed a lease thereof to the lessee named in the said agreement."

11. April 2nd, 1768. *Newcastle Chronicle.*
Bishop Wearmouth Pans.

"To let immediately and entered upon 13th February 1769, the Bottle Glasshouse at Bishop Wearmouth Pans, &c., now in the possession of the Company of Ayres-Key glasshouses. N.B. May have good firestone quarry, supplying the said works with firestones; enquire of George Sparrow Esq. at Washington."

12. September 16th, 1769. *Newcastle Journal.*

"To be sold at the New Glass Houses, Sunderland, all sorts of Double flint glass, white enamel, fine blue and green glass, &c. Apply to Mr. John Hopton, Sunderland."

13. June 27th, 1772. *Newcastle Journal.*

"Runaway: Matthew Betson, lawfully hired and bound apprentice to Messrs. Wilson and Russell, at the Glass-Houses at

Ayres Key, near Sunderland by the sea, in the County of Durham, has absented himself and deserted their employment in the said glasshouses, without any just cause." [Notice of, reward for his apprehension.]

14. July 3rd, 1778. *York Chronicle.*

"Runaway from the Glass Manufactory at Aire Key nigh Sunderland two apprentices, the one named Timothy Pimperton and the other Joseph Liddell: they are supposed to be employed (particularly the former who has been absent above 12 months) at some glass works in Yorkshire.*

July 25th, 1778. *Newcastle Chronicle.*

[Repeats the above notice as to Liddell.]

15. December 1st, 1781. *Newcastle Chronicle.*

"Glasshouses: to be let to the highest bidder at the house of Robert Farimond at Aires Key nigh Sunderland on 19th Dec. 1781. Two Glass houses at Aires Quay, aforesaid, with all the premises thereto belonging for the term of 14 years to commence the 14th Feb. 1783."

16. April 14th, 1787. *Newcastle Courant.*

"Glasshouses. A clerk as an assistant to the present agent wanted at the glassworks at Aires Quay. A man that has been accustomed to business, by having been some time in a merchant's office, or if he has been employed about a glass manufactory, would be more approved of. None need apply but those who have an unexceptionable character. Apply at the Company's Office at Aires Quay, aforesaid, or to Mr. Edward Clarke, Gateshead."

17. November 14th, 1789. *Newcastle Advertiser.*

---

* Several glass-makers of the name of Pimperton worked at the Rothwell Haigh Glasshouse near Wakefield.

"To be sold to the highest bidder, on the 20th November at Reay's in Sunderland. All that good Brigantine or vessel called the 'Ayres Key,' now lying in Sunderland. This ship was built by the Proprietors of the Ayres Quay Glass-house, at Ayres Quay."
[18] August 15th, 1789. *Newcastle Advertiser.*

"Arrived at Sunderland. The Margaret and Jane [Carter] from Lynn, with sand for the glass-works."
19. October 23rd, 1790. *Newcastle Chronicle.*

"Died, early on Monday (18th) at Ayres Quay near Sunderland, greatly lamented, Mr. William Barras, one of the proprietors of the glassworks there."
20. July 25th, 1795, *Newcastle Chronicle,* and August 8th, 1795, *Newcastle Advertiser.*

"To be lett to the highest bidder at the house of Phillis Pearson at Ayres Quay on 13th August next and to be entered upon at Candlemas 1797. All those the Broad and Bottle glasshouses at Ayres Quay aforesaid, with all and every the houses, buildings, &c. which are now in the occupation of certain persons under the firm of 'The Proprietors of Ayres Quay Glass Works.' Together with several of the utensils and materials used by the said proprietors in carrying on the said Glassworks. For further particulars apply to Mr. Edward Clark of Gateshead."

APPENDIX II.

*Sunderland Imports**

2.1.90.	*Advertiser.*	"Hannah" from London with glass.†
10.3.92.	,,	"Providence" from London with broken glass.

---

* References to Newcastle papers.
†I.e., "Broken glass" presumably.

13.9.00. *Chronicle.* "Neptune" from Bridlington with broken glass.

*Sunderland Exports**

13.10.70. *Journal.* "Minerva" to St. Petersburg with bottles.
19.6.84. *Chronicle.* "Mayflower" to Dantzig with bottles.
4.4.89. *Advertiser.* "Fortitude" to Dunkirk with bottles.
25.4.89.   ,,   "Freedom" to Ostend with glass bottles.
11.7.89. *Chronicle.* "Freedom" to Ostend with glass bottles.
25.7.89. *Advertiser.* "Friendship" to Amsterdam with bottles.
27.2.90. *Chronicle.* "Hannah" to Ostend with bottles.
17.4.90.   ,,   "Providence" to Rotterdam with bottles.
4.9.90. *Advertiser.* "Freedom" to Ostend with glass bottles and glasses.
7.5.91.   ,,   "Freedom" to Ostend with glass bottles.
9.7.91.   ,,   "Robert & Sarah" to Ostend with glass bottles.
13.8.91. *Chronicle.* "Success" to Riga with glass bottles.
12.11.91. *Advertiser.* "Mary" to Amsterdam with glass bottles.
3.3.92.   ,,   "Jenny" to St. Valery with glass.
14.4.92. *Chronicle.* "Peggy" to Amsterdam with glass bottles.
3.6.92.   ,,   "Betsey" to Amsterdam with glass bottles.
30.6.92. *Advertiser.* "Union" to Rotterdam with bottles.

Glasshouses on the Tyne in the Eighteenth Century
By Francis BUCKLEY

The newspaper record of glass-making on the Tyne has proved disappointing. There are in the Municipal Library at Newcastle-on-Tyne more than a hundred volumes of newspapers printed in the town during the eighteenth century; but a prolonged search through their files has produced few results. The reason may be that glass-making was very much a family affair on the Tyne; and instead of the usual cut-throat competition, it was apparently the custom for the local glass-makers of the same branch of the industry to combine for special purposes.[10, 11, 18, 38, 45, 60, 87] perhaps as everyone in "the North" knows everybody else, they did not take the precaution (as they did, for example, in the Bristol area) of advertising changes in the partnership firms. Nor has any advertisement of a Newcastle glasshouse yet been found in the old newspapers of any other town. We have, therefore, to rely a good deal on the general and family historians of Newcastle.

The history of glass-making at Newcastle during the seventeenth century has been written so often that it seems unnecessary to do more than refer to the accounts given by H. Bourne and J. Brand, and latterly by A. Hartshorne and H. J. Powell. The present inquiry starts in the year 1696, at which date there were six window glasshouses, four bottle-houses, and one flint glasshouse on the Tyne.* And the glasshouses may be arranged conveniently according to locality; the Skinner Burn glasshouses to the west of the old town, the Ouse Burn glasshouses to the

---

† The numbers refer to Appendix 1.

cast, the South Shields glasshouses, and the other (more scattered) glasshouses.

The Skinner Burn Glasshouses

It is said that this district, about the Forth Bank and outside the old Close Gate, was the spot selected by the first Huguenot glassmakers before they finally settled in Newcastle.† But permanent glass-making was really started here by the family of Dagnia, of whom a comprehensive record has been written recently by Mr. H. M. Wood.‡ Three brothers, Onesiphorus, Edward and John, settled in Newcastle in the later years of the seventeenth century; and the following separate glasshouses near the Closegate are recorded as owned by these members of the Dagnia family or by their descendants.

(1) A glasshouse "near Closegate" for making white glass and bottles was founded in 1684, and a lease of 999 years obtained, by Onesiphorus and John Dagnia, B. Durant and J. Wall.§ In 1691 the two latter partners had dropped out, and thereafter "great quantities of glass bottles were sent beyond seas or coastwise."[6]

(2) A glasshouse, also near Closegate, was taken by Onesiphorus and John Dagnia, with John Harrop as partner, in the year 1701. ||

(3) A white glasshouse, in the same district, was transferred by Edward Dagnia to his brother John in 1710.¶

---

* J. Houghton, *Letters on Trade*.
† Bourne, *Newcastle*, pp. 145 ct seq.
‡ *Arch. Aeliana*, (1920), 3rd Series, Vol. xvii.
§ Welford, *Arch. Aeliana*, 2nd Series, Vol. xxiv.
|| H. M. Wood, *loc cit*.
¶ Welford, *loc cit*.

(4) A glasshouse "near the Forth Bank" was held by Onesiphorus Dagnia, son of John, under lease from Mr. Swinburne. In this glasshouse George Spearman may have been a partner holding a third share.**

By 1717 the three original Dagnia brothers were dead, and at this point it will be seen that there were two groups of Dagnia glasshouses near the Closegate; the first was held jointly by the descendants of Onesiphorus and John, the second group entirely by the descendants of John. But apart from the legal title, the actual working of the Dagnia glasshouses at Closegate passed, after 1731, largely into the hands of John Williams.* Williams came from Stourbridge about 1730, and in 1731 married Margery Dagnia, the widow of Onesiphorus (son of John), mentioned above. In this way he gained (in right of his wife, and during her life) a share in the two partnership houses, (1) and (2) above, and a more considerable share in the ether two houses, (3) and (4) above. He had been trained as an iron-founder; but like most Stourbridge men he took readily to the glass business. Consequently it is not surprising to find John Williams and Co. in possession of at least two glassworks at Closegate which had been founded by the Dagnia family. The later history of the Dagnia glasshouses near the Closegate is considered under the headings "Flint glasshouse without Closegate" and "Bottle-House without Closegate," although the latter represents at least two of the original Dagnia glasshouses.[20]

1. *The Flint Glasshouse Without Closegate*

This, "the white glasshouse at Closegate," was situated near the River,[43] and it was probably the flint glasshouse recorded by

---

** J. C. Hodgson, *Proc. Soc. Antiq. Newcastle*, 3rd Vol., vii, 207.
* J. C. Hodgson, *Proc. Soc. Antiq. Newcastle*, 3rd Vol., vii, 207.

Houghton in 1696, then the only one on the Tyne. In 1749, James Dagnia, the eldest of the grandchildren of Onesiphorus and John, offered the glasshouse for sale;[27] and the same year all these grand-children joined in transferring the glasshouse to John Williams and Co.† It is possible that Francis Rudston was one of the partners in this firm until he became bankrupt in 1751.‡ John Williams died in 1763,§ and he left his interest in this glasshouse to at least two of his sons. After his death the firm continued under the name of Williams and Co.; and the glass-house was one of the two flint glasshouses on the Tyne recorded in 1772 and 1776.[50,56] "In 1764, the glasshouse was damaged by fire but not destroyed."[43] In 1778, Williams and Co. appear in the earliest Newcastle Directory with a glass warehouse near the Closegate. But in 1782 the glasshouse was totally destroyed by fire.[61] And it can never have been rebuilt, for there is no further trace of the firm.

2. *The Bottle-house Without Closegate*

These glassworks were, after 1724, vested in Christopher and John Dagnia (grandsons of the original John), subject in part to a life interest of their Aunt Margery, who married John Williams. The names, therefore, of Christopher and John Dagnia appear on the granting of leases,[20,41,55,76] and for this reason the identity of the glassworks in the advertisements is clear. In 1743, a half share was offered on lease;[20] and eventually John Williams and Co. took a lease of the works[41] and appear as bottle-makers in the Closegate in 1758.[38] John Williams, as we have seen, died in 1763; the "Bottle-house" was then offered on lease by C. and J.

---

† Welford, *loc. cit.*
‡ J. C. Hodgson, *Proc. Soc. Antiq. Newcastle*, 3rd Sories, IV, 98.
§ *Newcastle Courant*, rob. 8th, 1763.

Dagnia and taken over until 1775 by John Cookson and Co.[41,55] The glassworks [still more than one house*] were afterwards leased to a Cookson company called "The Owners of the Closegato Bottle-house."[64] In 1785, however, Isaac Cookson announced that he would in future carry on the business himself, and, in 1788, the lease came to an end.[76] The Directories show that the Cooksons retained possession of these works; John Cookson made crown glass and bottles here in 1795, and Isaac Cookson bottles in 1801.

3. *The Close Glassworks*

The following records may throw a little light on the early history of these flint glassworks

(a) Brand† states that "in the street that leads from Closegate to Skinner Burn are several glasshouses; one of these was formerly a meeting house of protestant dissenters." This old meeting house was advertised to be sold 6th April, 1728.‡

(b) Joseph Airey, who (died 1749, "established glasshouses in the Close." *Sharp's MSS.*§

(c) Isaac Cookson's son John was apprenticed to Joseph Airey, 1728.§

(d) Isaac Cookson and Joseph Airey were amongst the joint trustees of the new meeting house of the Protestant Dissenters.||

(e) Isaac Cookson died in 1743, and was then known in London as "one of the most considerable glass manufacturers" in Newcastle.[21]

---

* H. M. Wood, *loc cit.*, p. 241.
† *Newcastle*, I, 411.
‡ *Newcastle Courant.*
§ *Ambrose Barnes*, Surtees Soc., 1866, II 73.
|| *Ibid.*, p. 473.

It is probable that Joseph Airey founded the Close Glassworks some time about 1728, partly on the site of the old meeting house. It is also probable that Isaac Cookson was financially behind this concern; although, not being a member of a Newcastle company, his financial interests may have been kept out of sight. He was obviously a friend of Joseph Airey, and both were connected with the Protestant Dissenters. These glassworks were the second of the two flint glass manufactories mentioned in 1772 and 1776.[50,56] From 1783 onwards, the firm name was Airey, Cookson and Co.*[87] In the early nineteenth century the Northumberland Glass Company acquired the works.*

THE OUSE BURN GLASSHOUSES

If the families of Dagnia, Williams and Cookson were supreme in the west, the Huguenot families of Henzell and Tyzack were for many years the leading glass-makers on the east side of the town. They had been, of course, the pioneers of glass-making on the Tyne, and perhaps for this reason the Ouse Burn glasshouses were often called "the glasshouses in Newcastle,"[12] and the district east of the Ouse Burn acquired the place name "The Glasshouses."† Bourne gives the following list of the Ouse Burn glasshouses in 1736:

4. The Western Glass House.
5. The Crown Glass House.
6. The Middle Bottle House.
7. The Middle Broad House.
8. The Eastern Glass House.
9. St. Lawrence's, or, the Mushroom Glass House.
10. St. Lawrence's Bottle House.

---

* See *Directories*.
† *Newcastle Courant*, March 20th, 1725.

Of the above, Nos. 4 and 5 were known at first as the "Western Glasshouses," latterly (in 1789, at any rate) as the "High Glass-houses." Nos. 6 and 7 as the "Middle Glasshouses." Nos. 8, 9, and 10 as the "Eastern Glasshouses," but by 1725 as the "Low Glasshouses,"‡ and possibly sometimes as the "Mushroom Glass-houses."§

In 1736 only the St. Lawrence Bottle House was worked by a firm not obviously connected with the Henzell-Tyzack families; the latter were now concerned with the making of window glass and bottles, especially the former.

In 1696 Peregrine, John and Jacob Henzell, and Peregrine Tyzack were leading men in this family glass-making business,[3] whilst in 1736 the late Peregrine Henzell was said to have been "the principal person then remaining of his Family and one of the chief owners of these works."|| It is probable that Henzell and Co. were responsible for all the earlier advertisements relating to Newcastle broad glass,[1,2,11] and they had an agent in Norwich between 1730 and 1732 for the sale of their bottles.[12] In 1757, the window glass-makers of this family traded under the name of "The Newcastle Company of Glass Owners";[34] the bottle glass-makers under the name of "'Thomas Henzell and Company."[35] In 1762, they offered a share in the Mushroom Glasshouse for sale; 39 but the control of the works seems to have remained for a time in their hands .[44]

It appears from the local records that one John Henzell was "formerly part-owner and first founder of the Crown glass manufactory in this town." Also that the Crown glasshouse near the Ouse Burn was, in 1734 a joint undertaking by "the owners of

---

‡ *Ibid.*, March 6th 1725.
§ *Newcastle Journal*, April 28th, 1744.
|| *Bourne*, pp. 155 *et seq.*

the five several Broad Glass Houses" (including the Broad Glasshouse at Howden Pans). This was of course the Newcastle Company of Glass Owners.[34,47,68]

Joshua Henzell, who died in 1769, had survived from the seventeenth century, and is reported to have acquired a very handsome fortune.[47] His namesake, Joshua Henzell, however, mentioned in 1771 as residing at the Glasshouses[48] was not so fortunate. He had many shares in the Broad and Crown glasshouses, an interest in a new flint glass company, R. T. Shortridge and Co. (started about 1785 on the north shore), and also a flint glasshouse on the south shore.[63,68,69] But he and two of his partners, James and Joseph King, became bankrupt in 1786.[66,67]

This disaster must have been a severe blow to the Henzell glass-house owners; and they never afterwards had the same predominating position at Newcastle. But we still hear of Paul Henzell Esq., as "one of the principal glassowners here" in 1789;[77,80] and of Catherine Henzell and Co. in 1791,[81] stated by Baillie in 1801 to be owners of "extensive works." The Directories give William Henzell and Co. as glassowners at the Low Glasshouses 1787–1811. But the Mushroom glasshouse was held in 1787 by William Elliott who made bottles; and in 1795 by Sir M. W. Ridley and Hewitson. In 1787, John Tallentire made bottles at "Glasshouse Bridge," presumably the High or Western Glasshouses.*

It would appear, therefore, that the Benzell family lost much of their former monopoly on the eastern side of Newcastle by the end of the century. This family has, however, continued to own glass-works at Newcastle until comparatively recent times, a wonderful record.

---

* See *Directories*.

10. *The St. Lawrence Bottle House*

In 1697 Joshua Middleton was one of the leading bottle-makers in Newcastle,[5,7] and it is almost certain that this was his glass-house; for in 1736, Bourne states that it was held on lease by Mrs. Middleton, and that one of the proprietors was Mr. Richard Ridley. This is the first mention of the Ridleys as glass-makers; and they gradually acquired a large interest in the window and bottle glass trade. Sir Matthew Ridley worked the St. Lawrence Bottle House in 1758 [38] and in 1769; and "there were great rejoicings at the Low Glasshouses" on his re-election to Parliament at the latter date.[48] Matthew Ridley is also mentioned in 1745,[23] and in 1790, Sir Matthew White Ridley and Hewitson are mentioned as one of the principal firms of bottle-makers in Newcastle.* Mr. Middleton Hewitson (note the name) was "principal agent of the Bottle-glasshouses near the town" in 1766.[48] In 1795, Ridley and Hewitson were making crown and broad glass on the North Shore."† The Ridleys also for a time owned the Howden Pans Glasshouse (see below).

THE SOUTH SHIELDS GLASSHOUSES ‡

It has been stated that glass-making was carried on at South Shields during the seventeenth century. This is probably true enough, but there is little positive evidence on the point. Between 1671 and 1676 an Edward Henzell resided at South Shields, but his trade is not stated.§ Even the reference[4] to debentures on glass exported from "Newcastle and Sheels" in 1696 is not quite conclusive; for there was a glasshouse at North Shields,

---

* *Universal British Directory.* † *Directory.*
‡ See generally, G. B. Hodgson, *History of South Shields*, (1924), 357–370.   § *Local records*, H. M. Wood.

about which very little is known.³² It is, however, quite likely that window glass and bottles were made at South Shields towards the end of the seventeenth century. The original Onesiphorus Dagnia set up a glasshouse here some time before 1712;‖ probably before 1707, when his son, the famous "John Dagnia of South Shields, glass-maker," went to reside there,¶ and after that there are several references to glasshouses at South Shields in the hands of the Dagnias.

11. & 12. *The Bottle Houses at Mill Dam*

On Fryer's *Plan of the Tyne*, 1773, are marked two "Bottle Houses" rather to the west of Mill Dam, South Shields. This was the name and use of these two glasshouses in 1773; and the "Bottle Houses" are mentioned again in 1790 (see below). Their history from 1737 onwards is now fairly clear.

On Nov. 22nd, 1737, a lease for twenty-one years was granted to John Dagnia by the Dean and Chapter of Durham, in connection with two glasshouses "now in the tenure of John Dagnia" and "lately erected."* At this time only one of the glasshouses was used for making bottles; the other was known as the " South Shields Broad glasshouse"† in 1737, and in 1756 its use was the same.³³ John Dagnia (died in 1743; ‡ and his family carried on the two glasshouses until 1756. But in order to do so they had to mortgage the glasshouses to John Cookson (the neighbouring glass-owner) for more than £3,000.³⁸ Evan Deer, who married

---

‖ H. M. Wood, *Arch. Aeliana*, loc. cit.
¶ C. E.. Adamson, *Proc. Soc. Antiq. Newcastle*, VI, 163–168.
* *Vict. C. H., Durham*, II, 309; and see reference No. 33.
† Brand, *Newcastle*, 11, 46.
‡ C. E. Adamson, *loc. cit.*

Sarah, daughter of John Dagnia, appears to have had a half share in the works. In 1756, the other half share was offered for sale, not a very hopeful proceeding in view of the heavy charges upon it,[33] and at this point it is quite evident that John Cookson entered into partnership with Evan Deer, and with him took over the glass-houses, probably used henceforward as a bottle factory. Thus, in 1758 " John Cookson and his partners" of South Shields are included in the agreement by the Tyne bottle-makers.[38, 40] In 1760 the rate books give "Cookson and Deer"; ‡ and in 1777 "Messrs. Cookson and Dear's glasshouses in South Shields" are mentioned.[58] Evan Deer died 17th April, 1790, and his memorial in St. Hilda's church, South Shields, describes him as "a proprietor of the Bottle Houses in this place for many years." ‡ The Cooksons remained until the middle of the nineteenth century the leading partners in these glassworks. §

13. & 14. *Cookson's Crown and Plate Glasshouses*

Isaac Cookson (born 1679, died 1743), the head of the great glass-making family of Cookson, came to Newcastle about 1700 from Penrith.|| Although his name does not appear in any of the local glass firms, he was (as we have seen) known in London as one of the most successful glass manufacturers on the Tyne.[21] He acquired a large fortune in various business enterprises, of which glass-making was only one. The difficulties in the way of a stranger merchant, in those early days of City guilds and companies, may not be fully appreciated to-day. Thus, the name of Isaac Cookson was not openly associated with any of the various glass businesses

---

‡ C. E. Adamson, *loc. cit.*
§ See Directories.
|| See Newcastle Daily Chronicle, May 20th, 1897.

which he founded or financed. His connection with the famous Crown and Plate Glasshouses at South Shields is a case in point. His son, John Cookson, was apprenticed in 1728 and admitted to a City company in 1738. In anticipation, one would imagine, of the latter event, Isaac Cookson took a lease of a site in South Shields in March 1737,¶ on which he built a glasshouse on behalf of his son. In 1738, John Cookson and Thomas Jeffreys entered into partnership for making crown glass here.[15]

There is ample evidence that the crown glass made at Cookson and Co.'s Glassworks in South Shields was from the first widely known and of excellent reputation. In 1740, a London warehouse was established, first near London Bridge, later on at Black Friars Stairs and then in Fleet Street.[15] In 1741, Cookson's crown glass was being sold in Leeds, and the glasshouse was described already as one of "the two best window glasshouses in England,"[16] Newcastle crown glass, probably from the same factory, was frequently advertised in Norwich between 1741 and 1746, being rather cheaper than the crown glass from London.[17,25]

A plate glasshouse is mentioned also in 1742.[19] It must then have been only recently erected; for in 1773 it was stated before a Parliamentary Committee that the Cooksons had been making plate glass for thirty years.[52] This statement disposes of the suggestion, sometimes made, that plate glass was made by Cookson in the seventeenth century. Newcastle plate glass made at these glassworks is referred to in a pamphlet called "The Plate Glass Book," 1757, written by a "Glasshouse Clerk"; and a discount form is given as used by their London agent, "at Blackfriars, now Fleet Street."* It is even said that in 1773 east plates of a large size were

---

¶ *Vict. C. H., Durham*, II, 309.
* See *Appendix*, No. 15.

occasionally made at these works; but most of the plate must have been blown.[52] This plate glasshouse is the one referred to in the lists of glasshouses 1772 and 1776.[50, 56] A potential rival at Howden Pans was destroyed a few months after its conversion into a plate house in 1772.[51,53] As the business at these glassworks increased the partnership grew in size; thus, in 1746, there were six partners. But in 1776 John Cookson bought out all his partners except Dixon, his London agent."† John Cookson died ill 1783, and the business passed to his son Isaac, who is mentioned in connection with these works in 1787 and 1796.[70,84]

14. *The West Holborn Flint Glassworks*

Richard Turner Shortridge and Co. are said to have established flint glassworks at South Shields in the year 1797. ‡ This company had previously made flint glass on the North Shore, Newcastle,[63] In April, 1797, a notice was issued on behalf of the company by William Harrison from South Shields,[86] and it is therefore possible that Shortridge and Co. moved to South Shields before 1797. A further notice was issued by the company in 1800;[87] and the following year they are stated to have been among the principal glass-makers on the Tyne.*

OTHER GLASSHOUSES

15. *The Howden Pans Glasshouse*

Situated on the north bank of the Tyne, rather to the east of Wallsend, this glasshouse is recorded by Brand as standing in

---

† *Vict. C. H., Durham*, loc. cit. ; see reference No. 89.
‡ *Vict. C. H., Durham*, loc. cit.
* Baillie, *Newcastle* (glass manufactures), where the firm is given as J. Shortridgo and Co.

1692, and as making broad glass in 1737.† Its early history is supplied entirely by the Wallsend Registers, Durham Marriage Bonds and Wills.‡ From these records it is fairly clear that the families of Henzell and Tizack worked a glasshouse at Howden Pans at least as early as 1686, and probably from 1670. Members of the former family seem to have been the principal co-owners for many years. The record is equally clear that broad glass was the manufacture at these works. Thus, in 1734 Edward Henzell bequeathed one-sixth of the Howden Pans Broad glass-house to his wife and afterwards to his son Edward, who in 1747 is described as "glass-owner at Howden Pans." In 1700, John Tyzack was "chief workman in the Howden Pans glasshouse," and there is a record of Joseph Tyzack, broad glass-maker there in 1781, at a time when the ownership of the glasshouse had changed hands. For some years before 1772, the broad glass-house was worked by Matthew Ridley and Co.,[51] and the local registers seem to fix the date of the transfer of the business between 1754 and 1760; for, at the former date, the Wallsend Henzells were described as glass-makers at Howden Pans, but after 1759, without exception, as glass-makers at Newcastle.

In 1772, Ridley and Co. converted the glasshouse into a plate glass factory, and claimed that their plate glass was "equal to any manufactured in England." [51] It is probably the glasshouse referred to in 1773 in the evidence before a Parliamentary Committee, where it was stated that the largest plate made at this house was 65 × 38 inches.[52] But the new venture at Howden Pans was doomed to failure. In June, 1773, the glasshouse was badly damaged by fire.[53] That it was intended at the time to proceed with the business, we may assume from an advertise-

---

† Newcastle, H, 46.
‡ References kindly supplied by H. M. Wood, Esq.

ment, issued about ten days later by John Reed, a local cabinet-maker, who purposed "to serve his customers of the produce of the New plate glass manufactory at Howden Pans."[54]§ We know that plate glass was not being made here in 1776; for there was then only one plate glasshouse on the Tyne, viz., Cookson's.[56] The reference to Joseph Tyzack, broad glass-maker in 1781, suggests that the old manufacture was restarted. But beyond this, no other reference has been found relating to the glasshouse.

16. *The Bill Quay Glasshouse*

This glasshouse was situated on the Haining shore, on the south side of the Tyne, about 2 miles east of Gateshead. It was founded in 1694 and used as a bottle-house in 1737.* Perhaps Mr. Broome was glass master here, in 1697.[5] In July, 1726, there is a reference in the Register of Durham Marriage Bonds to one Thomas Thompson of Gateshead, glass-maker, who married Margaret Henzell. Later on, in 1758, at any rate, Joseph Airey and Company (including several Cooksons) were in possession, and they were parties to the agreement made with King in that year.[38,40]

Sir Benjamin Rawling seems to have been the landlord and to have granted the leases, and in 1771 the remainder of a term of sixteen years, with right of renewal, was offered for sale,[49] presumably by Joseph Airey and Company. It was still used as a bottle-house. In 1777, Robert Dodds was the agent;[57] but the glass-makers are not yet known. In 1811 and 1833, Cookson and Co. are found in possession;† and it is quite possible that they took over the works in 1771.

---

§ John Reed retired from business, May 11th, 1776, *Newcastle Journal*.
* Brand, *Newcastle*, 11, 46.
† *Directories*.

17. *The Northumberland Glasshouse, Lemington*

The Lemington glassworks, some miles to the west of Newcastle, on the north bank of the Tyne, were in the nineteenth century famous for flint and crown glass. They started, however, with a single glasshouse used for making flint glass and called the "Northumberland Glasshouse."

Mackenzie says of Lemington as follows:‡ "Till the year 1787 this village was very inconsiderable. About that time a company of enterprizing gentlemen cantered into the glass trade in Newcastle under the firm of the Northumberland Glass Company." They were at first, we are told, treated with hostility and jealousy by the other glass-makers and could find no site for their glassworks. But eventually the Duke of Northumberland granted a lease of a site at Lemington, where their first glasshouse was erected. The glasshouse, called "the Northumberland Glasshouse,"[72,74] is shown on Gibson's *Tyne Colliery Plan* of 1788; but the firm appears for the first time in the Newcastle Directories in 1787. Mr. Joshua Henzel* was agent for the glasshouse until his death in 1788.[72] He was succeeded by John Dyson, who signed a notice on behalf of the firm in 1797.[85] †

In 1788, Thomas Colbeck had some connection with this glasshouse, possibly as proprietor.[74] The company joined with, the other flint glass companies in issuing a notice in 1800.[87] Although the members of this glass business are not yet known, the business must have flourished exceedingly; for in 1811 the Northumberland Glass Company had taken over the Close Glass-

---

‡ Mackenzie, *Newcastle*, II, 382.
* This Joshua Henzell was descended from the Howden Pans glass-makers. [*Wallsend Epitaphs*, per Mr. H. M. Wood.]
† See also *Directories*.

works; and Mackenzie states that at Lemington there were four glasshouses eventually, one of remarkable shape and size. In 1833, three glasshouses are recorded at Lemington owned by Joseph Lamb and Co.‡

18. *The Salt Meadow Bottle-house*

Wood's Plan of Newcastle, dated 1827, shows a large glass manufactory, a little south-east of Gateshead, marked "Tyne Glass Works, [C. Attwood.]"

It is not unlikely that the earliest, predecessor of these works was the Salt Meadow Bottle-house, situated near the south bank of the Tyne.§ First mentioned in 1753,[29] it was perhaps built during the first half of the eighteenth century by Joseph Liddell, who was dead in 1753. It was then offered on lease, and a lease of nineteen years from Nov. 11th, 1753, was granted to James King.[38] In 1758, however, the other leading bottle-makers of Newcastle wished to have this glasshouse closed; and they arranged with King to pay him £50 per annum for the rest of the lease, and to buy the stock and implements at the glasshouse. King, however, agreed to keep the glasshouse in repair.[38] The glasshouse, then, is net to be reckoned in the list of five bottle houses recorded in 1772 and 1776,[50,56] for obviously it was not then at work. Nothing further has been learnt of the subsequent history of this glasshouse.

19. *The South Shore Flint Glasshouse*

A more immediate predecessor of the Tyne Glass Works was the "South Shore Flint Glasshouse," built by Joshua Henzell and

---

‡ *Parliamentary Papers*, 1833.
§ A Scotch ship is mentioned as "now lying at the Key near the Salt Meadow Glasshouse," *Bath Journal*, September 16th, 1754.

partners shortly before 1786. In that year Henzell because bankrupt,67 and in 1787 part of the stock, etc., of the glasshouse was offered for sale.[69] In 1788, the glasshouse itself, described as "new-built," was also offered for sale,71 and it is quite possible that it is "the Glasshouse situate near Newcastle," which is mentioned in 1795.[82] Messrs. John Barber and John and Francis Banner, trading as "the Tyne Glass Company," took over the last-mentioned glasshouse. But disputes between the partners arose,[82] and in 1796 John Barber became bankrupt.[83] The name, however, survived; and the Directory of 1801 gives Shutts and Co., the Tyne Glass Manufactory, Gateshead.

The exact connection between the Salt Meadow Bottle-house, the South Shore Flint Glasshouse and the Tyne Glass Works has yet to be traced; they are all situated in the same general area.

20. *The Bottle-house in the Dock*

A bottle-house of this name, "adjoining upon the Tyne," was in 1758 in the hands of Sir Matthew White and Company.[38] It cannot be said where "the Dock" was situated, but it was probably on the north shore, somewhere west of Glasshouse Bridge. Possibly this glasshouse is connected with the glasshouse next mentioned.

21. *The North Shore Flint Glasshouse*

In 1784, Joshua Henzell, Richard Turner Shortridge, John Grey, and James and Joseph King set up or acquired a flint glass factory on the north shore at Newcastle, trading as Richard Turner Shortridge and Co. Their original advertisement appears on Jan. 8th, 1785.[63] On the bankruptcy of Henzell and the Kings in 1787,[66,67] this partnership must have been dissolved; but the firm name evidently survived.[86,87] Perhaps R. T. Shortridge took over the glasshouse on his own account, as there is no mention of its sale. John Grey appears in the *Universal British Directory* of 1790 as a "cut glass manufacturer," but at present no further or other trace of him can be found. As already mentioned, Shortridge and Co. prospered, and are found after 1796 in South Shields (see above).

The possibility of this glasshouse on the north shore being identical with the "Bottle House in the Dock," mentioned in 1758,[38] should not be overlooked.

General

Some idea of the areas at home and abroad, which were served by the Tyne glass-makers, will be obtained from Appendices I and II. London received large quantities of crown,[15] plate[15] and broad glass[1,2,9-11] made on the Tyne; and in 1764 bottles also were advertised in London.[42] Agencies also for "Castle window glass" and bottles were established in such places as Norwich,[12,17,25] Faversham,[14] Leeds[16] and Woodbridge.[88] Of flint glass made on the Tyne very little is said in the newspapers of other towns; in fact, the only advertisements of Newcastle flint glass, outside Newcastle, occur in Irish papers. In 1727, London, and not Newcastle, was supplying the Scottish market with flint glass. At the end of the century the Sheffield plate-makers gave much work to the Birmingham and Dudley glass-makers, but not, so far as is known, to the Tyne glass-makers. It is probable, therefore, that Newcastle flint glass, although of good quality, was for the first sixty years of the eighteenth century designed mainly to serve the local market and for places in Ireland and abroad. Much even of the table glass of high quality which was used by the gentry of Northumberland must have come from London along with expensive kinds of china and earthenware. Towards the end of the eighteenth century and in the earlier part of the nineteenth century the production of fine table glass about Newcastle increased enormously. But until 1775, at any rate, this was not by any means the main product of the Tyne glass-makers.

Acknowledgment

The author's best thanks are due to J. C. Hodgson, Esq., for much kind and valuable help with the family history of many Newcastle glass-makers, and for supplying several valuable references to glass-houses in the local records, notably No. 38 in the first Appendix. Also to Herbert M. Wood, Esq., for 'the loan of three valuable MSS. notebooks, in which are recorded numerous references to the families of Henzell, Tyzack, and Tittery, extracted from the registers, etc., of many parishes in Northumberland and Durham; and to Mr. James McGarrigle for carrying out a lengthy search through many files of Newcastle newspapers.

TUNSTEAD, GREENFIELD,
   YORKSHIRE.

APPENDIX I

1. 25th June, 1691. *London Gazette*.

"Newcastle Cut-Glass, good and sizeable, may be had by all Merchants and others at 13s. per Hundred Foot. Apply yourselves to John Tyzacke at the Glass-Warehouse near Old Swan stairs."

2. 17th March, 1692. *London Gazette*.

"Newcastle Glass cut into Quarries, good and sizeable, may be had at 10s. per Hundred Foot. Apply yourselves to John Tyzacke, &c."

3. 7th January, 1696. *Journals H. C.* xi, 386.

A petition of Peregrine Henzell, John Henzell, Jacob Henzell, and Peregrine Tizack, on behalf of themselves, and the rest of the Glass-makers upon the North side of the River Tine, was presented to the House of Commons against the War Tax on Glass and Coals. [6 & 7 William & Mary, e. 18].

4. (?) December, 1696. *Tracts relating to Trade, Brit. Mus.*, 816-M. 12-117.

An account of the produce of the Glass Duty From Michaelmas 1695 to 17th Nov. 1699 £17,642 1s. 5d.

"For debentures at London £840.
  „ „ „ Bristol £2,976.
  „ „ „ New Castle and Sheels £1,020."

[The "debentures" represent the amount of duty returned on glass exported from England.]

5. 17th February, 1697. *Journals H. C.* xi, 707.

Upon the Petition of the Glass-makers in and the Town of Newcastle upon Tyne Mr. Broome and Mr. Middleton gave the evidence there mentioned. "Notwithstanding the great quantities of ales that are returned from Newcastle to London and other Parts, which, used to take off great Quantities of Bottles before the Duty enhanced the price of them, that now the said ales are chiefly returned by Cask."

6. 4th November, 1697. *Treasury Papers*, xc, 112; xciv, 82.

Onesiphorus Dagnia, a glass-maker of Newcastle, was fined £200 and costs for having fraudulently concealed over 2,679 dozens of glass bottles.

7. 21st May, 1698. *Journals H. C.*, xii, 281.

"Upon a petition of the Glass-makers of Newcastle against the War Tax on Glass—

Joshua Middleton, Owner of a Glass-house, said That he has endeavoured to strive with the burden of the said duty; and to that end kept his fire in and worked for twenty weeks, and employed his poor servants; but was forced to lay down, not being able to sell the bottles he made, by reason of the addition the duty puts upon the price thereof; which puts so great a restraint upon their consumption; besides the loss they sustain in flying and breakage, after the duty is paid to the King. John Colt, Workman, said, He has left his wife and children behind him at Newcastle, whilst he came to seek for work in London; and has not had one day's work these 19 months, the fires being all out in the Country; but used to got 40s. a week when he was fully employed."

8. 10th March, 1701. *English Post*.

"Window-Glass: All merchants &c. may be furnished with well coloured, clean and beautiful German Window Glass—which in all respects is better than Newcastle Glass, and shall be at cheaper rates. John Hopgood, Glasier, in Basing Lane."

9. 1703. R. Novo, *Builder's Dictionary*, 1st edon. p. 149 &c.

"Newcastle Glass.

This sort of glass is of a Kind of an ash colour, 'tis the glass that is most in use here in England, but 'tis subject to have specks and blemishes and streaks in it, and 'tis very often warped crooked."... [Here follows a description of the packing of tables of glass in cases].... "These cases are brought to London in the coal ships, they being sot in end in the Coles more than half its depth, by which means they are kept steady from falling and being broke by the motion and rowling of the ship. Mr. Leybourn saith, the price of Newcastle glass is uncertain, for when coals are plenty then glass is cheap, and when the coals arc dear at London, then Newcastle glass is so likewise, not that they want coals at Newcastle; but because they have no other conveyance for it to London. So that sometimes it is at 30s. per case, and other times 40s."

10. 22nd October, 1709. *Post Man*.

"The agreement between the glassmakers of Newcastle and

the Glass Cutters* of London being expired, any Broad glass makers that are willing to supply the glasiers in London for the future with common Broad Window Glass, or workmen to make the same, arc desired to treat with Mr. John Page at Cole's Coffee house in Birchin Lane."

11. 5th November, 1709. *Post Man.*

"Whereas an advertisement was put in the Post Man insinuating that because the contract between tile Glassmakers and Glass Cutters was expired, the Glaziers could not be furnished with Newcastle glass as heretofore, which insinuation is altogether groundless, for that the said Glassmakers are as capable as ever to serve the Glaziers, either from Newcastle or from their Warehouses at London, with as good a commodity and at as reasonable rates; the design of the said advertisement thereof is only the project of some men to make confusion in the Trade, and to draw in (by specious pretences) men not knowing the true circumstances of the Glass Trade."

12. 19th September, 1730. *Norwich Gazette.*

"Mrs. Elizabeth Tizeck, next door to the Widow Rowley in St. Margaret's parish in Norwich, has a large quantity of quart glass bottles at reasonable prices."

3rd October, 1730. (*Ibid.*)

(as above) adding " glass bottles at 17s. a gross."

29th April, 1732. (*Ibid.*)

"At Mrs. Elizabeth Tyzack's, at the Sign of the Six Bottles, in St. Margaret's, Upper street, is a large parcel of glass bottles, now to be sold, and she intends to carry on the said business, and will sell them as reasonably as anyone in Norwich, being one of the Owners of the Glass Houses in Newcastle."

---

* An old name for "Glaziers."

13. 1st January, 1736. *General Advertiser*.

"Newcastle. Dec. 27 (1735). Yesterday was se'nnight, in the afternoon a man going accidentally into the Mushroom Glasshouse, near this Town, with a charged fowling-piece in his hand carelessly laid it down; when Zachary Tyzack, one of the workmen, taking it up, mortally wounded William Randal, another of the said workmen."

14. 12th June, 1736. *Kentish Post*.

"Christopher Pratt of Feversham having a quantity of Newcastle Bottles, sells them to any person at a reasonable rate; common Quarts at 16s. per Groce; eight-square or long-necked quart bottles at 18s. per Groce; common pints at 14s., eight-square and long-necked pints at 16s., to be fetched from the Storehouse, and paid for."

9th March, 1743. (*Ibid*.)

"Christopher Pratt Jun. of Faversham sells Coals, Coke, Bottles and Grindstones &c."

24th May, 1755. (*Ibid*.)

"Sold by Christopher Pratt at Faversham, ... Newcastle Bottles, common quarts at 25s. per grose: champagne quarts at 27s. per grose."

15th December, 1759. (*Ibid*.)

"Christopher Pratt &c. sells Newcastle Champain quart Bottles at 26s. per groce; common Bottles at 24s. ditto: delivered at the Storehouse at the King's Head Key."

15. 17th January, 1740. *London Evening Post*.

"From the new Glasshouse, lately erected by Cookson and Jeffreys at South Shields near Newcastle, the best Crown Glass is to be sold at their warehouses at tile Old Swan near London Bridge."

16th July, 1740. *General Advertiser*.

"Removed since Mid Summer Day, from the Old Swan to

tile Great House at Black Fryar's Stairs: Where daily attendance is given for the sale of Crown Glass made by Cookson and Jeffreys from their new-erected Works at South Shields.

N.B. Glazier's and Dealers in Glass who live in or near Seaport Towns that trade to Newcastle are desired to send their orders to John Cookson Merchant in Newcastle."

6th March, 1756. *London Evening Post*.

"Glass Warehouse, late at Black Fryars, is removed over against St. Bride's Church in Fleet-street; where tile Trade may be supplied with Plate and Crown Glass as usual."

16. 5th May, 1741. *Leeds Mercury*.

"The best Crown Glass from Mr. Bold's* Glasshouse in London or the best Crown Glass from Mr. Cookson's Glasshouse in Newcastle and Company; any day in the week at the house of Richard Butler, nigh Woodhouse Bar, Leeds. Sash glass is 6d. to 8d. a foot; clock faces and pictures 8d. to 10d. a foot; cut glass for setting in load from 2d. to 4d. a foot. Which far exceeds any glass made in this country, for fine and streight; cut out of the shoot by Richard Butler aforesaid; two of the best window glass-houses in England."

17. 5th June, 1741. *Norwich Mercury*.

22nd May, 1742. *Norwich Gazette*.

"Daniel Pycroft, St. George's of Colegate, Norwich, Glazier, sells :-Best London Crown Glass at 9d. per foot.

Castle do. at 7d. a foot."

11th July, 1741, Norwich Mercury.

"in the Fleece Yard, in St. Simon's, Norwich, is continued to be sold. ... Ratcliffe or Newcastle Crown Glass, or Broad Glass, by the case or cut, by John Simpson."

---

* Error for "Mr Bowles's."

18. 10th September, 1741. *Newcastle Journal*.

"Whereas three current going glasshouses on the River Wear are advertised to be lett on October 2nd next, the several proprietors of the Broad Glasshouses and Bottle Houses on the River Tyne are desired to meet at the Crown Tavern on the Key on Wednesday next betwixt the hours of 2 and 3 in the afternoon, to consider of the same; at which time, if any of the said owners be prepared with proposals for putting the glass and bottle trade on a better footing than at present, he is desired to communicate them."

19. 28th January, 1742. Richardson, *Table Books* [*Hist.*], I, 406.

"The roof of Cookson's plate Glasshouse at South Shields was set on fire."

20. 23rd April, 1743. *Newcastle Journal*.

"To be lett immediately and entered on May Day next for a term of years, situate without the Close-gate in Newcastle-on-Tyne, A moyety of a bottle and flint glass-house with a complete set of tools and workmen for each house. For further particulars enquire of Messrs. Christopher and John Dagnia at the said glass-house office."

21. 30th April, 1743. *Craftsman*.

"Dead, Mr. Isaac Cookson of Newcastle, one of the most considerable Glass Manufacturers in those parts."

22. 6th July, 1743. *Daily Advertiser*.

Notices of dissolution of partnership between Thomas Jeffreys, Richard Jeffreys and James Dixon, of Snow Hill … in "transactions relating to the glass trade."

23. 4th May, 1745. *Newcastle Courant*.

" To be lett at Blyth in Northumberland, a fire stone quarry for Glasshouse Furnaces. Enquire of Matthew Ridley Esq. in Newcastle."

24. 23rd November, 1745. *London Gazette*.

"An express just arrived from Marshal Wade dated 22nd at Newcastle brings advice that the Army under his command was received and lodged by the Magistrates and Inhabitants in the Publick Halls, Glasshouses, Malt-houses, and other empty buildings."

25. 5th April, 1746. *Norwich Mercury*.

Notice by 20 Norwich Glaziers of rise in prices, owing to the duty on Window Glass.

London Crown, in sashes or lead 1s. 6d. a foot.

Castle Crown   „   „   „   „   1s. 3d. „   „

26. 3rd October, 1747. *Newcastle Journal*.

"Made and sold by John Radcliff Jr. Sieves and Riddles of all sorts for Glasshouses."

27. 10th June, 1743. *Newcastle Journal*.

"To be sold. Together or Separate A Glasshouse and several dwelling houses Without the Closegate, Newcastle-on-Tyne, Freehold. Enquire of James Dagnia at Cleadon. Mr. Thomas Hilton, Without the Closegate will show the premises."

28. 16th March, 1751. *Newcastle Journal*.

Mentioned in a subscription list . . . John Cookson Esq. Mr. Peregrine Tyzack. Messrs. Thomas, John & Joseph Airey.

29. 27th January, 1753. *Newcastle Journal*.

"To be lett, the Glass House, late belonging to Mr. Joseph Liddell deceased with the Buildings lands and grounds thereunto belonging, situated on the South Shore upon the River Tyne near Gateshead in the County of Durham. Enquire at Mr. Airey's office, Westgate Street, Newcastle."

30. 6th October, 1753. *Newcastle Journal*.

"To be sold Mr. Dagnia's House at Cleadon."

31. 1754. Thomas Dockwray, *Sermon on Consecration of Infirmary Chapel*.

The subscription list to Newcastle infirmary includes: The

Middle Bottle House, and The Eastern, The Middle, The Western, and The St. Lawrence Broad Glasshouses.

32. 25th October, 1755. *Newcastle Courant.* [per J. C. Hodgson.]

"Tuesday was married at the Quakers' Meeting house at North Shields, Mr. James King, one of the owners of the Glasshouse there."*

33. 28th February, 1756. *Newcastle Journal.*

"To be sold to the best Bidder, A moiety or full Half Part of two Glass-Houses in South Shields in the County of Durham, the one a Bottle-House and the other a Broad Glass House. The whole of the said Glass-houses are subject to two several annuities of £50 and £25 for two several lives in being. Which said premises are held by several leases from the Dean and Chapter of Durham for 21 years lately renewed, and were late the estate of Mr. Dagnia deceased, and stand charged with payment of the sum of £3,182 11s. 7d. to John Cookson of the Town of Newcastle. Messrs. Deer and Miller both of South Shields will show the premises."

34. 12th March, 1757. *Newcastle Journal.*

"The Newcastle Company of Glass Owners hereby give notice that William† and John Keenlyside being dismissed from all employments under them, they have appointed John Nesbit their agent and cashier.

All Persons favouring the said Company with their orders for Broad and Crown Glass are desired to send them to John Nesbit at the Company's Office at the Glass-Houses, by whom

---

* Zachariah Tyzack, was "glassman" at North Shields in 1737, and Isaac Henzell "glassmaker" at North Shields in 1749. *Registers.* (H. M. Wood.)

† Mentioned 4th January, 1746, *Newcastle Journal.*

they will be duly executed."

35. 12th March, 1757. *Newcastle Journal*.

"All persons indebted to Thomas Henzell and Company for bottles are hereby desired to pay their debts to no other person than Mr. Paul Henzell or his order from this day."

36. 4th July, 1757. *Newcastle Journal*.

"William Featherstone, glazier, puts in Crown Glass at 11d. per foot, and Common Glass at 5d. per foot."

37. 11th February, 1758. *Newcastle Journal*.

"To be let lying near Shotley Field, Northumberland, a fine clay mine which is fit for the Glasshouses."

38. 6th April, 1758. J. C. Hodgson, *Proc. Soc. Antiquaries Newcastle*, 3rd Series, VII, 207.

A deed of this date recites the following glasshouses:-

(a) "James King stands possessed of the Salt Meadow bottle house for remainder of a term of 19 years commencing 11th Nov. 1753."

(b) "Matthew Ridley and partners are joint proprietors of the St. Lawrence bottle-house."

(c) "Sir Matthew White and partners are joint owners of a glasshouse adjoining upon the Tyne called the Bottle-house in the Dock."

(d) "John Cookson and his partners are joint proprietors of the South Shields Glasshouse."

(e) "Joseph Airey and partners are joint proprietors of the Bill Key glasshouse."

(f) "John Williams and partners are proprietors of the Closegate glasshouse."

In effect King agreed to cease working the Salt Meadow glasshouse and to sell the stock of potts, materials &c. to the other glassmakers named, who agree each to pay £10 per annum to James King during the remainder of his lease.

39. 16th January, 1762. *Newcastle Journal*.

"To be sold to the highest bidder at Kary's Coffee house 2nd February next. One third of St. Lawrence Broad Glass House, without the walls, but within the liberties of Newcastle, held by lease under the Mayor and Burgesses of the same town. Apply to Air. Jonathan Tyzack, Attorney-at-law, Newcastle."

40. 4th January, 1763. *London Gazette*.

"Pursuant to a Decree of the Court of Chancery at Durham in a cause wherein George Hall and others are complainants, and John Cooksoon Esq. and others are Defendants. The creditors of Isaac Cookson, late of Sherburne in the County of Durham, Gentleman, deceased,* are to come in and prove their several Debts &c. Also the several Estates of the said Isaac Cookson hereinafter mentioned are to be sold entire ... several parts or shares of Glass Houses at South Shields and Bill Key in the said County respectively."

41. 9th July, 1763. *Newcastle Journal*.

"To be let immediately. All that Bottle House with the several necessary Conveniences thereto belonging, situate without the Closegate, Newcastle. Now in the possession of John Williams Esq. and Company. Complete set of workmen. For further particulars enquire of Messrs. Christopher and John Dagnia."

42. 5th June, 1764. *London Evening Post*.

"At the Royal Northumberland Glass and Bottle Warehouse, in the Upper Ground, facing Black-Fryars, Southwark, Wine Merchants, Captains of Ships, Taverns, and others, may be carefully and expeditiously supplied with all sorts of Glass Bottles, either for Home Consumption, or exportation, on the most reasonable terms.

---

* This Isaac Cookson died 1761, presumably a son of the original glass manufacturer of that name.

N.B. Country Orders and Penny Post letters will be duly attended to, by directing for Edward Williams, at the said warehouse."

43. 15th December, 1764. *Newcastle Journal.*

"Thursday evening† a fire broke out in Mr. Williams's glasshouse in the Close, Newcastle, occasioned by the foulness of the chimney, which taking fire, some of the sparks got in between the Pantiles and kindled the ceiling; but as the House stands near the River, and it was then High Water, the Workmen without much other assistance got the Fire extinguished before any considerable damage was done."

44. 20th April, 1765. *Newcastle Journal.*

"Mr. Jonathan Tyzack, having resigned the agency of St. Lawrence Broad Glass House. It is desired that all persons who have any demands on that Glasshouse, may send in their accounts immediately to Mr. Peregrine Henzell at the Low Glass House."

45. 17th May, 1766. *Newcastle Chronicle.*

"Married, at the Quakers' Meeting House in North Shields, Mr. Middleton Hewitson, principal agent of the Bottle-glass-houses near this town."

46. 4th March, 1769. *Newcastle Chronicle.*

"On Sunday the bells were set a ringing here on the arrival of the news of Sir Matthew Ridley keeping his seat in Parliament for Morpeth; and on Monday there were great rejoicings at the Low Glass-Houses, at Myth &c. on that occasion."

47. 18th March, 1769. *Newcastle Chronicle.*

"Thursday died at the Low Glass Houses Mr. Joshua Henzell in the 82nd year of his age, a very worthy, friendly and honest man. Though he was esteemed the most corpulent person in this part, of the country, yet (till within a few years of his latter

---

† i.e., 13th December.

end) be always displayed himself in the manual execution of his business, a glass-maker, as possessing the abilities of an able workman, united with the alacrity of youth, and has thereby acquired a very handsome fortune."

18th March, 1769. *Newcastle Courant* (per H. M. Wood).

"Died, ... Mr. Joshua Henzell, the oldest proprietor of the Crown and Broad Houses in England, and who continued a constant worker till within the last six years."

48. 6th April, 1771. Newcastle Journal.

"The Fire Clay brick-works, South Shore, Newcastle. The Proprietors have now removed their works to a quay on the North Side of the River Tyne, near to the Glass-houses, and greatly enlarged thorn. Orders taken for bricks by Mr. Joshua Henzell,* ono of the Proprietors at the glasshouses, Newcastle."

49. 18th May, 1771. *Newcastle Journal.*

"To be sold to the best bidder, the 20th June next. The Lessee's Term and Right of Renewal of that well known Glass-bottle house, situate at Bill-Key, on the South-side of the River Tyne, in the County of Durham, held of Sir Benjamin Rawling by lease, whereof 16 years are yet to come; and all the stock of bottles, materials and utensils thereto belonging. Mr. Jacob Wilson, of Bill-Key, will show the premises. N.B. There is a complete set of workmen belonging to the said Bottle-house."

50. 13th January, 1772. Hutton's *Plan of Newcastle.*

"There are at present constantly and fully employed on the River 16 large Glassworks: viz. 1 for Plate Glass, 3 Crown Glass Houses; 5 for broad or common Window Glass, 2 for White or

---

* Mr. Joshua, Henzell, an owner and principal agent to the Glasshouse Company at the Ewesburn. *Newcastle Courant*, 19th August, 1775.

Flint Glass, and 5 Bottle Houses. The Products of which are sent to most parts of the world."

51. 19th December, 1772. *Newcastle Journal.*

"Last week the Plate-glass House at Howdon-pane was finished by Matthew Ridley Esq. and Company, where plate glass has already been made equal to any manufactured in England."

52. 24th February, 1773. *Journals H. C.*, xxxiv, 149.

The Committee, on Petition for a Company to make Cast Plates,† reported as follows:- "It appeared by the evidence of Mr. Dickson, that at Mr. Cookson's Manufactory for Plate Glass, the largest Size made is 84 × 52 inches, which he believes were cast. This Manufactory has been carried on for 30 years, but as-there is no call for them (the French underselling us) very few had boon made, and he could not tell the Price."

"A member present* informed your Committee, that he had received a letter lately, wherein he was informed, that at a Manufactory he was concerned in, they had just begun to blow Plate Glass; and had made one Plate 65 × 738 inches:"

53. 22nd June, 1773. *Leeds Mercury.*

"Early on Tuesday a fire broke out in the Plate Glass-house at Howdon-Pans, which burnt with such violence that in a few hours all the timber work therein was entirely consumed. This house had been converted into a plate Glass-house but a few months and was, like the other glass manufactures in Northumberland, from the excellency of their manufacture, in a very flourishing way."

54. 3rd July, 1773. *Newcastle Journal.*

"John Reed cabinet-maker, Newcastle, having begun the business of grinding &c. Plate glass, purposes to serve his Cus-

---

† This company became the famous British Cast Plate Glass Manufactory of Ravenhead near St. Helens.
* Probably Sir Matthew Ridley, M.P. See Nos. 51 and 53.

tomers of the produce of the New plate glass Manufactory at Howdon-Pans."

55. 25th February, 1775. *Newcastle Chronicle.*

"To be let immediately and entered upon the 12th May next, All that Bottle-house, with the Warehouses &c., situate without the Close-gate, Newcastle, now occupied by John Cookson Esq. and Company. For further particulars enquire of Mr. Christopher Dagnia or Mr. John Dagnia, or Mr. William Peters, Attorney at Law."

56. 1776. Hutchinson, *A view of Northumberland*, Vol. II., 473.

"There are upon the river Tyne, 5 Glass Bottle Houses, 3 Broad Glass Houses, 2 Crown Houses, 2 Flint Glass Manufactories, and 1 Plate Glass House."

57. 8th March, 1777. *Newcastle Chronicle*,

"Married, Mr. Robert Dodds, agent to the Glass works at the Bill-Key."

58. 3rd May, 1777. *Newcastle Chronicle.*

Advertisement of 3 Salt-Pans. "The whole adjoining close by Messrs. Cookson and Dear's glasshouses in South Shields."

59. 25th October, 1777. *Newcastle Courant* (per J. C. Hodgson).

"Tuesday at the Glasshouses on the North Shore died Mr. James King Junr., son of Mr. James King, one of the people called Quakers."

60. 1st April, 1780. *Newcastle Chronicle.*

"To be sold by Mr. Joseph Harris, Bigg Market, (under consignment from the proprietors of the glass-houses of this town) all sorts of flint glass, plain, engraved and cut, of the most modern patterns and best quality, as low as manufactured for ready money."

61. 27th February, 1782. Richardson, *Table Books* [Hist.], Vol. II, 27

"A very high wind blew down the roof of the flint glasshouse belonging to Messrs. Williams & Co. in the Close, Newcastle, which falling upon the furnace, soon caught fire and burnt with great violence, until the whole building except a gable end was destroyed."

62. 22nd November, 1783. *Newcastle Courant.*

Advertisement by Mr. Joseph King of the Lower Glasshouses, near the Mushroom Gate.

63. 8th January, 1785. *Newcastle Chronicle, Courant.*

"To the Public and all dealers in Flint Glass. Henzell, Shortridge, Grey, King & Son, Flint Glass Manufacturers on the North Shore, Newcastle, sell wholesale and retail, all kinds of flint glass and phials, at the customary prices, and usual discount for prompt payment. Orders directed to Richard Turner Shortridge & Co., will be executed with punctuality and expedition. N.B. Watch crystals of all sizes after the 20th Inst., by wholesale."

64. 26th March, 1785. *Newcastle Courant. Newcastle Chronicle.*

"Close-gate Bottle Glass-house. The Copartnership carried on under the firm of the Owners of the Close-gate Bottle-house being dissolved, the friends of the house are hereby informed, that it will in future be carried on by Isaac Cookson, to whom all letters and orders for Bottles or Crown glass, at the Warehouse in the Close, will be punctually attended to."

65. 14th January, 1786. *Newcastle Courant. Newcastle Chronicle.*

"Wood Mongers, who can supply the following articles, viz. Birch and Alder Posts from 38-40 inch, Ash laths 42 inch, Ash laths 18 ins. Rods 54 ins. long, all for the purpose of making crates for packing window glass, are desired to send their proposals to Joseph Kirkup, at the Crown glass house, South Shields, or to Samuel Wilson, at the Bottle and Crown glass warehouses, in the Close, Newcastle. N.B. They are to be delivered at South Shields."

66. 22nd April, 1786. *Newcastle Courant*.

"To be sold by auction by order of the Assignee of James King and Joseph King, Bankrupts, their estates &c."

67. 9th May, 1786. *London Gazette*.

"Bankruptcy Notice. Joshua Henzell of the Low Glass-house Newcastle, Glass-manufacturer."

68. 23rd September, 1786. *Newcastle Courant*.

"To be sold to the highest bidder by the order of the assignees of Joshua Henzell, a Bankrupt, 614 shares of the Broad and Crown Glass-works, with stock in trade."

69. 17th March, 1787. *Newcastle Courant*.

"To be sold by auction, by order of the assignees of Joshua Henzell, a bankrupt, on 27th March, five sixteenth parts or shares of the stock in trade of the South Shore Flint Glasshouse, consisting of a large assortment of manufactured glass-wares, working utensils &c. &c."

70. 11th August, 1787. *Newcastle Courant*.

"Whereas William Glister, employed as a Teazer in the glass-works at South Shields belonging to Isaac Cookson Esq., to whom he was bound by indenture for 7 years, did on the 8th July abscond himself from his master's service." [Notice against employing him.]

71. 19th January, 1788. *Newcastle Courant*.

"To be sold by auction by order of the assignees of Joshua Henzell, a Bankrupt, all that new built Glass-house &c., situate on the South Shore below the town of Newcastle and adjoining the River Tyne, very suitable for carrying on various branches of the business."

72. 19th July, 1788, *Newcastle Courant*.

"Died, Mr. Joshua Henzell, Agent for the Northumberland Glass House, at Lemington."

73. 23rd August, 1788. *Newcastle Courant*.

"Married, Mr. George Tyzack of the Low Glass-houses."

74. 13th September, 1788. *Newcastle Courant*.

"Thomas Colbeck, of the Northumberland Glass-house situate at Lemington, in the Parish of Newburn, Northumberland," makes a public apology for an infringement of the licensing laws.

75. 20th September, 1788. *Newcastle Courant*.

"Glass makers: A few good hands in the Crown glass branch, not under an engagement to any company or person, will meet suitable encouragement to their abilities by applying to Thomas McCabe, Newcastle."

76. 29th November, 1788. *Newcastle Chronicle. Newcastle Courant.*

"To be let immediately and entered upon the 12th May next. All that Bottle glasshouse, with the several necessary conveniences, situate without the Closegate, Newcastle, now in the possession of Isaac Cookson Esq. For particulars, enquire of Mr. John Dagnia, or Mr. Peters, attorney, in Newcastle."

77. 21st February, 1789. *Newcastle Advertiser*.

"Married, Miss Henzell, only daughter of Paul Henzell Esq., one of the principal Glass-owners here."

78. 2nd May, 1789. *Newcastle Chronicle*.

"Died, at the Mushroom Glasshouse, Mr. John Soulsby, in his 49th year."

79. 3rd October, 1789. *Newcastle Advertiser*.

"King of the Glassmakers.

On Saturday last came on, at the house of Mr. Robert Elliot, in the Close in this town, the Election for a King of the glassmakers. The candidates for this high honour were the Hon. Sir John Turner and the Hon. Sir James Sanders, Glassmakers. During the poll the votes on each side were nearly equal: but at the close, Sir James obtained a majority. The following is the state of the poll:-

For Sir James	. . . .	500
„ Sir John	. . . .	498
Total	. . . .	998

Majority in favour of Sir James 2."

80. 18th September, 1790. *Newcastle Advertiser*.

"Deaths. At Tynemouth, Mr. Paul Henzell, an eminent Glass-owner in the 77th year of his age."

81. 19th March, 1791, *Newcastle Chronicle*.

"Joshua Henzell's Bankruptcy. The creditors are requested to take notice that his assignees will attend at the office of Catherine Henzell and Company at the Glasshouses on 22nd Inst., in order to pay the dividend of 7s. 6d. in the £."

82. 19th September, 1795. *Newcastle Chronicle*.

"Tyne Glass Company. We, John Banner and Francis Banner, partners in the Glass-house situate near Newcastle, with Mr. John Barber of that place, hereby give notice that we will not pay bills &c drawn by the said John Barber &c. And we request that all persons to whom the said Tyne Glasshouse Company now stand indebted, will send in an account to the office of Purvis & Surtees in Newcastle. 16th Sept. 1796."

19th September, 1796. (*Ibid.*),

"Tyne Glasshouse.

[After referring to above notice] John Banner and Francis Banner have not yet been able to advance their shares in the house; in June last, when their note to me for £1,000 became due, they could not take it up, and I gave them further time to pay that sum by instalments; a further large sum is due to me from Mr. John Banner on an account settled the 9th Instant, for which I have given directions to attach his property in London. I therefore refused to execute any deed of copartnership with them &c. &c.   JOHN BARBER"

26th September, 1796. (*Ibid.*)

Tyne Glass house. Rejoinder by Messrs. John & Francis Banner.

83. 11th June, 1796. *Newcastle Chronicle*.

Bankruptcy notice. John Barber, late of Newcastle, glass manufacturer.

84. 3rd September, 1796. *Newcastle Chronicle*.

"To be let and entered upon immediately the conveying of the Ballast from Mr. Isaac Cookson's Ballast Quay in South Shields. Apply to Mr. Samuel Wilson, at the Crown Glass House, South Shields."

85. 22nd April, 1797. *Newcastle Advertiser*.

"Alkaline Salts, Chrystals of Mineral Alkali or of Soda, Dried Chrystals of Alkali, Barilla Salts, Chrystals of Dried Pot Ash, Pearl Ashes of the usual strength, as are now preparing in large quantities at the Works established near Newcastle, from whence plate, flint, and crown glass manufacturers, Soap-makers, and Bleachers may be supplied with the article which suits their purpose: I hereby certify that I have made trial of the Pearl Ashes made by Lord Dundonald in making of flint glass and find it to answer the same as foreign pearl ashes.

Northumberland Glass Co. (Signed) John Dyson."

86. 29th April, 1797. *Newcastle Advertiser*.

"To the Northumberland Alkali Company. Gentlemen, I herewith send you a sample of flint glass made from the Pearl Ashes manufactured by Lord Dundonald, which for colour and plainness is equal if not superior to any I over saw made from foreign Pearl. I have pleasure in saying this sample was taken from the first and only essay I have made of his Lordship's Pearl Ashes.

I am For R. T. Shortridge and Co. and self, William Harrison, South Shields."

87. 4th October, 1800. *Newcastle Chronicle*.

"Being satisfied of the necessity of prosecuting any servant employed in our different manufactories stealing or embezzling glass and offering it for sale, we do hereby agree to prosecute at our joint expense any such offenders, or any person purchasing such glass, knowing it to be stolen, to the utmost rigour of the law.

 Airey, Cookson & Co.

 Northumberland Glass Co.

 R. T. Shortridge & Co."

88. The following probably relates to Newcastle glass, as the Tyne Glass-makers obtained broken glass from Woodbridge in 1788 (*Newcastle Courant* 31st May, 1788):-

 13th July, 1771. *Ipswich Journal*.

 "Glass Bottles will be sold until Michaelmas next at J. Stow's Bottle Warehouse on the Common Key, Woodbridge.

 Best Champagne Quarts at 24s. per gross or 2s. 1d. per doz.

 Common Quarts at 22s. per gross and 2s. per doz.

 Gentlemen may be supplied with square, octagon, or marked bottles, 'with name or arms' on shortest notice, all fruit bottles in proportion."

89. The following has been found recently:-

 23rd June, 1748. *Whitehall Evening Post*.

 "Mr. James Dixon is appointed by all the Partners receiver of what money is due to the Glass Company, late in the name of Cookson and Jeffreys, at the Glass-warehouse at Black-Fryars, London. The trade for Crown and Plate Glass is carried on there as formerly, in the name of John Cookson and Co."

APPENDIX II

Tyne Exports of Glass and Bottles

(1) Between 21st July, 1743 and 21st July, 1744 the following cargoes are recorded in the Newcastle Journal as leaving the Tyne:-

Destination	Cargoes Bottles	Glass
Rotterdam......	10	-
Hamburg......	2	6
Emden......	-	1
Dort......	6	1
Guernsey......	-	3
Boston [N.E.]......	1	3
Sound......	16	6
Dantzig......	1	-
Stralsound......	1	-
Oporto......	-	1
Christiansands......	-	1
Marseilles......	-	2
Ostend......	1	-
Lisbon......	2	1
Dunkirk......	1	-
Total......	40	2

(2) 1776. Hutchinson, *A View of Northumberland*, Vol. ii, pp. 464 *et seq*.

N.B. Probably the return for the purposes of the Excise Act, 1745; therefore "White Glass" means Crown, Plate and Flint Glass, "Green Glass" means Broad Glass and Bottles.

	Exported from Newcastle			
	White Glass		Green Glass	
	cwt.	qr.	cwt.	qr.
Africa......	31	2	565	2
Denmark and Norway	75	-	96	3
Germany......	298	-	41	3
Gibraltar	-	-	203	1
Guernsey......	4	3	248	1
Holland......	544	2	4,284	2
Jersey......	55	0	213	2
Ireland......	1,184	2	418	1
Portugal......	-	-	457	3
Russia......	58	2	3,002	3
Sweden......	20	1	-	-
West Indies......	46	0	-	-
Totals	115 tons 18 cwt.		476 tons 12 cwt. 3 qrs.	

APPENDIX III

Tyne Imports of Broken Glass

After 1788 numerous cargoes of broken glass were brought to the Tyne. The following imports appear during one year in the *Newcastle Chronicle*:-

Broken Glass

Date	Ship	Port of Export.
2.5.95	Nimble	London
30.5.95	,,	,,
13.6.95	Staff of Life	Yarmouth
27.6.95	Hope	Bridlington
4.7.95	Nimble	London
25.7.95	Traveller	,,
1.8.95	Nimble	,,
8.8.95	Hawk	Boston
15.8.95	Unity	Yarmouth
29.8.95	Traveller	London
,,	Concord	,,
12.9.95	Southampton	Southampton
10.10.95	Traveller	London
2.1.96	,,	,,
5.3.96	Nimble	,,
26.3.96	Concord	,,
30.4.96	Traveller	,,

The Early Glasshouses of Bristol*
By Francis BUCKLEY

The importance of Bristol as a glass-making centre during the 18th century has long been recognised; but hitherto very little has been said about the men who actually made the glass and carried on the business in this district. The names of the master workmen, who actually fabricated the glass during the century, are still preserved in the Bristol Poll Books, which contain lists of the burgesses voting at Parliamentary elections, together with their trade occupation. These lists, however, say little about the merchants and glass-masters of Bristol, who owned the Bristol glassworks, and who pushed the fame of Bristol glassworks to the four corners of the earth. The history of these glass-making firms, famous enough in their day, has had to be dug out of the old Bristol newspapers; a task that has been accomplished to a large extent by the author's brother, Dr. G. B. Buckley, M.C., who is, therefore, responsible for most of the recent discoveries in Bristol glass history.

The earliest record of glass-making in Bristol occurs about 1651, when Edward Dagney † (or Dagnia), an ingenious Italian, had a glasshouse at Bristol, of which the master was John Williams.‡ By the end of the 17th century the glass trade was firmly established in Bristol (1); in 1698 there were six glasshouses for bottles and four for making flint glass (2), one of the

---

* Note: The numbers in brackets refer to extracts in the Appendix.
† The Dagnias had glassworks at Newcastle and South Shields between 1697 and 1749 at any rate.
‡ D. Dudley, *Metallum Martis*, p. 22.

bottle houses also made window glass.§ In 1722, there were fifteen glasshouses in Bristol,|| in 1761 also fifteen,** and in 1794 "about 12." †† The latter statement is perhaps misleading; the Bristol Guide Map of 1815 shows fourteen glasshouse cones in the map area, two others are known just outside this area, and others not far from Bristol.

Matthews states that in 1794 there was no decline in Bristol glass-making, but rather an increase. The "12 glasshouses" of 1794 probably then refer to twelve glass concerns or firms. Towards the end of the century there were various' combines of glass firms, of which the most notable' result was the famous Phoenix Glass Works. The four Bristol glasshouses mentioned in the Parliamentary return of 1833 probably give no idea of the extent of the glass business, even at that date.

Glass-making did begin to decline in Bristol during the early part of the 19th century; and the following reasons may be given for the gradual loss of the trade. The glass-makers, generally, preferred to have their works nearer to the great coalfields in the north of England; and Bristol had only a moderate supply of coal from Kingswood (8), &c. The increase after 1780 of glass-making in Ireland and the prosperity of the Irish glasshouses deprived Bristol of its old market in Ireland and the Farther West. The people of Bristol seem about this time to have lost some of their former business enterprise; for example, they neglected to enlarge their docks and so lost to the city much of its former importance as a great seaport.

---

§ Houghton, *Letters on Trade*, 1696.
|| Defoe.
** Evans.
†† Matthews.

At first Bristol was chiefly famed for its fine window glass and bottles. R. Neve,* writing in 1703, says that Bristol window glass was better than most kinds, but was seldom seen in London owing to the difficulty of getting it there. This difficulty was not really removed until 1792, when the Thames and Severn Canal was opened (74, 83).

Bristol is also famed to-day for the special kinds of flint glass that were produced there. Enamel and coloured glasses were made perhaps in greater quantities in Bristol than anywhere else; and this kind of Bristol glass is now much prized. But Bristol lagged behind at first in the production of the popular cut glass, and the glass-makers had in consequence to meet in the city itself a serious competition on the part of the London cut-glass makers between 1763 and 1785. The City Poll Books show that the men of Bristol owed little during the 18th century to foreign or outside glass-makers; most of the names in these lists are typical of the West Country; but the glass-makers of Bristol took their special knowledge of enamel glasses into Ireland, Lancashire, and elsewhere; and in these places prosperous glassworks were founded by Bristol men.

The Glasshouses Without Templegate

Two glasshouses are shown in the Bristol Guide of 1815, standing about 100 yards apart in Red Lane, or, as it was called more generically in the old days, "Without Templegate." It is quite possible that both were included in the Phoenix Glass Works, which are said to have been commenced here in, 1785. If not, then it seems that the older glasshouse was abandoned before the end of the 18th century, as there is no trace of it in any

---

* Builder's Dictionary.

record after 1785. The earlier glasshouse Without Templegate must have been in existence before 1752, for in that year it was let to Messrs. Taylor at the heavy rent of £125 per annum, and the inference, therefore, is that it was then a going concern and able to command a heavy rent (25). This was known as "the Glasshouse Without Templegate," and it stood in close relation to the Phoenix Inn (33). The head of the firm of Messrs. Taylor was Daniel Taylor, senior, who took a residence (23) in Bedminster on long lease in 1716 and was probably lessee also of the Bedminster Glasshouse. But in 1734 and 1739 the Taylors are found to be voting in the Parish of St. Phillip and Jacob, and they may then have had an interest in the Hoopers glasshouse. When they took a 21 years' lease of the Glasshouse without Templegate they came to a going concern; but it cannot be said who the previous proprietors were or what they made. It is known, however, that the Taylors were window glass- and possibly also bottle-makers (53) until 1783. Daniel Taylor, senior, died (24) in 1755. He was probably succeeded by his sons Samuel and Daniel Taylor, who are mentioned as owners (32) in 1762. Daniel Taylor, junior, died in 1796. Samuel Taylor was alive, probably a child (23), in 1712. The twenty-one years' lease of the glasshouse came to an end (25) in 1773; and it seems to have been renewed to the firm of James Taylor and Brothers (53). In 1783, this partnership was dissolved, or at least Samuel Taylor dropped out (53). In 1785, the two other partners, James and George Taylor, founded a large flint glass manufactory on a neighbouring site.* This became the nucleus of the celebrated Phoenix Glass Works, and it stood on the site of the Phoenix Inn (63). Its original name was, however, "The Phoenix Flint Glass-House." The Taylors soon disposed of their interest in the new glasshouse, and we hear of them no more. Their successors in 1789 were Wadham, Ricketts and Company (63). The partners were probably John Wadham, senior (who also had a glass business in Horse Street and died in 1796), Richard Ricketts, David Evans, and Jacob Wilcox Ricketts (89, 90, 96). In 1797, the firm name had become Ricketts, Evans, and Ricketts; and in 1801 Richard Ricketts dropped out and the firm became, Ricketts, Evans, and the Phoenix Glass Company (96). The junior partners were probably those who had previously been interested in' the Redcliff Backs Glasshouse, which was now absorbed. This group of glasshouses is described in the Bristol Guide of 1815. The making of flint glass cannot be traced after 1830, and the 'works were closed before 1874.*

The St. Thomas Street Glasshouse

This glasshouse, situated 200 yards north of St. Mary Redcliff Church, was probably one of the 17th century glasshouses; and it was well known at an early date for its fine window glass and bottles. It was for many years in the hands of the family of Warren. In 1712, Richard Warren and Co. advertised their crown window glass and bottles in a London newspaper (3). To do this they must have had time to acquire a considerable local reputation. John Warren voted as a freeholder in the parish of Temple in 1739, and he was probably connected with this glasshouse. In 1752 Thomas Warren and Co. were making some of their bottles here with brass moulds (18); an interesting departure in bottle-making, worthy of note at this early date. The next firm name is J. and T. Warren, and in 1768 the family took in outside partners, and the firm became J. and T. Warren, Richard Cannington, Richard Reynolds, and William Cowles (43). In 1770, Cannington and Reynolds seem to have gone to the Temple Street

---

* Hugh Owen, Two Centuries of Ceramic Art in Bristol, p. 386.

Glasshouse. Owen* states (possibly in error) that Vigor and Stevens were making flint glass here between 1775 and 1787, if so, the glasshouse soon returned to the manufacture of crown glass, and it is thought that the principal manufacture was always crown glass (64).

In 1778, the full firm name was Vigor, Stevens, and Hill (49), and in 1789 it was Vigor, Stevens, Randolph, and Stevens (68). In 1790, William Stevens and Son,† and shortly afterwards William Stevens, James Stevens, John Cave, and George Daubeny (76) or shortly Stevens, Cave and Co. James Stevens dropped out (77) in 1793, and a little later the whole partnership was dissolved (79). The business was, however, continued under the name of William Stevens and Glass Company (82) until William Stevens became bankrupt about 1798, when the Glasshouse was offered for sale. It would appear that at this time, besides William Stevens, George Daubeny, and John Cave, junior, were other parties interested in the business (92).

After this there is no trace of the St. Thomas Street Crown Glass House, although it is marked on the map of 1815. One is bound to conclude either that it was abandoned, or that it was taken over by the Phoenix Glass Works.

The Redcliff Backs Glasshouse

There was a glasshouse on the Redcliff Backs, about 150 yards north-west of St. Mary Redcliff's Church, in the first half of the 18th century, if not earlier. The manufacture was of flint and green glass. It was owned before 1750 by the firm of Jones, who were prominent Bristol glass-makers (15). In 1750, it passed to

---

* Owen, loc. cit.
† Directory.

Messrs. Crosse and Berrow, who became, bankrupt (29) in 1760.

Although unsuccessful from a business point of view, it is probable that Crosse and Berrow were the first in Bristol to make the celebrated Bristol enamel glass (30), The expression "white and flint glass" has no meaning, unless it includes white enamel glass (35). On the sale of this glasshouse, Messrs. Little and Longman went into possession;, from 1762, at any rate, and onwards,: enamel glass was being made here * In 1767 the firm was Longman and Vigor.*

The subsequent history of the glasshouse is for a time connected with that of the St. Thomas Street Glasshouse. Between, 1774 and 1786, the firm was Vigor and Stevens or possibly Vigor, Stevens, and Hill (45, 49, 57).

In 1789, Vigor, Stevens, Randolph, and Stevens (64, 66, 67, 68). In 1790, probably William Stevens and Son (*Directory*), and shortly afterwards Stevens, Cave and Co. (76). In 1793, William Stevens and Glass Company (79, 82). In spite of the bankruptcy of William Stevens (92) in 1798, this branch of the .business seems to have been continued in his name. In the Directory of 1801, we find William Stevens "glass concern," Redcliff Backs. But in 1801 the works carried on at Redcliff Backs, known by the firm name of "Stevens Glass Concern," were consolidated with and became part of the Phoenix Glass Works (96).

The Temple Street Glasshouses

There were at least two glasshouses in Temple Street, and another hard by in Portwall Lane which might be included in the regional description of "Temple Street."

---

* Owen, loc. cit.

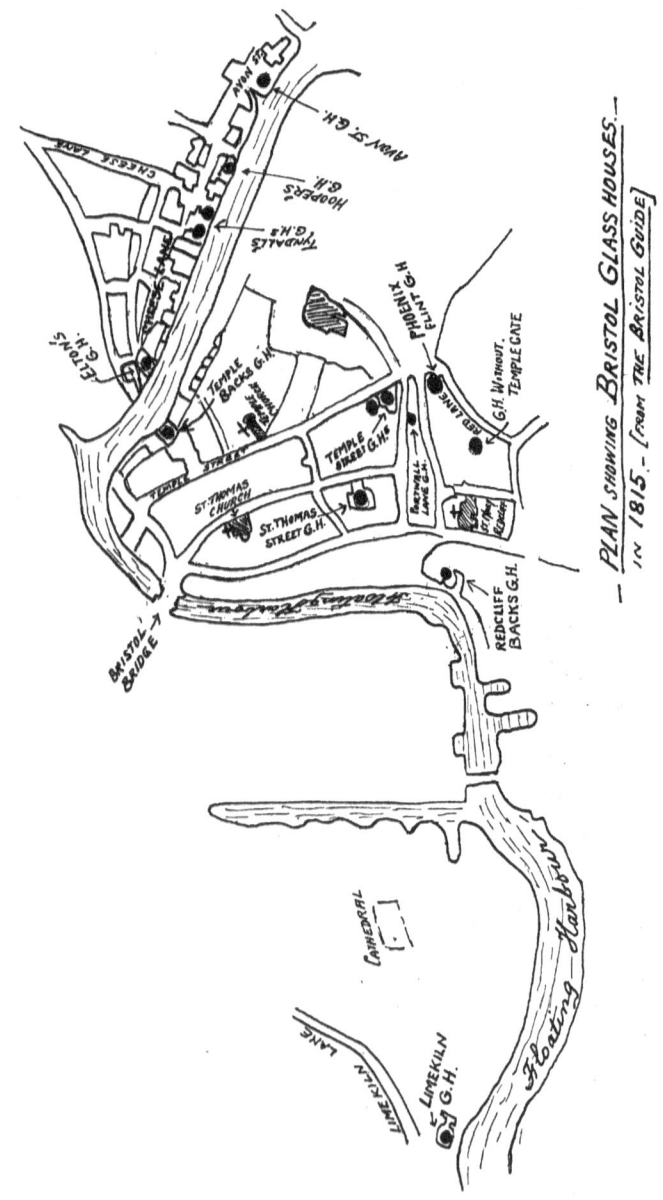

(a) The Glasshouse at Temple Gate

This was probably always a flint glasshouse; it was certainly such during the last quarter of the 18th century. "For many years" prior to 1741 it was worked by Messrs. Collier Cook and Co., and in 1741 the partnership was styled Francis Cook and Co. (11). In 1755, Francis Cook voted as "glassman" in the Parish of Temple; but shortly afterwards the glasshouse passed to the firm of Richard Cannington and Co. Richard Cannington had interests about this time in several glasshouses. The Temple Street firm was Richard Cannington, Richard Reynolds, and Cornelius Fry (56); and it is first mentioned (44) in 1772. Sketchley's *Directory* of 1775 gives the firm name as Richard Cannington and Co. In 1786, Cannington bought out his two partners and continued the business under the old name. In 1789 he made over the business to William Fry, James Jones, John Mayo Tandey and Co., who, however, continued to trade as Richard Cannington and Co. (65). Matthews,* writing in 1794, implied very strongly that this glasshouse had been taken over by and was worked as part of the Phoenix Glass Works; and this idea is corroborated by the subsequent description of the Phoenix Glass Works as "at Temple Gate" and not merely "Without Temple Gate." Richard Cannington died in 1793 (80).

(b) Perrott's Glasshouses

It is melancholy to record the fate of an ingenious but commercially unsuccessful glass-maker. Humphry Perrott, maker of crown window glass, has long been known to fame as the inven-

---

* *New History of Bristol*, pp. 40 et seq.

tor of improved glass furnaces and kilns.† His family came from Stourbridge way.‡ For some years prior to 1734 he had been experimenting with new furnaces and kilns in connection with the crown glass industry, and on February 15th, 1734, he was granted a patent for fourteen years in respect of his new inventions. Unfortunately, however, shortly before his invention came out or was accepted, namely, on November 10th, 1733, he was advertised as a bankrupt (6). He had a residence, and "glass-houses" in Temple Street, which were advertised for sale (13) on September 8th, 1744. So far as we can judge at present, one of these glasshouses was the one immediately north of Cook's glass-house, the other was probably that in Portwall Lane. Probably in consideration of his patent the creditors waited for ten years before deciding to sell up his effects. Perhaps no one took the glass-house in Portwall Lane, or perhaps Perrott occupied it till his death in 1757; for this glass-house is offered for sale, "formerly in the possession of Humphry Perrott," in 1766 (40). Perrott's will is preserved in the Bristol Registry of Wills. As the Portwall Lane glasshouse was subject only to a yearly chief rent of 20s., the presumption is that Perrott had erected it himself. There is something to be said for the suggestion that the owners of the St. Thomas Street Glasshouse eventually took over the Portwall Lane Glasshouse and used it in connection with their business there. There were certainly in 1798 two glass-house cones' in connection with this business, "situate in Portwall Lane and St. Thomas Street" (92); but the old description of the premises is not sufficiently definite to enable us to come to a certain opinion upon the point.

---

† Hartshorne, p. 458.
‡ See Grazebrook, *Worcestershire Families*.

With regard to Perrott's Glasshouse in Temple Street, Owen states that Lazarus Jacobs (who in 1775 was working as a glass-cutter and engraver at 108 Temple Street) had a flint glasshouse in Temple Street at any rate between 1785 and 1787. Later on he moved to Great Gardens, where he died (87) in 1796. Here his son and successor, Isaac Jacobs, won fame and became glass-maker* to the King.

Nothing is known of the subsequent history of this glasshouse; as it was apparently next door to Cannington's glasshouse, it was probably absorbed first into, that concern and then, into the Phoenix Glass Works.

The Temple Backs Glasshouse

In the first half of the 18th century Robert Bradley and Co. had a glasshouse, probably for making bottles, on Temple Backs, near the present bridge over the Harbour. It was offered (16) on lease in 1750; after this nothing definite is known before 1801, when Thomas Jones and Co. are stated to have been making black bottles there.†

It is quite likely that when Messrs. Jones left the Redcliff Backs glasshouse in 1750, they transferred their business to this glass-house. James Jones was interested for a time in Cannington's Temple Street glasshouse (67), and later on in a bottle house at Crewshole (see below). The firm name of Farrell and Jones occurs (49) in 1778.

The Limekiln Glasshouse

This glasshouse was situated near Limekiln Dock, in the parish of St. Augustine's, the only glasshouse in this parish. To give a

---

* Powell, *Glassmaking*.
† Directory.

modern description, it stood on the north bank of the Floating Harbour, due south of Brandon Hill, a little to the west of the present gas works. It must have been founded before 1722, for in that year William Wood "glassmaker" voted in St. Augustine's parish. In 1745, the Limekiln Glasshouse was offered on lease with immediate possession (14), apparently by John Clement, Esq. Perhaps Mr. Hill took over the glasshouse; at any rate he is found in possession (31) in 1761. He died in 1762.*

In Sketchley's *Directory* of 1775 a number of glass-makers are recorded living about the Limekilns; for example, Cornelius Rogers, Edward Williams, and William Child; and Thomas Short on Brandon Hill. They may have been partners. In 1780, John Short was one of those in occupation of the Glass House (52); and the death of Mr. Child, a proprietor, is mentioned in 1790 (71).

In 1790, John Nicholas and Co. took over the glasshouse and used it as a bottle works, which it probably always was (78). The firm consisted at first of John Nicholas, Richard Stratton, and John Robert Lucas (the latter of Nailsea fame). In 1793, Lucas dropped out (78), and in 1795 Stratton also withdrew (85). From this date to 1833 at any rate, John Nicholas and Co. made bottles at the Limekiln Glasshouse. In 1816, it seems to have been one of the principal bottle houses of Bristol.†

The Cheese Lane Glasshouses

Cheese Lane lies along the north bank of the Floating Harbour and was outside the old City, in the parish of St. Phillip and Jacob. In the middle of the 18th century there were four or five

---

* *Bath Chronicle*, October 21st, 1762.
† Corry and Evans, *History of Bristol*, II. p. 307.

glasshouses here, some of which must have been established between 1734 and 1739. In 1734, only eleven "glass-makers" voted in this parish; but in 1739 their numbers had increased to twenty-eight, nearly twice the number voting in any other parish in Bristol. Owing to this concentration of glasshouses, it is often difficult to disentangle their history from the old advertisements.

(a) Elton's Glasshouse probably the St. Phillip's Glasshouse

The Eltons were an important family in Bristol and continually held office in the City corporation, etc. Their glasshouse stood near the Ferry in St. Phillip's. During repairs the glasshouse collapsed (7) in the year 1736. This indicates that it was already an old glass-house. It was owned at the time by Sir Abraham Elton, Bart. (in 1738 Sheriff of Bristol and in 1741 M.P.), who died in or before November, 1742.‡ It is mentioned again in 1751 as "Mr. Elton's glasshouse" (17). In 1790 and in 1794, the firm was Elton, Miles and Co., and in 1801 Elton, Miles, and Wilcox. The manufacture was of crown glass and bottles.

Elton's glasshouse stood near the present passage over the Floating Harbour, and was probably that known as "St. Phillip's Glasshouse" (59).

(b) Tyndall's Glasshouses

Going south-east along Cheese Street (or Lane), about 350 yards from Elton's Glasshouse, there was a group of three glasshouses. The first two are believed to be those known in 1751 as "Mr. Tyndall's Glasshouses" (17). An advertisement of this date mentions the sale of certain property, which lay between Mr. Elton's glasshouse and "Mr. Tyndall's first glasshouse." Apparently Tho-

---

‡ *Daily Post*, November 30th, 1742.

mas Tyndall had a long lease of these two glasshouses; and he seems to have assigned the beneficial interest in them before 1766 to a firm called William King and Co., including William King, Thomas Harris, and James Allcott. The manufacture here was of crown glass and bottles; and it is probable that the glasshouses were erected by Thomas Tyndall between 1734 and 1739.* In 1766, disputes occurred between the partners; and Messrs. Tyndall Pennington and Rogers (not necessarily a firm, of glass-makers) intervened and took over the winding up of the partnership concern (38, 39, 42). After this, the actual history of the two glasshouses is obscure, but Messrs. Coghlan, Peach and Co., who had a glass-house in 1790 in St. Phillip's (70) and were importing large quantities of kelp in 1778 and 1779 (49), probably took over one of Tyndall's glasshouses.

Robert Hurst, a Bristol bottle-maker in 1785, is known, but not the place of his glasshouse, and the Bristol Directory of 1794 gives Hester Hodder and Edward Smart as glass-makers in Cheese Lane. Any of these may have worked at the second of "Tyndall's Glasshouses."

(c) The Hoopers Glasshouse

The third of the group of glasshouses mentioned above was probably the Hoopers Glasshouse, which is always described as in St. Phillip and Jacob. Messrs. Hooper Brothers are known to fame as bottle-makers of Bristol.† They were in all probability the founders of this glasshouse, which was called the Hoopers Glasshouse at any rate between 1744 and 1765. At the latter date it was offered for sale as a going concern (36); and a careful study of the advertisement allows certain inferences to be fairly drawn

---

* See Poll Books.
† Powell, *Glassmaking in England*, p. 99.

as to its previous history. "The present lease has fifty-five years to come and is subject to aground rent of £12 per annum." We can deduce from this that a lease was granted for ninety-nine years in the year 1721, and also that there had been a former lease. The glasshouse was, therefore, probably founded towards the close of the 17th century by the Hooper family. It is almost certainly referred to in 1744, although it is called (presumably by a printer's error) the "Coopers Glasshouse"(12).

In 1752, two shares in the Hoopers Glasshouse were offered for sale (20). The Taylors may have had an interest in the concern up to this date; for they voted in St. Phillip's in 1734 and 1739, and just after the offer of the two shares they got their lease of the Glasshouse-Without-Templegate (25).

In 1765, the partnership at the Hoopers Glasshouse came to an end, and the glasshouse and stock were offered by the proprietors as a going concern (36). It was taken over probably at this point, by the firm of Cannington, Lawson and Co. (46), the leading men being Richard Cannington and Robert Lawson. In March, 1775, Cannington sold his share, and the firm became Cowles, Dowell, Lawson and Co.*

In 1786, the firm was Lawson, Fry, Frampton and Co.†; and the firm appears in the Directory of 1790 as Lawson, Fry and Co. of Cheese Lane; and in that of 1801 as Fry, Frampton and Co. of St. Phillip's, Robert Lawson having died (46) in 1794.

In 1812, the Cooksons (Joseph and Septimus) took over the glass-house, appearing in the Bristol Guide of 1815 as Cookson and Co. In 1824, the firm became Cookson and Powell, and in.

---

* William Cowles, Richard Reynolds, John Dowell, Richard Frampton, Cornelius Fry, and Robert Lawson (46).
† Powell, p. 99.

1831 Powell Brothers and Co.‡ In the Directory of 1838, a change of address from Cheese Lane to Avon Street may be noticed; the latter was a continuation of Cheese Lane, and a glasshouse stood in Avon Street in 1815.

The Crewshole Glasshouse

A bottle glasshouse called the Crew's Hole Glasshouse stood on the north bank of the Avon about two miles to the east of the old City. It was one of Thomas Tyndall's group of three glasshouses, which he held on long lease, and assigned before 1766 to William King and Co. (39, 51).

In spite of the disagreements between William King and his partners (38, 39, 42), William King carried on this glasshouse until his death in 1777 (47, 50, 51). It was then, for a while, worked by G. Bowser on behalf of King's executors, until it was sold in 1778. At this time, Mr. Charles Powell was manager of the works (51). The name of Powell was later on to be associated with some of the principal glassworks in Bristol. The Crew's Hole glasshouse seems have been bought by Mr. James Jones, a member of a well-known Bristol glass-making family, and carried on by him until he died in 1795 (84, 88, 95). After that it was advertised for sale six times before 1800, and nothing further has been learnt of its history except that it was working in 1798, probably under the executors of James Jones.*

Bedminster

There is clear evidence of one glasshouse in this suburb of Bristol. In the four Polls between 1722 and 1754 glass-makers voted

---

‡ see generally Powell, Glassmaking in England.
* F. F. Bristol Journal, April 7th, 1798.

in this area; and in 1789 William Barrett† says that a glasshouse in Bedminster occupied the old site of the former Hospital of St. Catherine (61). Daniel Taylor, senior, took a long lease of premises in Bedminster in 1716 (23), and voted for the district in 1722; and it is therefore most probable that he was for some years about this time working the glasshouse. The Taylors, it will be remembered, were makers of window glass and probably of bottles.

In 1830, Daniel Wilmot had a glasshouse here.‡

The Chepstow Glasshouse

Although some sixteen miles from Bristol and across the Severn in Monmouthshire, this glasshouse was a Bristol trading venture. We are told by Owen that the glasshouse was founded by a Bristol firm; and it certainly had a warehouse in Bristol. The product was the enamel and flint glass, for which Bristol was famous. Here Williams, Dunbar and Co. set up a glasshouse and started work in October, 1764 (35). For about a year the glasshouse was continually advertised in *Felix Farley's Bristol Journal*; a fact which somewhat discounts the glowing description of the "hands" employed. It is thought that Williams probably, left the firm to take up the glass business in Ireland; as this family in 1764 obtained a premium from the Dublin Society for flint glass.§ Whilst in June, 1766, Dunbar and Co. (Dunbar and Bradley) opened a warehouse in Dublin (37).

A further change took place in November, the same year, when Bradley left the firm, and Isaac Hays Dunbar announced that in future he would carry on business by himself (41). Mr.

---

† *History of Bristol.*
‡ *Directory.*
§ Westropp, *Irish Glass* (1913), p. 28.

Westropp has pointed out that Dunbar also went to Ireland as a glass-maker; for he appears as "glassmaker Dublin" in a list of insolvent debtors under a Relief Act of 1778. The venture at Chepstow was probably, therefore, short-lived.

The Nailsea Heath Glasshouses

Nailsea, situated a few miles south-west of Bristol, has become famous of late years for a certain kind of fancy bottle glass once made there, but the glassworks were founded for more serious purposes. John Robert Lucas, who was the moving spirit in the establishment of these works, had for many years before 1788 been engaged in the beer and cyder business in Nicolas Street, Bristol (60). He was also a partner in the Limekiln Bottle House, which he left in 1793 (78).

In 1788, J. R. Lucas, Henry Pater, and William Coathupe established the first Nailsea Glasshouse for making crown glass and bottles (75). Shortly afterwards, a second crown glasshouse was erected here, which was damaged by a fire (69) in May, 1790. On March 30th, 1793, the firm name changed to John Robert Lucas, William Chance, Edward Homer, and William Coathupe (75). From the first this firm had their warehouse in Nicholas Street.* The crown glass-making flourished here so well that in 1835 the Nailsea glassworks were considered one of the four most important window glass factories in England.† It was probably a family affair from first to last, although in the Directories the names change rather abruptly. For example, the Bristol Guide of 1815 gives Lucas, Chance and Co.; 1830 Lucas, Coathupe, and Homer; 1833 and 1853, Coathupes and Co. The factory

---

* *Directories.*
† Powell, p. 106.

closed in 1873. The association of R. L. Chance (later on of Spon Lane) with the Nailsea glassworks, where he learnt the business, is an indication of their efficiency.

Chelwood

Chelwood, about nine miles from Bristol, was the site of an old-established glass-making business about which very little is definitely known. It is mentioned by Houghton in 1696 as making window glass, but nothing further is heard of it until January 6th, 1787 when the bankruptcy notice of John Adams was inserted in the London Gazette. Adams was described as glass-maker of Chelwood. Apparently he was allowed to continue the business until his death, for on January 16th, 1796, there is a notice in the Bristol papers of a renewed commission of bankruptcy against John Adams, glass manufacturer, deceased (86).

Acknowledgment

The author is glad to express his hearty thanks to his brother, Dr. G. B. Buckley, for his great assistance in unearthing much of the newspaper record of glass-making in Bristol.

APPENDIX

Sources of Information
Extracts from Newspapers, etc.

(1) 29th January, 1698. *Journals H. C.* xii, 74.

A petition against the Glass Tax was presented to the House of Commons by William Clark, owner of glassworks in or near Bristol.

(2) 21st May, 1698. *Journals H. C.* xii, 281-283.

Henry Dixon, a workman at a Bristol glasshouse, gave evidence in the House of Commons that there were 6 Bottle Houses at Bristol, and 4 "white-houses" at work there.

(3) 17th May, 1712. *Post Man*.

"At Mr. Richard Warrens and Company's Glasshouse in St. Thomas Street, Bristol are to be sold all sorts of very good Crown Glass, wholesale or retale; and at the same house are made all sorts of very good Bottles; all sold as cheap as at any place in England."

(4) 8th June, 1720. *Daily Post*.

"Whereas several eminent merchants and tradesmen in the City of London and Bristol have mutually engaged to enter into a copartnership for making of glass bottles and glass. Books will be opened, &c."

(5) 18th July, 1722. *Freeholders' Journal*.

"Bristol Water for sale in Bottles. The empty bottles at 2s. per dozen. N.B. The bottles are large and London-shaped."

(6) 10th November, 1733. *London Gazette*.

"Humphry Perrott of the City of Bristol, glassmaker, bankrupt."

(7) 8th June, 1736. *General Advertiser*.

"They write from Bristol that on Friday last [4th June] about 11 o'clock in the forenoon a large Glasshouse belonging to Sir Abraham Elton Bart. near the Ferry in St. Phillips', suddenly fell down; happy it was for the Glass-men that the Fire was out, and only some few masons were employed in the repair of it."

(8) 17th October, 1738. *General Advertiser*.

It is stated that the glasshouses of Bristol were supplied with small coal by the colliers of Kingswood.

(9) 14th November, 1738. *Daily Post*.

"Bristol, Nov. 11. Yesterday the Prince .and Princess of Wales paid their promised visit to this City ... The Companies of the City made a magnificent appearance in their formalities, marching two by two, preceding the Corporation and the Royal Guests. The Company of Glassmen went first dressed in white Holland shirts, on horseback, some with swords, others with crowns and sceptres in their hands made of glass."

(10) 29th March, 1743. *Daily Advertiser*.

"Bristol, March 26. Last week a Glassman in Temple Street died."

(11) 26th November, 1743. Bristol *Oracle*.

"Whereas a partnership was for many years carry'd on in a Glass-House in Temple Street Bristol in the names of Collier, Cook & Co. But about 2 years ago the style of the said partnership was altered to Francis Cook & Co. and hath ever since so continued. Now these are to desire all persons who are or shall be indebted to the said Copartners not to pay such debts to any person except the said Francis Cook or his order.

"Francis Cook for self and company."

(12) 16th June, 1744. *Bristol Oracle*.

"To be sold 4 messuages situate near the Coopers (? Hoopers) Glass House in the Out Parish of St. Phillip and Jacob near this city."

(13) 8th September, 1744. *Bristol Oracle*.

"To be sold the dwellinghouse, glasshouses &c Late of Humphry Perrott, a bankrupt, situate in Temple Street Bristol."

(14) 2nd February, 1745. *Bristol Oracle*.

"To be lett and entered upon immediately the Limekiln Glasshouse, dwellinghouse and premises, together with or without some meadow adjoining. Enquire of John Clement Esq."

(15) 18th August, 1750. *Bristol Weekly Intelligencer*.

"The glasshouse on Redcliff Backs (late Jones's) is now carried on by Messrs. Crosse and Borrow. Where all sorts of the best flint and green glass are made and sold wholesale and retail at reasonable rates."

(16) 1st December, 1750. *Bristol Weekly Intelligencer*.

"To be lett and entered on immediately a convenient glasshouse with proper warehouses, situate on Temple Backs, late in the possession of Robert Bradley & Co."

(17) 1st June, 1751. *Bristol Weekly Intelligencer*.

"To be sold the following houses in Cheese Lane … near Mr. Elton's glasshouse. Three houses opposite Mr. Tyndall's first glass-house … All situate within the Parish of St. Phillip in Bristol."

(18) 15th August, 1752. *Felix Farley's Bristol Journal*.

"On Thursday James Watkins was committed to Newgate for stealing one Brass Bottle-mould, value 18s., the property of Mr. Thomas Warren & Co. from the Glasshouse in St. Thomas Street in this City. It seems the said Watkins worked at the glasshouse, and sold the mould to a Brazier of this City at a market price." [N.B. 16th Sept. 1752. *F. F. Bristol Journal*. James Watkins for stealing 2 brass bottle-moulds – acquitted.]

(19) 22nd August, 1752. *F. F. Bristol Journal*.

"Among the several causes try'd at our Assizes before Mr. Baron Smythe was one of great consequence to the trade of this City, concerning a drawback of 2s. 4d. per cwt. on Bottles exported full of liquor, amounting to £5,000 per annum in this City alone."

(20) 29th August, 1752. *Bristol Weekly Intelligencer*.

"To be sold two shares in the Hoopers Glasshouse, situate in the Parish of St. Phillip and St. Jacob."

(21) 8th February, 1755. *F. F. Bristol Journal*.

"Married at Temple Church Mr. John Painton "glass-man" to Miss Keinton."

(22) 8th March, 1755. *F. F. Bristol Journal*.

"To be sold, a messuage in St. Thomas Street in Bristol, now in possession of Edward Parker " glass-man," under rent £7 16s. 0d. per annum."

(23) 29th March, 1755. *F. F. Bristol Journal*.

"To be sold [in Hartingham near Red-Cliff in the Parish of Bedminster] the following premises having a commodious messuage and garden thereon, with several structures and other edifices now held by Mr. Daniel Taylor, glassmaker, for the remainder of a lease granted in 1716 for 99 years determinable on the death of his sons Samuel and Benjamin Taylor."
(24) 19th April, 1755. *F. F. Bristol Journal.*

26th April. "Monday last died Mr. Daniel Taylor, Senior, glass-maker."
(25) 2nd December, 1758. *F. F. Bristol Journal.*

"To be sold by auction a messuage situate without Temple-Gate in the parish of St. Mary Redcliffe in Bristol. And also the Glasshouse, Warehouses, Pot-Chambers, Mill, Stable, Compting-House and Edifices, situate near the said messuage, together with an Horse Engine for raising water, and the feathers and shutes to the same belonging, which said premises are now lett to Messrs. Taylor for 21 years whereof 15 are yet to come, under yearly rent £125."
(26) 23rd December, 1758. *F. F. Bristol Journal.*

"Yesterday morning a fire broke out in a Pot house adjoining to the Glasshouse in St. Phillips."
(27) 9th February, 1760. *Bristol Chronicle.*

Bridge Committee.
"Resolved that a tax on coal be taken. That nine-tenths of what shall be paid as a duty on coal used in the glass manufactory shall be returned; and also one half of what shall be paid by other manufacturers."
(28) 8th March, 1760. *Bristol Chronicle.*

"The Bridge Committee included Robert Vigor and John Peach."
(29) 17th May, 1760. *Bristol Chronicle.*

"Bankrupt, – John Crosse and John Berrow of Bristol,

glassmen."

(30) 7th June, 1760. *Bristol Chronicle*.

"Notice is hereby given that the Glass House on Redcliff Backs, late Crosse and Borrow, on which there is a term of about 8 years yet to come, together with the utensils and materials for carrying on the trade will be disposed of on advantageous terms … The Stock in trade, consisting of every sort of the best White and Flint Glass Wares, is now selling on the very lowest terms."

(31) 18th April, 1761. *Bristol Chronicle*.

"Whereas a report generally pervades that Mr Hill * at Lime Kiln Glass-House had received from my shop on St. Augustine's Back a composition, instead of Glauber's Salts, &c."

(32) 5th June, 1762. *F. F. Bristol Journal*.

"Eloped from his Masters Samuel and Daniel Taylor (after having forged their hands to Messrs. Lloyd, Elton & Co.'s Bank) Thomas Holden. Information to Samuel and Daniel Taylor glassmakers Without-Temple-gate Bristol."

(33) 3rd July, 1762. *F. F. Bristol Journal*.

"To be lett, the Phoenix Inn Without Templegate, lately filled up Enquire of Daniel Taylor at the Glasshouse."

(34) 15th October, 1763. *F. F. Bristol Journal*.

"Lost or stolen out of the China Warehouse Broad Street Bristol (inter alia) 'two blue and gold glass toilet bottles without the stoppers; a bellied pomatum pot with enamell'd flowers, not the proper cover with it.'"

(35) 20th October, 1764. *F. F. Bristol Journal*.

"This is to acquaint the public that there is now opened at Chepstow South Wales a flint and enamel glass manufactory, where merchants &c. may depend on being supplied with all

---

* Mr. Hill died in 1792. *Bath Chronicle*, 21st October, 1762.

sorts of the best flint glass. Also apothecaries' green phials; and every other article made in the neatest manner and on the best terms by

Williams, Dunbar & Co.

As the above company have spared no pains nor expence to procure the best Hands in England they flatter themselves that their goods will give general satisfaction."

[N.B. – This advertisement was repeated for many weeks, and a warehouse was opened in Bristol.]

(36) 28th September, 1765. *F. F. Bristol Journal.*

"For sale by auction The Hoopers Glasshouse, situate in the Parish of St. Phillip's; with all the Buildings Outhouses and Materials, together with large quantities of Sand, Kelp, Clay, Pots, Glass, 16 tons of Hay, 6 horses &c &c. This glasshouse is known to be well situated and commodious for this manufactory, has lately had a very thorough repair and lies convenient to the River with a very good wharf. The present lease has 55 years to come and is subject to a ground rent of £12 per annum."

(37) 14th June, 1766. *Faulkner's Dublin Journal.* [per Mr. M. S. D. Westropp.]

"Dunbar & Co., Glass Manufacturers, Chepstow near Bristol, have opened a warehouse at the lower end of Fishamble Street (Dublin) where are sold wholesale, Jellies and Whips, Wine glasses, Decanters, Globes, Lamps and Shades, Square Garde-vins."

(38) 16th August, 1766. *F. F. Bristol Journal.*

"Bristol., Aug. 15, 1766. Notice is hereby given that the late partnership between William King and Thomas Harris is dissolved. And such persons as have any claim thereon are to deliver the same to the said Harris, to whom all partnership debts are to be paid and to no other person."

(39) 4th October, 1766. *F. F. Bristol Journal.*

"4th Oct. 1766. For sale by auction The Stock Implements

Utensils Kelp Fret Sand Ashes Pots Bricks Clay and a great number of other things commonly used in making Crown Window Glass and Glass Bottles, belonging to 2 glasshouses in Cheese Lane within the parish of St. Philip and Jacob in the County of Gloucester, and to one other glasshouse at Crew's Hole within the parish of St. George in the same County, lately occupied by William King and Company. Also a parcel of Crown Glass and Glass Bottles. Also one undivided third of the last mentioned glasshouse for the remainder of a term of years determinable on the life of James Smith.

"Also one third of the equitable right and interest in the two glass-houses in Cheese Lane for the remainder of the lease."

"3rd October, 1766. I the under written James Allcott being a Co-assignee with Thomas Harris Esq. in the sale of the above-mentioned premises do hereby certify that I have not agreed thereto."

(40) 25th October, 1766. *F. F. Bristol Journal.*

To be sold by auction a glasshouse in Port-Wall-Lane, formerly in possession of Humphry Perrott, on yearly chief rent of 20s."

(41) 22nd November, 1766. *F. F. Bristol Journal.*

"Whereas the partnership between Messrs. Dunbar and Bradley glass makers of Chepstow in the County of Monmouth is now by mutual consent dissolved. This is to inform the public that the said business is still carried on by Dunbar only.

Isaac Hays Dunbar.

Chepstow, 17th Nov. 1766."

(42) 6th December, 1766. *F. F. Bristol Journal.*

"Creditors of the late partnership between Messrs. Thomas Harris and William King in the glass trade are to leave the account of their demands on such partnership directed to Messrs. Tyndall, Pennington & Rogers."

(43) 23rd January, 1768. *F. F. Bristol Journal.*

"J. &. T. Warren, Richard Cannington, Richard Reynolds and William Cowles, have entered into a partnership in the Crown Glass trade (which has heretofore been carried on by the said J. & T. Warren) and will continue the same in Thomas Street in this city.

"Symonds Dyer* who was some years ago a servant to Warrens is not in the service of this Company."

(44) 19th March, 1772. *Bristol Gazette.*

"Saturday last was committed to Newgate W. Harris, for stealing several pieces of glass-ware, the property of Messrs. Cannington, Reynolds and Fry, within this city."

(45) 19th May, 1774. *Bristol Gazette.*

"Sunday, a man belonging to Vigor and Stevens' glasshouse on Redcliff-Backs dropt down in a fit and expired immediately."

(46) 23rd March, 1775. *Bristol Gazette.*

"Bristol, March 14th, 1775. Richard Cannington having sold his share in the Bottle Trade at the Hooper's Glass-House, known by the firm of Cannington Lawson & Co., the trade is now carried on by William Cowles, Richard Reynolds, John Dowell, Richard Frampton, Cornelius Fry and Robert Lawson† under the firm of Cowles, Dowell, Lawson and Co."

(47) 13th December, 1777. *F. F. Bristol Journal.*

"Notice is hereby given that the Glass Bottle and Vitriol Trade and other businesses that were carried on by the late William King will be continued at the same place for his executors, by Mr. George Bowser."

---

* 6th February, 1768. *F. F. Bristol Journal.* Advertisement by Symonds Dyer of Crown Glass.

† "Robert Lawson died June, 1794. He was a Quaker and a man universally esteemed." *Bristol Gazette*, 5th June, 1794.

(48) 17th January, 1778. *F. F. Bristol Journal.*

"For sale by auction, an Estate near Temple Gate in the City of Bristol ... A glass bottle trade may be carried on there to advantage. A loomy sand being to be dug there with which and Lime and Kelp, Bottles are generally made, except in this City, where on account of the former cheapness of Soaper's waste ashes they are made chiefly with soaper's ashes kelp and sand; but soaper's ashes being now used as a manure for land are advanced from 6d. to 2s. 6d. a cart load and as it gets more in use for manure will probably get dearer. For further particulars apply to Mr. Cannington at the Glass Warehouse near Temple Gate Bristol."

(49) *Bristol Import Books,* 1778–1780 (selected).*

Date.	From.	Importer.	Articles.
4 Feb., 1778	Belfast	Vigor, Stevens & Hill	Pork
27 March, 1778	Galway	”	Pork, &c., 30 tons kelp
13 June, 1780	”	”	2 hogsheads broken glass
25 Feb., 1778		Thos. Keefe	40 tons kelp
2 Nov., 1778	Waterford	”	7 tons kelp, 3 hhds broken glass
27 Nov., 1779	Galway	”	50 tons kelp
12 June, 1778	”	Farrell & Jones	110 tons kelp
12 June, 1778	”	Coghlan Peach & Co.	60 tons kelp
28 June, 1779	”	”	70 tons kelp, 5 bags old rags
10 Nov., 1778	”	Sam Span	90 tons kelp
10 May, 1779	”	Pennington & Biggs	15 tons kelp

* Some of these Bristol importers may have been glasshouse clerks or agents for the Bristol glassmakers. In 2 years 1,173 tons of kelp were imported from Ireland.

(50) 14th February, 1778. *F. F. Bristol Journal.*

11th April, 1778. The late Mr. William King of St. Phillip's glass-maker; late of Avon Street, St. Phillip's is mentioned.

(51) 13th June, 1778. *F. F. Bristol Journal.*

"The Glass Bottle House or Works at Crew's Hole in the Parish of St. George, late in the working of Mr. William King, glassmaker deceased for sale by auction.

"These works are deemed the most complete and conveniently situated of any in or about this City, being on the center of the Avon and near the Coal Works (a great advantage to a Glass House factory) and a good set of hands ready for employment so that the house may be immediately set to work ... Also 2 acres at Abbott's Hill adjoining or contiguous to the Glass House, also 10 acres called Noble's Hill at Crew's Hole aforesaid contiguous to the above ...

"All the above estates are held by lease under Thomas Tyndall Esq. for the remainder of several terms of 99 years &c.

"Also a yard lately occupied by the sd. William King as a bottle yard to the above works in Cheese Lane.

"Also a quantity of materials for making of Glass Bottles and pots, consisting of sand ashes, clay, and other things &c.

"For a view of the premises apply to Mr. Charles Powell (late manager of the Works) at Crew's Hole."

(52) 28th October, 1780. *F. F. Bristol Journal.*

"The Lime Kiln Glasshouse is mentioned."

4th January, 1783. (ibid.)

"Stolen out of the Lime Kiln Glasshouse some time last week
4 Bottle Pipes about 5 ft. 4 inches long
2 ,, 4 ,, 10 ,, ,,
1 ,, 4 ,, 6 ,, ,,
and several other working tools belonging to the said Glass-House. Whoever will discover the offender shall receive a Guinea

reward by applying to John Short at the said Glass-House."
(53) 11th January, 1783. *F. F. Bristol Journal.*

"The partnership between Samuel, James and George Taylor of this City, Glass Manufacturers (under the firm of James Taylor and Bros.) being dissolved by mutual consent, and the stock in trade equally divided; Samuel Taylor takes this method of informing his friends and the public that he will dispose of his share which consists of Window Glass in great variety of sizes, for exportation and home consumption (the quality of which, from the well-known reputation of their House for making good glass, needs no recommendation). Application may be made at his Warehouse in St. Thomas Street (late Tandey's Sugar House) or at his dwelling-house in No. 15 Cathay near Redcliff Church."
(54) 24th January, 1784. *F. F. Bristol Journal.*

"For sale the estate and premises of Mr. James Keys, Glassmaker, situate in Pipe Lane near Temple Gate."
(55) 20th March, 1784. *F. F. Bristol Journal.*

"For sale by auction 200 boxes of Window Glass, cut into proper sizes fit for exportation and well worth the attention of any merchant in the Quebec trade."
(56) 7th January, 1786. *F. F. Bristol Journal.*

"The partnership term between Richard Cannington, Richard Reynolds and Cornelius Fry in the trade of making glass at the Glass-House near Temple Gate in Bristol, carried on in the name of Richard Cannington and Co., being expired and the partnership terminated; and Richard Cannington having bought of Richard Reynolds and Cornelius Fry their parts and shares in everything belonging to the partnership, [Richard Cannington to be treated as sole member of firm]."
(57) 23rd September, 1786. *F. F. Bristol Journal.*

"Last Saturday two men broke into the counting house of Messrs. Vigor and Stevens, glass manufacturers on Redcliff Backs."

(58) 16th December, 1786. *F. F. Bristol Journal.*

"Robbery was committed near the Limekiln Glass-House, at the West End of the Ropewalk leading to Hot-wells."

(59) 12th May, 1787. *F. F. Bristol Journal.*

"John Glew and Edward Crossman, glass-founders belonging to St. Phillip's Glass-House in the City of Bristol are mentioned."

(Probably "Elton's Glasshouse.")

(60) 2nd August, 1788. *F. F. Bristol Journal.*

"John Robert Lucas, intending to confine himself solely to the Crown Glass and Glass Bottle Manufactures wishes to dispose of the Beer and Cyder business which he has many years carried on in Nicolas Street."

(61) 1789. William Barrett, *History of Bristol.*

"The hospital of St. Catherine was in Bedminster where now a glass-house is built."

(62) 15th August, 1789. *F. F. Bristol Journal.*

The Commissioners in a renewed commission of bankrupt awarded and issued against John Adams late of Chelwood, glass-manufacturer &c issue a notice.

(63) 22nd August 1789 to 10th October, 1789. *F. F. Bristol Journal.*

"Phoenix Flint Glass House Wadham, Ricketts and Co. at the Phoenix Flint Glass-House, without Temple Gate, Bristol (late the Phoenix Inn) most respectfully inform their friends and the Public, that they have begun to work said Glass-house; where will be kept a complete assortment of every article of flint-glass, which will be sold on the most reasonable terms."

(64) 19th September, 1789. *F. F. Bristol Journal.*

"Messrs. Vigor, Stevens & Co. of this city glass-makers and copartners do hereby apprize their friends and the public that John Thomas and Mattew Hill late clerks at their Flint Glass

Manufactory on Redcliff Backs and John Mayo Tandey, late clerk at their Crown Glass Manufactory in St. Thomas Street, have been for some time past dismissed from their respective employments."

(65) 19th September, 1789. *F. F. Bristol Journal.*

"Messrs. Fry, Jones, Tandey and Company beg leave to inform their friends and the public that they have succeeded to and carry on the Flint-Glass Works of Messrs. Richard Cannington and Co. in Temple Street in this City, and request a continuance of their favours which will be executed on the best terms and with strict attention."

(65) 19th September, 1789. *F. F. Bristol Journal.*

[Notice by John Mayo Tandey objecting to the notice of his dismissal by Messrs. Vigor Stevens & Co. and referring to Mr. William Stevens Senr. as member of that firm.]

[No reference 66]

(67) 19th September, 1789. *F. F. Bristol Journal.*

[Notice by Matthew Hawkins Hill objecting to the notice of his dismissal by Messrs. Vigor, Stevens & Co.] "In July last Messrs. William Fry, James Jones, John Mayo Tandey and Co., proceeded to work a glass-house in this city." ...

Mr. James Stevens of Vigor, Stevens & Co. is mentioned.

(68) 19th September, 1789. *F. F. Bristol Journal.*

"Mr. John Thomas* presents his most cordial respects to Messrs. Vigor, Stevens, Randolph & Stevens, and is highly obliged to them for their unkind "advertisement in the *Bristol Gazette* of the 16th Instant, after so many years of faithful service. He is now established in the Phoenix Glass-House Temple-Gate carried on by Wadham Ricketts and Co."

---

* Died November, 1789. *Bristol Gazette*, 5th November, 1789.

(69) 6th May, 1790. *Bristol Gazette.*

"On Thursday last a fire broke out in the new glasshouse at Nailsea belonging to Mr. J. R. Lucas, which burnt part of the roof, but by timely assistance, the other parts of the buildings belonging to both crown glasshouses were preserved."

[Glasshouses at Nailsea mentioned 12th June, 1790. *F. F. Bristol Journal.*]

(70) 13th May, 1790. *Bristol Gazette.*

"Tuesday morning about 3 o'clock fire broke out in a pot-house belonging to Messrs. Coghlan and Co.'s glasshouse in St. Philip's, which by timely assistance was prevented from doing any very material damage."

(71) 30th September, 1790. *Bristol Gazette.*

"Friday last Mr. Child, one of the proprietors of the Limekiln Glasshouse, suddenly dropped down and expiring immediately."

(72) 31st March, 1791. *Bristol Gazette.*

"Tuesday died Mr. Child at the Limekiln Glass-house."

(73) 25th February, 1792. *F. F. Bristol Journal.*

"Wanted a manager for Black Bottle House and another manager for a Flint Glass House. Replies to A. B. at the Post Office." 3rd March, 1792. (ibid.)

"Wanted partner in Black Bottle House. Wanted partner in Flint Glass House. Replies to W. D. at the Post Office."

(74) 7th April, 1792. *F. F. Bristol Journal.*

"Inland Navigation to London, in 14 or 16 days. Through the Thames and Severn Canal. Severn barges meet the Thames boats for London at Brimscombe Port in the Thames and Severn Canal in Gloucestershire. Rates black glass bottles to Brimscombe Port 7s. 6d. per ton. From Brimscombe Port to Brooke's Wharf in London £1 7s. 6d. per ton."

(75) 30th March, 1793. *F. F. Bristol Journal.*

"John R. Lucas, William Chance, Edward Homer and William Coathupe inform the public that they shall on the 1st April next succeed Messrs. John R. Lucas, Henry Pater and William Coathupe in the Crown Glass and Bottle Manufacturers."
(76) 13th April, 1793. *F. F. Bristol Journal.*

"The Partnership between William Stevens, James Stevens, John Cave and George Daubeny of the city of Bristol, glassmakers and manufacturers, is by mutual consent dissolved so far as respects the said James Stevens."
(77) 13th April, 1793. *F. F. Bristol Journal.*

"James Stevens acquaints the public that he is now forming a connection in the above line which will be announced in a few days."
(78) 27th July, 1793. *F. F. Bristol Journal.*

"The partnership lately subsisting between John Nicholas, Richard Stratton and John Robert Lucas of the City of Bristol, Manufacturers of Glass Bottles was dissolved by mutual consent on the 13th March last, and the business is carried on by the said John Nicholas and Richard Stratton only under the firm of John Nicholas & Co."
(79) 24th August, 1793. *F. F. Bristol Journal.*

"Notice is given that the' Copartnership in the Glass Manufactory, lately carried on in St. Thomas Street and on Redcliff Backs in Bristol under the firm of Stevens, Randolph and Company and afterwards of Stevens, Cave and Company, and which concern was lately dissolved as to James Stevens, one of the Co-partners, is now wholly dissolved. And notice is given that the same business will be continued by a firm which will be shortly announced to the public."
(80) 26th October, 1793. *F. F. Bristol Journal.*

"Thursday se'en night died Mr. Cannington Senr. late a glass manufacturer in this city."

(81) 2nd November, 1793. *F. F. Bristol Journal.*

"We hear that all the Glass Bottle Manufacturers in Bristol and its neighbourhood are obliged to discontinue their works in consequence of some late determinations in the Excise tending to their prejudice. The Houses in the North feel themselves equally aggrieved, so that we fear this extensive branch of manufacture which employs such numbers of labouring poor &c will be totally lost to this country."

(82) July, 1794. *F. F. Bristol Journal.*

"To be let and entered upon immediately sundry warehouses, together with a yard adjoining the river; all situated near the Glass-House on Redcliff Backs. Enquire at the Compting House of William Stevens and Glass Company."

(83) 28th February, 1795. *F. F. Bristol Journal.*

"Thames and Severn Canal Navigation. List of Goods declared light and hazardous Window and Plate Glass List of Goods declared heavy Black Glass."

(84) 4th April, 1795. *F. F. Bristol Journal.*

"To be sold or let by reason of the Proprietor's death the Capital Glass, Bottle Manufactory and Trade thereof at Crewshole about 2 miles from this city; in excellent repair and full working with a set of good hands and a large stock of prime pots."

Advertised also, 18th April, and 23rd May, 1795, and see 88 and 95 below.

(85) 5th December, 1795. *F. F. Bristol Journal.*

The Co-partnership in the Glass Bottle Manufactory lately carried on at the Glass-house at the Limekilns and elsewhere, under the firm of John Nicholas and Co. was dissolved on the 31st March last, so far as respects Richard Stratton, who withdrew therefrom, but the same business will be still continued under the former firm."

(86) 16th January, 1796. *F. F. Bristol Journal.*

Notice by commissioners in a renewed commission of bankruptcy against John Adams, formerly of Chelwood, glass manufacturer &c deceased.

(87) 21st April, 1796. *Bristol Gazette.*

"Died Thursday in the Great Gardens, after a short illness, Mr. Lazarus Jacobs, a Jew and an eminent glass-merchant."

(88) 7th January, 1797. *F. F. Bristol Journal.*

"Glass Bottle Manufactory to be sold by auction by reason of the proprietor's death ... For further particulars apply at the Counting House in Pennywell Lane of the late Mr. James Jones."

(89) 11th March, 1797. *F. F. Bristol Journal.*

"List of Citizens who agree during the present emergency to accept promissory notes of the several bankers of the city in lieu of cash &c.

Lucas, Chance & Co.

Pater & Williams.

Ricketts Evans & Ricketts."

(90) 1st April, 1797. *F. F. Bristol Journal.*

"All persons having any demands on the private estate of *John Wadham late of Queen's Parade in this city deceased; or in the late copartnership firm of John Wadham & Son are requested to send in their accounts to John Wadham junr. John Wadham continues his Glazing and Plate Glass Manufactory at his Warehouse in Horse Street as usual. N.B. Merchants, Glaziers and others supplied with Crown and Green Glass for exportation and Home Consumption."

---

* Mr. John Wadham, glassman in Horse Street is mentioned 15th March, 1777. *F. F. Bristol Journal.* On the 5th March, 1796 (ibid.) John Wadham, junr., advertises for "a few glass bottle hands," probably as agent for a Bottle-house.

(91) 7th April, 1798. *F. F. Bristol Journal*.

"Last week died at his house at Crewshole Mr. Samuel Crinks, many years a master potter and furnace builder at St. Philip's Glassworks."

(92) 20th October, 1798. *F. F. Bristol Journal*.

"A capital Glass Manufactory to be sold by auction by order of the Assignees of William Stevens glassmanufacturer a bankrupt.

"All that capital Crown and Flint Glass Manufactory situate in Portwall Lane and St. Thomas Street in the said city of Bristol, which promises were lately worked by Messrs. Stevens Cave and Company. The ground on which one of the Cones of the said Glass Manufactory stands is held by a lease under the Feoffees of St. Mary Redcliff Church Lands granted in 1792 for the term of 99 years. The Cone of the other Glasshouse stands on ground held by lease from the said Feoffees granted in 1785 for a term of 40 years.

"For a view of the promises apply to Mr. William Stevens. For particulars apply to George Daubeny & John Cave Junr."

(93) 20th July, 1799. *F. F. Bristol Journal*.

"The Counting House of Messrs. Ricketts Evans & Co. without Temple Gate was broke open and robbed of cash. Phoenix Glass House. Reward Offered."

(94) 16th November, 1799, *F. F. Bristol Journal*.

Messrs. Lucas Chance & Co. insert notice about their waggons using the Ashton & Nailsea roads.

(95) 22nd November, 1800. *F. F. Bristol Journal*.

"Crewshole Glass Bottle Manufactory advertised to be sold by auction. Apply to the counting house of the late Mr. James Jones."

(96) 13th February, 1802. *F. F. Bristol Journal*.

"Phoenix Glass-House. Bristol 4th November, 1801.

"Notice is given that the Copartnership between Richard Ricketts, David Evans and Jacob Wilcox Ricketts in the business of manufacturing making and selling Glass carried on at Temple Gate, Bristol under the firm of Ricketts Evans & Ricketts was by mutual consent dissolved on the 1st June last so far as relates to the said Richard Ricketts who retires therefrom.

"The works carried on at Redcliff Backs known by the firm of Stevens Glass Concern being now consolidated with the above the Proprietors inform the public that their Flint, Bottle and Cut-Glass Manufactory has been considerably extended on a new and improved plan, and that in future the firm will be Ricketts Evans and Phoenix Glass Company."

(97) 5th June, 1802. *F. F. Bristol Journal.*

"Having discovered an improved method of making all kinds of Glass by which the process is effected in a period of time very much shorter than by the usual mode, and thus created a saving of fuel, [Patent granted.] Any gentleman in the trade may have my permission to adopt the said improvements on liberal terms. Apply to me at Rickets Evans & Co.'s Patent Glass-Houses, Bristol. John Donaldson."

Sketchley's Directory, 1775 [a rare book, Bristol Museum].
Probably confined to certain parts of the present City.
Glassmakers.

Richard Cannington	89 Temple St.
Richard Cannington & Co.	91 „
William Child	38 Limekiln Lane.
John Encell.	22 Bristol Back.
Cornelius Fry	103 Temple St.
William Landening	2 Lewis Buildings.
Robert Marston	12 Tower St.
Cornelius Rogers	27 Limekilns

Thomas Rogers	8 Brandon Hill.
John Seager.	6 Tower St.
Thomas Short	9 Brandon Hill.
Thomas Sith	16 Jacob's Well.
Robert Vigor.	4 College Green
Jerry Whitehouse.	96 Hotwell Rd.
Edward Williams.	26 Limekilns.

Universal British Directory, 1790

Elton, Miles & Co.	Cheese Lane.
John Nicholas & Co.	Limekiln Glasshouse, Limekiln Lane.
Henry Payne	1 Bread St.
William Stevens & Son.	Thomas St.
Wadham, Rickets & Co.	Without Templegate.
Lawson Fry & Co.	Cheese Lane.
Lucas Pater & Coathupe	Nicholas St.
Robert Marston	Great Gardens.

Bristol Directory, 1794 (Matthews).
List of Glass Firms

Cannington & Co.	Temple St.
James Clark	”
Elton Miles & Co. (crown glass & bottles)	Cheese Lane.
Heater Hodder	” ”
John Nicholas & Co. (bottles)	Limekiln Dock.
George Norman	Thomas. St.
Henry Payne	St. Phillips.
Edward Smart	Cheese Lane.

Stevens, Cave & Co. (flint & crown glass)	Redcliife Backs.
Stevens, Cave & Co. (crown glass)	St. Thomas St.
Wadham Ricketts & Co. (flint glass)	Without Templegate.
William Walters	Lawrence Hill.
– Williams	Hotwell Road.

Bristol Export Books

Summary of Glass Wares exported from Bristol during the first six months of 1801.

Total Amounts

Bottles 364,796.

Also 1,376 baskets, 100 hampers, and 10 crates of bottles. Window Glass (mostly Crown Glass).

8,935 boxes, 830 sides, and 312 crates.

Flint Glass.

262 crates, 121 boxes, 44 cases, 23 hogsheads, 18 tierces, 12 casks, 7 puncheons, and 1 basket.

Ports of Consignment and Numbers of Consignments.

Cork(14)	Limerick(1)	Newfoundland(2)	Barbadoes (1)
Dublin (5)	New York (5)	Quebec (2)	Martinique (1)
Waterford (9)	Charlestown (1)	Guernsey (8)	Surinam (1)
Wexford (1)	Boston (2)	Jersey (9)	Lisbon (1)
Newry (3)	Maryland (1)	Jamaica (3)	Oporto (1)
Belfast (2)	Philadelphia (3)	Trinidad (1)	Madeira (1)
Galway (1)	Virginia (1)	St. Vincents (1)	

Old Nottingham Glasshouses
By Francis BUCKLEY

THE history of glass-making in Nottingham town is well authenticated; but unfortunately the situation of the glasshouses is seldom specified in the advertisements. Two glasshouses were standing and at work in 1741; for two smoking cones of glasshouses are shown, considerably apart, in a view of Nottingham, dated 1741, and reproduced in the preface to Dering's "History of Nottingham" (1751).

We start our inquiry with the following statement made in 1815 by Blackner*:-

"Formerly there were two glasshouses in this town; one at the east end of Snenton-street,† of very large dimensions, and one between Charlotte-street and York-street near the end of Glass-House Lane; but within about 50 years they have both disappeared, nor has glass ware of any consequence been made in them during that time."

The above fragment of local glass history is supplemented by Daniel Defoe, who, writing in 1727,‡ says as follows: "Fine flint glass, including all sorts of drinking glasses, cruets, apothecaries' and chymists' glass phyals, retorts, fine Bottles for cases, Decanters, &c., sconces, branches, and small ware, Toys, &c. Also watch glasses, &c. [made at] London, Bristol, Stourbridge, Nottingham, Sheffield,, Newcastle." And this statement is repeated in 1738;§ and again (but clearly in error as far as Not-

---

* "History of Nottingham," p. 251.
† Modern name "Sneinton Road."
‡ "The English Tradesman," Vol. II. p. 63.
§ "The Complete English Tradesman."

tingham is concerned) in 1787. II

In Houghton's list of English glasshouses in the year 1696, there are recorded one bottle house in Nottingham itself, another at Custom More, and two flint glasshouses at or near Awsworth. The making of flint glass at Nottingham town was probably started in the early part of the eighteenth century; but curiously enough the advertisements are very silent as to the kinds of glass (except bottles) produced here.

THE OLD GLASSHOUSE

The Old Glasshouse was probably the smaller of the two glasshouses shown in the sketch of 1741; presumably it gave rise to the place-names "Glass-House Lane" (now Street) and "Glass-House Court," in the Parish of St. Mary. The actual site of the Old Glasshouse is probably now occupied by part of Victoria Station.

This glasshouse was established rather before 1691;* and was then described as a "good new Brick Building."†[1] Mr. Lovett of Nottingham was a person interested in the letting of the glass house, and he may indeed have been the founder. After 1691 it was taken over by Peter Thompson, who joined in the petitions to Parliament, in 1697, against the unpopular War tax on glass. Some time afterward Christopher Wood bought the freehold of the glasshouse and appears to have carried on the business until he became bankrupt.[5] He died before February 1719,[3] and the Assignees in Bankruptcy sold the freehold in 1733.[5] Meanwhile

---

II "The Complete Tradesman," Wright, Dublin.
* Dering (p. 95) says that there was no glass-maker at Nottingham in 1641.
† The numbers refer to references in the Appendix.

the latter appear to have let the glasshouse, probably for the term of seven years, to John Bark, a Salter, and Richard Reeves, a working glass-maker.[3] The latter was "late servant of Mr. Bretnel" (a local name) ; and Mr. Bretnel may therefore have been working the glasshouse between C. Wood's bankruptcy and 1719. The partners Bark and Reeves seem to have rebuilt and enlarged the old glasshouse; and the lease came to an end in September 1724,[4] Richard Reeves then went into possession as lessee; and there is not much evidence yet to show when his occupation came to an end. The sale of the freehold in 1733 would not affect his rights as lessee; and this glasshouse was, as we have seen, standing and at work in 1741. But in 1751 Dering states that there was only one glass-maker in Nottingham;‡ and unless this man worked both glasshouses, which to judge from the advertisements is unlikely, the older establishment had been abandoned before 1751. Again, it is stated of Morley's Glasshouse in 1765, that there was no other glasshouse "so near as to interfere with it."[10]

MORLEY'S GLASSHOUSE

Another glasshouse was erected at Nottingham before 1740; probably indeed before 1727, when Defoe described Nottingham as one of the principal centres for the English flint glass manufacture. In 1740 it was described as " well-accustomed," and Charles Morley was working the glasshouse himself.[7] This seems to be the large glasshouse in Snenton Street, referred to by Blackner in 1815. Between 1740 and 1765, at any rate, the freehold remained in the hands of the Morley family.[7,8,10] In 1740 the glasshouse was offered on lease, and was taken over sooner or later by Adam Young.[8,9] He gave up the business in 1750, and the following year Buxton, Foxcroft and Co. commenced busi-

---

‡ "History of Nottingham," p. 95.

ness here, and continued in possession apparently for 14 years.[9,10] In 1765 the Morleys again offered the glasshouse, on this occasion either for sale or on lease, and we may conclude that they were no longer glass-makers.[10]

The glasshouse was probably not yet abandoned; but, as we have already seen, after 1765 "no glass ware of any consequence" was made in Nottingham. There is preserved in the Nottingham Museum a green glass jug, splashed with white spots, and fancy bottle glass, which is said to have been made by James Woodward, glass-blower of Nottingham, in 1769.

John Nodes, a glass-seller, attracted from London, perhaps by the success of the local flint glass works, was selling fine table glass in Nottingham and Derby between 1740 and 1746.[6]

The common practice of sealing glass bottles with dates and with the names or crests of the purchasers is referred to in one of the local advertisements;[9] and in the Nottingham Museum there is a pair of bottles with the seal "R. Hawley, 1750," made no doubt by Adam Young in Nottingham.

APPENDIX

1. 3rd August, 1691. *London Gazette.*

"At Nottingham Town, a large Glass-house, with all Conveniences thereunto belonging, of good new Brick Building will be Lent or Sold in April next. Enquire at Mr. Webb's over against the Coffee-house in Hatton-Garden London, or at Mr. Tho. Lovett's in Nottingham."

2. 8th January, 1697. *Journals H. C.* xi, 649.

A Petition of "Peter Thompson, Glass-maker, of the Town, and County of the Town, of Nottingham on behalf of himself and his Servants," was presented to the House of Commons against the War Tax on Glass 1695. [6 & 7 William & Mary, c. 18.]

3. 19th February, 1719. *Nottingham Mercury. Victoria County*

History Notts ii, 333.

"Whereas John Bark, Salter, and Richard Reeves, Glass founder (late servant to Mr. Bretnel), have taken the Glasshouse lately Mr. Christopher Wood's deceased at Nottingham."

4. 16th May, 1724. *London Journal*.

"At Nottingham. An old and well accustomed Glasshouse, new rebuilt and enlarged, with good accomodation of warehouses and dwelling house, to be let at Michaelmas next. Enquire at Mr. Parravicini's house in Nottingham."

5. 17th July, 1733. *London Gazette*.

"The real estate of Christopher Wood, late of Nottingham, against whom a Commission of Bankrupt hath issued, consisting of a Dwelling House, Glass-house, and Warehouse, Yard, Garden, and Close of Pasture, in the Possession of Mr. Reeves, and a Pot-house near the same in the Possession of Mr. Wier, in the Parish of St. Mary in Nottingham, Lett together at about £38 a year, will be sold to the best Purchaser, on or before the last day of August next."

6. 26th July, 1740. *London Evening Post*.

"John Nodes, China &c. Warehouse near the White Lyon Inn, Nottingham (late from Temple Bar, London), Selleth All sorts of Flint Glasses at 8d. per pound."

20th May, 1742. *Derby Mercury*.

"John Nodes of Nottingham will have a large sale of fine China ware, Glass and Toys in Derby."

7. 9th September, 1740. *London Evening Post*.

"To be let and entered upon any time at the Taker's option, a convenient and well-accustomed Glasshouse, now in the occupation of Charles Morley of Nottingham; and the stock on hand and working utensils to be sold, with a large stock of good Bottle Pots, many of the same sort having stood ten or twelve weeks each, and the compound of which they are made and the manner of preparing and working the same will be taught any person who takes the said house.

N.B. The said house will be worked by the said Charles Morley till let."

8. 20th September, 1750. *London Evening Post*.

"To be lett and entered upon at the Taker's Option, A convenient Glass-House, for both White and Bottle Glass, with large warehouses and other Conveniences thereto belonging. Enquire of Mrs. Anne Morley, Potter, in Nottingham aforesaid. N.B. Mr. Adam Young, late glass maker having left off business, has all sorts of working Implements, and divers other materials, to be sold a pennyworth."

9. 11th January, 1751. *Derby Mercury*.

"Nottingham. The business of making glass which has been lately carried on by Mr. Adam Young of this Town will still be continued to be carry'd on by Messrs. Buxton, Foxcroft & Co. All persons sending their orders shall have them fulfilled as soon as possible on the best terms. We expect to begin to make goods in two months. N.B. Mr. Young is ready to deliver all Gentlemen's Crests on the first notice."

10. 28th January, 1765. *Aris's Birmingham Gazette*.

"To be sold or let and entered upon immediately if required. A convenient Glass-House, Dwelling-House, Ware Houses &c. in good repair, situate in the Town of Nottingham (close by which runs the River Trent) with a Furnace now standing and fit for Use and also several valuable Pots. For particulars enquire of Mr. C. Morley in Nottingham. N.B. The situation commands a good Trade, there not being any other Glass House so near as to interfere with it."

TUNSTEAD, GREENFIELD,
 YORKSHIRE.

Cumberland Glasshouses
By Francis BUCKLEY

THERE were in the eighteenth century two glasshouses in Cumberland, neither of which appears to have survived to the end of the century.

The first was a bottle house at Whitehaven, founded in 1732 and held under a long lease from Sir James Lowther at a yearly ground rent of five guineas.[1]* Beyond the fact that Robert Verney was steward of the works in 1739, nothing is known of the glass-makers here. After seven years' work, the glasshouse came into the market for sale; and the only possible indication of glass-making at Whitehaven itself at a later date is the notice of a cargo of bottles "from Whitehaven" which reached Liverpool in 1757.[2]† The subsequent history of this glasshouse is not yet known; but it can scarcely be identical with the glasshouse next mentioned.

There was also a glasshouse on the south side of the harbour at Maryport, near Whitehaven.[6] George Monkhouse was for many years "sole proprietor"; but he seems to have let the glass-house, probably in 1752, to a company of glass-makers who manufactured broad glass and bottles.[3] The trade in glass made at Maryport was probably extensive; the goods were sent, not only to the adjacent parts of Scotland and Ireland, but along the English coast as far south as Liverpool and West Chester.[5] Thomas Aydon, who is mentioned in 1760, may have been a mem-

---

* The numbers refer to the Appendix.
† Unless the notice is very accurate, it might refer to a cargo from Maryport,

ber of the company, or perhaps merely steward of the works.[4] At about this date the glasshouse changed hands, and a further lease for seven years was granted, about 1759 or 1760. In 1767, the glasshouse was again advertised by Monkhouse for sale or lease, both in the Liverpool and Birmingham newspapers,[5] an indication that it was an important work and by this time well known. It is probable that a new firm took possession at this point, for crown glass-making was adopted in addition to broad glass and bottles.[6] A lease was again granted for seven years, and fell in on June 17, 1773.[6] The glasshouse was then advertised for sale; and it may be inferred that George Monkhouse either was dead or had sold the freehold. After this, there is no indication of further glass-making at Maryport. Indeed, by 1790 there were no manufactories at all being carried on here.[7]

APPENDIX

1. 25th August, 1739. *Newcastle Journal*.

"To be sold by publick auction at Whitehaven on 10th September next, for the remainder of a term of 999 years commencing in 1732, a large, convenient and well-built Glass-Bottle-House, with a Dwelling house, several Storehouses, Pot-lofts, a Mill and other proper Conveniences, situated at Whitehaven aforesaid; together with all the Utensils, Tools, Pots and Materials belonging to the Works.

Note:– There are upon the premises 90 dry, sound Pots, 10 tons of Kelp, 250 tons of Soap-ashes, a new Furnace, and the Iron Geer in good order. The Pot-lofts will contain above 200 pots. The premises pay £5 5s. per annum reserved rent to Sir James Lowther, Bart.

Enquire of … Mr. Robert Verney, steward at the said Works."

2. 6th May, 1757. *Liverpool Chronicle*.

"Arrived in Liverpool from Whitehaven, a cargo of Glass

Bottles."

3. 10th March, 1759. *Newcastle Journal.*
24th March, 1759. *Newcastle Courant.*

"To be let and entered upon immediately, situate at Mary-Port, otherwise Allenfoot in Cumberland, a Glass-House with warehouses and Dwelling house for the Workmen, with every conveniency of carrying on a work in the most extensive manner; also a number of Pots, and other utensils and materials for making of Broad Glass and Bottles. Enquire of Mr. George Monkhouse in Penrith. N.B. Very good coal and Pot clay within a mile."

4. 5th July, 1760. *Newcastle Journal.*

"To be sold to the highest Bidder on the 6th August 1760 at MARYPORT in the County of Cumberland. All the Utensils and Materials belonging to the late Company, fit and convenient for manufacturing of Broad Glass and Bottles.

At the same time will be sold or let for a term of years the said Glasshouse with all erections, also the Key or Wharf 60 yards in length on which the glasshouse is erected. Enquire of Geo. MONKHOUSE of PENRITH, or of Mr. THos. AYDON at MARYPORT.

N.B. Maryport is conveniently situated for carrying on an extensive Work, having coals at hand and sand on the spot for making Bottles, Broad or Crown Glass, and also Clay for making Pots within 2 miles."

5. 7th July, 1767. *Liverpool Advertiser.*
10th August, 1767. *Aris's Birmingham Gazette.*

"To be let or sold, A most compleat Glasshouse with every conveniency proper for carrying on a large Work, situate at Mary-Port near Whitehaven in Cumberland, having a number of good coal mines and an Iron work contiguous, commanding an easy and extensive trade to the west of Scotland, the North of Ireland

and Coast of England from Carlisle to Liverpool and West Chester. Apply to Mr. George Monkhouse of Penrith, the sole proprietor of the Work."

6. 27th March, 6th June, 1773. *Newcastle Journal*.

 "To be sold, on 17th June, at the house of William How, in PENRITH, all that commodious and convenient Glass-house, situated on the South-side of the harbour at MARY PORT, consisting of a Cone, or Round house, two large Pot-Chambers, Mill and Clay houses, bottle warehouse, and two Crown and Broad glass warehouses, Korker and Ash house, and dwelling houses for twelve families, and a very good dwelling house for an agent of the work."

7. 1790. *Universal British Directory*.

" MARYPORT. – There are no manufactories here at present."

TUNSTEAD, GREENFIELD,
　　YORKSHIRE.

Notes on the Glasshouses of Stourbridge 1700–1830
By Francis BUCKLEY

THE history of glass-making in the district about Stourbridge is still far from complete. The newspapers and directories of the 18th century have proved rather disappointing sources. This attempt, therefore, to piece together scattered items of information has been undertaken only in the hope that it may lead others to continue the inquiry by way of local and parochial records. It is a history that is well worth completing. The glass-makers of Stourbridge are still known all over the world for their productions; and in no other district has English glass-making had so long and so continuous a record.

One valuable statement about the glass-makers of Stourbridge has hitherto been overlooked by recent glass historians, including the present writer. And, as it is proposed to make this statement the basis from which to start the inquiry, it is here set forth in full. It is a statement due to Langford,* namely:

"In the year 1760, the glass manufacture of the Stourbridge district was in the hands of the following producers : Broad glass and bottles, Pidcock, Hill, Rodgers ; smooth enamel glass, Grazebrook, Denham ; flint glass, best and ordinary, Grazebrook, Denham, Bradley, Barrar, Rogers, Honeybourne, Russell, Little; phials, Pidcock, Grazebrook, Denham, Barrar, Rogers, Russell, Honeybourne."

We know from another source that Pidcock had a broad glasshouse and also a bottle house; whilst enamel glass would be made at a flint glasshouse, and phials at any glasshouse for bottles or

---

* *Staffordshire and Warwickshire, Past and Present*, Vol. 11, Appendix, p. lxviii.

flint glass. This list then gives 12 glasshouses at least in Stourbridge,* not counting those at Dudley, Worcester, Bilston, Birmingham, etc. A further list of owners and glasshouses is given in *Pigot's Commercial Directory*, 1829 (practically repeated in the Parliamentary Return in 1833) ; and as this list ,helps to locate some of the glass-masters in Langford's List of 1760, it is now set out in full.

    Executors of Richard Bradley Ensell, Wordsley.
    Ensells & Co. (plain and cut), Wordsley.
    George William Wainwright (plain and cut), Wordsley.
    Michael and William Grazebrook (flint), Audnam.
    Hill, Hampton & Co. (black bottles), Coalburn Brook.
    Benjamin Littlewood & Son, Holloway End.
    Pidcock, Cope & Co. (broad and bottles), Dial Glasshouses.
    Philip Rufford (plain and cut), The Heath.
    Silvers, Mills & Stevens (flint), Brierley Hill.
    Westwood Moore & Rider (black bottles), Brierley Hill.
    William Seager Wheeley, Brettel.

The Dial Glasshouses; the Platts[10] †

The original "Dyal Glasshouse" seems to have been founded in the year 1704 by Joshua Henzey the Younger for the purpose of making broad glass. He obtained, we assume, a lease of 99 years, which is mentioned as having 56 years unexpired in 1747. Robert Foley is mentioned as partner with him for a time; and when Joshua Henzey died in 1738 without issue, he was succeeded by his nephew, John Pidcock. The latter became one of the leading fig-

---

* Postlethwayt, *Dictionary of Trade* (1766), says there were "about" 10 glasshouses in Stourbridge.
† The numbers after each heading refer to the Appendix.

ures in the Stourbridge district. At first he appears to have gone into partnership with John Godwin; and these two probably erected the Bottle House at the Platts between 1738 and 1747.

In 1747 both these glasshouses were offered publicly for sale; but we may assume that this simply meant the termination of the partnership between Godwin and Pidcock, and that the latter bought out his partner's share; for in 1761 "Mr. Pidcock" applied from the Dial Glasshouse for workmen in both the broad glass and bottle glass trade. About 1790 the firm's name was "John Pidcock & Son." In the following year John Pidcock, J.P., died, at the age of 74, and the business passed to his sons, who traded under the firm of "John Pidcock & Co." Although mainly concerned with the broad and bottle glass trade, John Pidcock was for a time also associated as senior partner in an important flint glass-house at Wordsley.* In 1791 the firm of "John Pidcock & Co." was represented by John, Thomas and R. Pidcock; and later on, until 1814, John, John Henzey, George, and Thomas Pidcock were the partners. In 1829 the firm was Pidcock, Cope & Co.

The Amblecote Bottle-house; Coalburn Brook[20]

This bottle house was associated, from 1760, at any rate, with the family of Hill; and it was acquired or founded by them prior to 1760. The Hills were connected with the family of Waldron, glass-makers and bankers of Stourbridge. Thus, in 1771, Waldron Hill and Thomas Hill were in partnership at Amblecote with William Waldron.† In 1793 the firm was still Hill and Waldron;

---

* See below, also Appendix 17 (a).
† William Waldron was High Sheriff of Worcestershire in 1796. Grazebrook, *Heraldry of Worcester*, pp. 598, 690.

but by 1818 it had changed to Hill, Hampton & Co. One Robert Hill, a great glass-maker about Stourbridge, gave evidence before a Parliamentary Committee in 1785. It is possible that this is one of the three glasshouses owned by Joshua Henzey, senior, in 1664, and misread as "Coleman's Glasshouse" (i.e., Coalburn Glasshouse).

The Heath Glasshouse[2,9,29]

One Rodgers, presumably distinct from Thomas Rogers the flint glass-maker, had a glasshouse for making broad glass or bottles, or both, in 1760. This may well have been the Heath Bottle House; and for this reason a note on it is given at this point.

It is thought that this may have been one of the three glasshouses owned by Joshua Henzey, senior, in 1664, and misread from manuscript as "Hood's Glasshouse" (i.e., Heath or Heath's Glasshouse). Either there were two glasshouses on the Heath or else the old glasshouse was rebuilt some time before 1734.

The following items may have some bearing on the earlier ownership of the Heath glasshouse. John Jeston, a bottle-maker at Stourbridge, appeared in connection with the petitions against the glass tax in 1696 and 1698. In 1699 it is stated that Mrs. Hunt had a glasshouse on the Heath at Stourbridge.‡ In 1734 Humphry Jeston, "of the Heath, near Stourbridge," became bankrupt, and the Commissioners (including Francis Hammerton) appear to have worked the glasshouse till 1736, when it was offered for sale as "Heath's New Glasshouse."

It is likely that Rodgers, as the only unplaced bottle-maker in Langford's list of 1760, took over the business here, and that he was succeeded, perhaps in 1781,* by Serjeant Witton, of Old

---

‡ *Victoria County History of Worcestershire*, II. p. 280.

* See Appendix No. 23. Witton may have made flint glass.

Swinford. The latter is mentioned twice in 1793, and became bankrupt in 1801. It is probable that Francis Rufford & Sons then acquired the Heath Glasshouse. They are mentioned here as makers of plain and cut glass in 1818, being succeeded in 1829 by Philip Rufford.

The Audnam Flint Glasshouse[26]

Throughout the 18th century this glasshouse was in the hands of the family of Grazebrook, whose history has been written up long ago.† The most interesting new item about this glasshouse is the fact that it was one of the two glasshouses about Stourbridge making "smooth enamel" glass in 1760.

 1713 Michael Grazebrook.
 1756 Michael Grazebrook, Jr.
 1789 Sarah Grazebrook.
 1793 Thomas & Michael Grazebrook.
 1818 M. Grazebrook & Sons.

Denham's Glasshouse

In 1760 this was one of the two glasshouses making both flint and enamel glass. Possibly it was one of the glasshouses at Brettle Lane. But no further information has yet been obtained to connect it with the 19th century glassworks.

Bradley's Wordsley Flint Glasshouse[8,17]

The Birmingham Journal, 31st May, 1851, states that this glasshouse was "at Brettle-Lane"; but all the earlier records describe it as at Wordsley. The Bradleys were making glass about Stourbridge for many years. In 1727 Henry Bradley, of Audenbrooke, became bankrupt; and in 1743 Edward Bradley, of Wordsley,

---

† See the works of H. S. Grazebrook.

"white glass-maker," is mentioned as insolvent. For a time Pidcock, presumably the famous John Pidcock, joined the Wordsley business; and in 1769 the firm was Pidcock, Ensell & Bradley.

But in 1760 Bradley, Ensell & Co. are mentioned as the owners. Later on, Pidcock dropped out; and in 1789 Richard Bradley, J. Bradley, and George Ensell appear to have been the principal owners.* In 1796 Richard Bradley died, and the firm continued as Bradley & Ensells. About 1800 it changed to Bradley, Ensells, & Holt. Shortly afterwards J. Bradley seems to have dropped out, and the business was continued by Richard Bradley Ensell & Charles Ensell in partnership with John Holt. On the death of John Holt his widow, Mary Holt, became a partner, and she continued as such until she married G. W. Wainwright, who took over her share. At this point there seems to have been a combination of three glass establishments at Wordsley: Bradley's Flint Glasshouse, Bradley's Bottle Glasshouse, and Wainwright's Flint Glasshouse. But in 1827 all these partnerships were dissolved, and in 1829 Bradley's Flint Glasshouse was worked under the firm of Ensells & Co.

Bradley's Wordsley Bottle House[17]

This was founded in 1796 by Bradley, Ensell, Paget & Co.; and became part of the " Wordsley Glass Works," mentioned in 1818 as owned by Bradley, Ensells, & Holt. After the dissolution of the combine in 1827, Richard Bradley Ensell seems to have taken over these bottle works on his own account, and he died before 1829; for in 1829 the Directory gives "the executors of Richard Bradley Ensell" as owners of glassworks at Wordsley, the only

---

* See Tunnicliffe's *Survey of Worcestershire* (1789).

works there not described as making flint glass.

Wainwright's "Wordsley Flint Glass Works"[17g]

The history of these works is given by Powell, *Glassmaking in England*. It seems clear that they were founded by George William Wainwright rather before 1827, and that between 1829 and 1833 the firm of Thomas Webb & Co. had taken possession. G. W. Wainwright was a member of this firm.

Barrar's Amblecote Glasshouse[8,16]

In 1723 one Benjamin Batch, a glass-maker of Amblecote, is mentioned as insolvent. He was possibly a predecessor of Elijah Barrar. The latter was making flint glass and phials in 1760; and we learn from his bankruptcy notice in 1767 that he worked at Amblecote. No further trace of this glasshouse has yet been found.

Rogers's Amblecote Glasshouse[11]

The family of Rogers came from Wales in the 17th century and owned several glasshouses about Stourbridge.† But the greatest of the family in the 18th century was Thomas Rogers, who became Sheriff of Worcestershire in 1750. In 1768 his glassworks (at Holloway End, Amblecote) were offered on lease, and probably a seven years' lease was granted to some glass-maker unknown. In 1775 the celebrated scientist James Keir became interested in these glassworks, and although he left them in 1778 to take charge of the Soho. Iron Works at Birmingham, it would seem that he remained a partner; for in 1789 the glass-making firm of Scott, Keir, Jones & Co. is recorded at Stourbridge.

---

† See H. S. Grazebrook's works.
* Scott, Stourbridge (1832), p. 107.

It is definitely recorded that Benjamin Littlewood succeeded this firm at Holloway End,* but the exact date is difficult to ascertain. Benjamin Littlewood, who was also a banker, appears at Stourbridge in 1793, and in 1793 the names of Scott (2) and Jones (1) appear in lists of Stourbridge tradesmen. Probably the change was made between 1793 and 1800 (certainly before 1818); but this is a matter still open to doubt. Benjamin Littlewood died between 1829 and 1833 and was succeeded by his son Thomas. The latter then went into partnership with Berry, the firm being Littlewood & Berry in 1835 and 1841.

Russell's Glasshouse (? Amblecote)[11b]

Mr. Russell had a flint glasshouse near Stourbridge in 1760. If he was Edward Russell, then there is just one indication that it was situated at Amblecote. In 1767 Edward Russell was referred to in the advertisement of Rogers's Amblecote Glasshouse; in the absence of Mr. Rogers he was to show intending lessees over this glasshouse.

Little's Glasshouse

Again there is now nothing to connect this glass-master with any of the later firms. We do know, however, that a glass-maker called Little was working at Stourbridge at the end of the 17th century, for in 1691 and 1692 John Little of Stourbridge, glass-maker, apprenticed two of his sons to Bristol citizens,† and the name Little appears later on in connection with the ownership of two Bristol glasshouses. Mr. John Little was until 1752 proprietor of the flint

---

† A. C. Powell, Glass-making in Bristol, *Trans. Bristol, etc., Arch. Soc.*,
‡ *Bristol Weekly Intelligencer*, 18th July, 1752.
§ H. Owen, *Ceramic Art*, Bristol.

glasshouse at Bedminster,‡ and Messrs. Little & Longman worked another flint glasshouse on Redcliff Backs from 1760 to 1767.§

Brierley Hill Flint Glasswork[22]

We do not know where the "Mr. Honeybourne," flint glass-maker of 1760, had his glasshouse. He was in all probability Richard Honeybourne, who is stated to have founded the Brierley Hill Flint Glassworks in 1776.* The author's own impression is that these glassworks are referred to in 1780 as having been established by Honeybourne and Ensell for making German sheet and crown glass; and that Robert Honeybourne succeeded to the business but converted it into a flint glasshouse. Robert Honeybourne is mentioned in 1781, and as a flint glass-maker in 1793. He was succeeded at the Brierley Hill Flint Glassworks by the firm of Silvers, Mills, & Stevens, who dissolved partnership in 1828.

The Brierley Hill Bottle Works[19]

In the early 19th century there were two glassworks at Brierley Hill, or, as it was sometimes called, Moor Lane. The bottle works were apparently founded before 1771, and were offered on lease in that year by a man named Thomas Seager. They eventually came into the hands of Edward Westwood, who is mentioned as a "victualler" (not a glass-maker) in 1793.† In 1818 the firm was Westwood, Price & Co.; in 1829 Westwood, Moore, & Rider.

Brettle Lane Glassworks[7, 27, 28]

The "Glasshouse in Bottell," mentioned in 1664 as owned by Joshua Henzey, was probably a misreading of manuscript writ-

---

* Hartshorne, *Old English Glasses*, p. 176.
† See *Universal British Directory*.

ing for "the glasshouse in Brettell." Certainly the Henzeys had a Broad Glasshouse in Brettle Lane in 1717; the owners being Paul, John, and Joseph Henzey. About the same time William Andrews also had a Broad Glasshouse at Brettle Lane; but he became bankrupt in 1721. With the death of Joshua Henzey "the younger" in 1738, not only does the name Henzey disappear from the list of Stourbridge glass-makers, but the making of broad glass seems to have declined. The Henzey interest in this manufacture was acquired by the famous firm of John Pidcock, as we have already seen. It is not difficult to assume that one or more of the glasshouses at Brettle Lane were about this time converted into flint glasshouses; and if this is correct, then Denham and even Little may have worked at Brettle Lane in 1760. These suggestions are offered to future investigators. In 1793 we come across the firm of Coltman and Grafton (trade not stated), who are shown by a notice of 1811 to have been glass-makers. One of the partners was of Wordsley, another of Brettle Lane, and it is probable they had at least one glasshouse at the latter place; but this firm appears to have ceased before 1818.

In the 19th century the name of Wheeley is prominently connected with flint glassworks at Brettle Lane, and the original member of this firm of glass-makers, Thomas Wheeley, can be traced back into the 18th century, although not necessarily as a glass-maker.

In 1793 Thomas Wheeley, "Boat Owner," appears in a Directory; this means that his principal business was that of carrier on the canals, but it does not exclude a subsidiary glass concern. In 1796 Thomas Wheeley appears in partnership with Benjamin Littlewood, of Brettle Lane, where they had an "accounting house." The latter was both a banker and a glass-maker; and it is not perhaps a great assumption to make that they were partners in a glasshouse at Brettle Lane at this time. By 1816 Thomas Wheeley had been dead some time, for his share in the glass-making business was represented in the firm by Susannah Wheeley (probably his widow), one of his executrixes. T. and W. S. Wheeley, probably the sons of Thomas, took over the business from 1816, and by 1829 W. S. Wheeley appears as sole proprietor.

The Glassborough Glasshouse at Bilston[13]

Glass-making was probably carried on at Bilston many years before 1761. The place name alone suggests that, and "the new glasshouse" mentioned in 1761 suggests an earlier establishment. John Florry, of Birmingham, erected the new glasshouse at Glassborough on ground leased from Thomas Hoo, Esq. For a time he made bottles and broad glass in partnership with others; but, starting in 1761, various attempts were made to let or sell the glasshouse, which continued until 1765. At this point John Florry was made bankrupt, but had the commission superseded within a few months. He still appears to have carried on the glasshouse until 1774, when he sublet the premises to H. L. & Co., probably H. Loxdale & Co. Loxdale & Jackson were flint glass-makers here, at any rate from 1804 to 1810. After 1810 there is no trace of glass-making at Bilston.

The Longport Glassworks[31]

These were in existence at any rate between 1805 and 1807. At the latter date Thomas Kinnersley, John Davenport, and Edward Grafton, the proprietors, dissolved partnership. It is natural to identify the second partner with the famous potter of Longport. Edward Grafton was probably the expert glass-man, and he may have come from Stourbridge.

The Darlaston Glassworks[32]

Messrs. Rooker and Jackson, who had a glass manufactory at Darlaston in Staffordshire, dissolved partnership in 1807. Nothing further has yet been discovered about this concern.

Shropshire Glasshouses 33, 34

It is stated that there was a glass manufactory at Owestry for making green glass some time before 1751; but one of the glass-makers of Stourbridge bought the concern in order to close it.*

There was a glasshouse at Broseley in 1732, where they made both flint glass and bottles. The glass-makers, Benjamin Batchelor & Co., probably came from Stourbridge way.

And in the 19th century there are two notices of the Wrockwardine Glasshouse, giving the following firm names

1814 Richard Mountford.
1816 Cope, Biddle, Mountford & Cope.
1816 onwards Biddle, Mountford & Cope.

These names are connected with glasshouses both at Stourbridge and at Birmingham. To Wrockwardine have been credited various fancy glass products of the " Nailsea " type; but it is unwise to attribute these fancy articles to any particular glasshouse, as they were made all over the country.

General Notes

The following glass-makers appear in the Appendix or elsewhere, but their place in the history of Stourbridge glasshouses is not yet defined. The numbers refer to the Appendix.

c. 1640-1680 William Tristram.†
    1696 Thomas Cardo and Edward Baughton.[1]

---

* Dr. Pocock, Travels through England.
† Grazebrook, Heraldry of Worcester, p. 580.

1696	John Bague, bottle-maker.[2]
1697	Ananias Henzey and Elisha Batchelour[3]
1698	Edward Houghton, workman at a Bottle House.[4]
1723	Samuel Tizack, of Kingswinford.[8]
1762	William Ireland, of Kingswinford.‡
1774	William Rider, of Wordsley.[21]

The following glasshouses were offered on sale or lease, which cannot yet be fitted with any certainty into this history

1771	A well-established Flint Glass Manufactory.[18]
1781	A glasshouse near Stourbridge, fit for making any kind of glass.[23]
1789	A flint glasshouse in full work.[25]
1805	A flint glass manufactory 3e owned by " N. T." or "N. L" (? Nathaniel . . .).

Of the above, only the second was necessarily about Stourbridge ; there were glasshouses at Dudley, Birmingham, etc., but in the circumstances* all the above were probably situated near Stourbridge.

Acknowledgments

The author is indebted to his brother, Dr. G. B. Buckley, M.C., for valuable help in the research work here recorded; also to Mr. T. Duckworth, of the Victoria Institute, Worcester, for making a search in the Worcester newspapers to 1760; and to all librarians for their continual courtesy and assistance.

APPENDIX

STOURBRIDGE

1. 2nd December, 1696. *Journals H. C.*, xi. 605.

"A Petition of Thomas Cardo and Edward Baughton, on behalf of themselves and other Glass-makers, in and about Stourbridge in the County of Worcester, was presented to the

House, and read: Setting forth, That by a late Act of Parliament, there is a perpetual Duty laid upon all Glass Wares; since which the Petitioners have not had One day's Work: and if the same should be continued, the Petitioners and their Families must starve, or be maintained by their Parishes, though the said Duty is a very inconsiderable income to the Crown, as informed: And praying, That the said Duty may be taken off."
2. 10th December, 1696. *Journals H. C.*, xi. 621.

"A Petition of John Bague and John Jeston, on behalf of themselves, and other Glass-makers in and about Stourbridge in the County of Worcester, was presented to the House, and read; setting forth, That the Petitioners employed many Hundred Families in the making Glass-Bottles, till a Duty was laid upon Glass, which hath put a stop to the Petitioner's trade of making bottles; so that they have not wrought one Day since the Duty commenced."
3. 17th February, 1697. *Journals H. C.*, xi. 707-710.

"Upon the petitions of the glassmakers of Stourbridge, Ananias Henzey and Elisha Batchelour gave the evidence there mentioned."
4. 18th January, 1698. *Journals H. C.*, xii. 47.

"A petition of several Owners of Glass-works in or near Stourbridge in Worcestershire was presented to the House and read."
25th January, 1698. *Ibid.*, p. 60.

"A petition of the poor Working Glass-makers in and about Stourbridge, was presented to the House and read."
21st May, 1698. *Ibid.*, p. 281.

"Evidence upon the Petitions.

Upon the Petition of tile Glass-masters and Workmen in and about Stourbridge, John Jesson said, That he has not made one Bottle since the commencement of the Duty: having had 100

Dozen ever since by him, which he cannot sell, unless to Lose. Edward Houghton, a Workman, said, That there are Three more Work-houses for the Bottle-Trade at Stourbridge, which have not worked since the Duty: and that he has not had one Day's Work since. That one Bottle-house employs 100 People, when at work; and about 50 to a White-house. That there are 6 or 7 of the White Glass-houses at Stourbridge, and five Broad Glass-houses, which employ about the like Number to an House. That the said White and Broad Glasshouses, since the Duty, have worked but very little, viz. 7 or 8 weeks in the time they before used to work 40."

6th March, 1699. *Ibid.*, p. 551.

"A Petition of the Glass-bottle-makers, and other Glass-makers, in and near Stourbridge, was presented and read."

5. 1703. R. Neve, *Builder's Dictionary*, pp. 149 et seq.

"Staffordshire Glass. This sort of glass, which is made in Staffordshire, I could never learn any certain account of it; for 'tis a sort of glass but seldom used in these parts* of the Kingdom."

6. 27th July, 1710. *London Gazette*.

"Whereas several experienced and able workmen in the making of Broad Glass, now inhabiting in the Parish of Oldswinford in the County of Worcester, are willing to be partners, or to work as' journey-men at reasonable rates in any broad glasshouse within the Kingdom of Great Britain. If any persons shall think fit to join with them in any partnership or to employ them as Journey-men, they arc) desired to send word to Mr. Thomas Fryer at tile sign of the Crown in Stourbridge."

7. (a) 10th January, 1712. *London Gazette*.

"Whereas the price of Broad Glass or Window Glass in and about Stourbridge in the County of Worcester, for' many years

---

* I.e. the London area.

past has been 26s. the case. Now all Glaziers and others are desired to take notice that from this time the said Broad Glass or Window Glass will be sold by any of the Broadglass makers thereabouts at 22s. the case, either broad or cut."

(b) 12th January, 1717. *Ibid.*

"Whereas Broad Glass hath been lately sold at 18s. per case at the Glasshouses near Stourbridge; there is now Broad Glass to be sold at 16s. per case, by Paul Henzey, John Henzey and Joseph Henzey, at their Glasshouse in Brettle Lane near Stourbridge aforesaid. And when broad glass is raised in price, due notice shall be given in the Gazette."

8. (a) 12th December, 1721/27th July, 1723. *London Gazette.*

"Bankrupt, William Andrews, late of Brettel, in the County of Stafford, Broad glassmaker."

(b) 13th August, 1723. *Ibid.*

"Insolvent debtor, Samuel Tizack, late of Kingswinford, glassmaker."

(c) 24th August, 1723. *Ibid.*

"Insolvent debtor, Benjamin Batch, late of Amblecoate, glassmaker."

(d) 9th May, 1727. *Ibid.*

"Bankrupt, Henry Bradley, late of Audenbrooke, in the County of Stafford, glassrnaker."

(e) 21st June, 1743. *Ibid.*

"Insolvent debtor, Edward Bradley, late of Wordsley, in the County of Stafford, white glass maker."

9. (a) 19th November, 1731. *London Gazette.*

"Bankrupt, Humphry Jeston, of the Heath near Stourbridge, glass-maker."

(b) 31st August, 1736. *London Evening Post.*

"To be lett by the year, or any town of years, Heath's New Glass. House near Stourbridge, with all conveniencies late in the possession of Mr. Humphry Jesson."

10. (a) 9th October, 1747. *Weekly Worcester Journal*.

"To be sold, the remainder of a lease, being a term of 56 years, of the Dyal Glass-House, near Stourbridge, now in the occupation and possession of Messrs. Godwin and Pideock, together with all convenient outbuildings necessary for glassmaking, and in very good repair, at the yearly rent of £18 5s. 0d.

Also a lease for 3 lives (all now existing) of an estate called the Platts and Meadows, on which is erected a Bottle-House, with adjoining buildings &c. at the yearly rent of £38.

N.B. The stock in trade, together with tile utensils of the said business, will be sold to the purchaser, Enquire of Mr. John Godwin or Mr. John Pidcock at the said Dyal Glasshouse."

(b) 8th April, 1749. *Worcester Journal*.

"John Pideock, near Stourbridge," is mentioned.

(c) 6th January, 1761. *Birmingham Gazette*.

"Wanted, in the Broad Glass and Bottle Glass Trade, several hands, viz. Workmen, Blowers, Gatherers, Founders and Teezers. Any such by applying to Mr. Pideock at the Dial Glasshouse near Stourbridge, will meet with great encouragement and constant employment."

(d) 11th April, 1774. *Ibid*.

"Now in the hands of John Coates * at the Dial Glasshouse in Stourbridge," curtain property stopped on suspicion of being stolen.

(e) 7th November, 1791. *Ibid*.

"Died on Tuesday morning at tile Plats near Stourbridge, John Pidcock Esq., one of the magistrates of the County of Worcester."

(f) 1792. *Lowndes London Directory*.

---

* Possibly the manager or steward of the works.

"John Pideock & Son, bottle warehouse, Lambeth Hill, Thames St., London."

(g) 1st April, 1793. *Birmingham Gazette*.

"Merchants of Stourbridge using local bank-notes:- T. J. & R. Pidcock."

(h) 1798. *Kent's London Directory*.

"T. J. & R. Pidcock, bottle warehouse, 11 Bush Lane, Cannon St."*

(i) 5th November, 1814. *London Gazette*.

"The partnership between John Pidcock, John Henzey Pidcock, George Pidcock and Thomas Pidcock, in the business of glassmakers at Brettell-Lane-End near Stourbridge, trading under the firm of "John Pidcock & Co." was dissolved the 18th October, 1814, by mutual consent, so far as regards the sd. Thomas Pidcock who retired. The trade to be continued by the remaining partners."

11. (a) 12th November, 1750. *Birmingham Gazette*.

"Thomas Rogers, of Stourbridge, elected to serve as High Sheriff of Worcestershire."

(b) 4th April, 1768. *Ibid*.

"To be let and entered on immediately. The Glassworks belonging to Mr. Thomas Rogers near Stourbridge, with all accomodations necessary for carrying on the trade. Further particulars may be known of the said Mr. Thomas Rogers, or of Mr. Edward Russel, near Stourbridge."

(c) 1775. *Dictionary of National Biography*.

"In 1775 James Keir commenced business as glassmaker, and gave it up to take charge of the Soho Iron Works in 1778."

Scott, *Stourbridge* (1832), p. 107, says, "James Keir of Holloway End and Amblecote was succeeded by Benjamin

---

* In 1792 this warehouse was held by Benjamin Godwin.

Littlewood."

(d) 1789. Tunnicliffe, *Survey of Worcestershire*.

" Scott, Keir, Jones & Co., glass manufacturers, Stourbridge."

(e) 1st April, 1793. *Birmingham Gazette*.

The list of Stourbridge traders includes John Scott, William Scott and John Jones, but they were not necessarily glassmakers.

12. (a) 20th June, 1757. *Birmingham Gazette*.

"John Hancocks, in the High Street, (Birmingham) glazier, sells ... good London, Bristol or Stourbridge glass, white or green, cut into large or small squares. Also quart and pint bottles."

(b) 8th February, 1760. *Derby Mercury*.

"Stourbridge white and green glass, and bottles of all sorts, are sold by W. Richardson, glazier, in Derby."

13. (a) 11th May, 1761. Birmingham Gazette.

"To be lett and entered upon immediately, the New Glasshouse at Glassborough, which is now at work near Bilstone, in the County of Stafford, together with several houses for workmen to live in. The said glasshouse is advantageously situated for making of glass, and is also to be supplied with coals by contract on very reasonable terms. Enquire at the said glasshouse, or of Mr. John Florry of Birmingham, one of the present partners, who will be glad to hold a share in the said works. There is now a good set of workmen at the said house for making window glass and bottles."

(b) 16th March, 1762. *Ibid*.

16th March, 1762. *London Evening Post*.

"To be sold or let on 12th April next, the glasshouse at Glassborough, &c.

"N.B. There is now about 100 Pots on the spot, and a new furnace, all fit for immediate use; also all materials, for making window glass and bottles."

(c) 13th June, 1763. *Birmingham Gazette*.

20th June, 1763. *Gloucester Journal*.

"To be sold, the 12th July next, the Glasshouse at Glassborough, within 3 miles of Wolverhampton. All the premises are let under a lease of which about 20 years are unexpired. Window glass and battles."

(d) 18th February, 1765. *Birmingham Gazette*.

"To be sold or lett, the Glasshouse at Glassborough, &c. All which premises are held by lease under Thomas Hoo Esq. for a term of years yet to come and unexpired."

(e) 20th May, 1766. *London Gazette*.

"Whereas a commission of bankrupt, bearing date the 18th January last, was awarded against John Florry of Birmingham, Merchant, now the said commission is superceded."

(f) 11th July, 1774. *Birmingham Gazette*.

"Wanted, a partner in a manufactory of broad glass and bottles, now entering upon in a glasshouse lately erected by Mr. John Florry, and now under lease from him, together with an advantageous contract for coal. Further particulars by leaving a line with S. Aris, directed H. L. and Company."*

(g) 4th June, 1798. *Ibid*.

Elwell Jackson & Son appear in a list of Bilston traders, but the, name Loxdale does not appear.

(h) 1st January, 1811. *London Gazette*.

"Bilstone, Dec. 4, 1810: The partnership between Thomas Loxdale and George Elwell Jackson, as Flint Glass Manufacturers, carried on at Bilstone, Staffordshire, under the firm of 'Loxdale and Jackson,' was this day dissolved."†

---

* Possibly H. Loxdale & Co., who were in possession in 1804.
† These partners were also bankers until 1810 and coalmasters until 1816.

14 (a) 6th September, 1762. *Birmingham Gazette*.

William Ireland, of Kingswinford, "glassmaker and shopkeeper," advertises forbidding credit to be given to his wife Mary.

(b) 13th September, 1762. *Ibid*.

Mary Ireland made a spirited reply to the above, as comprehensive as it was annihilating.

15. (a) 28th July, 1767. *London Gazette*.

"Bankrupt, Samuel Benedict, now or late of Stourbridge, Engraver of Glass."

(b) 1st November, 1785. *Manchester Mercury*.

" S. Benedict, glass manufacturer (i.e. cutter) has arrived from London at Manchester with a large quantity of all kinds of cut glass, &c."

16. 29th September, 1767. *London Gazette*.

"Bankrupt, Elijah Barrar of Amblecot, in Old Swinford, glassmaker."

17. (a) 30th December, 1769. *Newcastle Chronicle*.

"Samuel Richards, apprentice to Pidcock, Ensell and Bradley, to the glass-engraving business, near Stourbridge, absconded his masters' service about 4 months since; went off with John Johnson, by trade a lapidary supposed to be at or near Newcastle-on-Tyne."

(b) 1st April, 1793. *Birmingham Gazette*.

The list of Stourbridge traders includes Richard Bradley and J. Bradley.

(c) 22nd February, 1796. *Ibid*.

"Messrs. Bradley, Ensell, Pagett & Co. have established a manufactory for Glass Bottles of all kinds at Wordesley, near Stourbridge."

(d) 7th March, 1796. *Ibid*.

"26th Feb. 1796. Stourbridge: Messrs. Bradley and Ensells take this opportunity to return their thanks for all favours con-

ferred on their late worthy relation, R. Bradley, and hope for a continuance of the same. The Glass and Coal trade, &c. will be carried on with the same punctuality and dispatch as usual."
(e) 10th March, 1796. *Bristol Gazette*.

"Died, Wednesday, R. Bradley Esq., an eminent glass manufacturer near Stourbridge."
(f) 19th January, 1801. *Birmingham Gazette*.

"Wanted, 3 or 4 overhand glass-cutters. Apply to Bradley, Ensells Holt, Wordsley near Stourbridge."
(g) 20th July, 1827. *London Gazette*.

"The trade formerly carried on by (the undersigned) Richard Bradley Ensell, senior, and by Charles Ensell deceased, and by John Holt, also deceased, at Wordesley under the firm of 'Bradley, Ensells and Holt,' and afterwards by the said R. B. Ensell, son., and J. Holt, since by the said R. B. Ensell, son., (the undersigned) Richard Bradley Ensell, the younger, and Mary Holt respectively under the same firm, and after the marriage of the said Mary Holt with (the undersigned) George William Wainwright, carried on as well in the firm of 'Bradley, Ensells & Holt,' as that of 'Ensells and Wainwright,' or 'Ensells & Co,' has been dissolved by mutual consent as and from the 11th April, 1827. Jeremiah Matthews of Stourbridge was appointed under the decree of the High Court of Chancery as manager for winding up the affairs of the late partnership concerns."

18. 1st April, 1771. *Birmingham Gazette*.

"A manufactory, to be disposed of and may be entered immediately, a well established trade in the Flint Glass Manufactory now in full work, with all the stock, materials, and tools belonging to the same. For further particulars enquire of the Printer."

19. (a) 27th May, 1771. *Birmingham Gazette*.

"To be let, a glasshouse, yard, pot-rooms, store rooms and

other conveniences suitable, and several dwelling houses for workmen, situated at Brierley-Hill in the parish of Kingswinford, very near to the turnpike road leading from Stourbridge to Dudley. Inquire of Mr. Thomas Seager at Brierley Hill aforesaid."

(b) 1st April, 1793. *Ibid.*

The list of Stourbridge traders includes : Edward Westwood.[*]

20. (a) 16th July, 1771. *London Gazette.*

"Thomas Willetts, clerk or agent to Waldron Hill and Thomas Hill of Amblecoat, glassmakers, was robbed of £125 2s. 6d. money of the said W. Hill and T. Hill and also of William Waldron of Stourbridge, glass-maker and copartner with the sd. W. Hill and T. Hill."

(b) 1789. Tunnicliffe, *Survey of Worcestershire.*

Stourbridge, Hill & Waldron, bankers and glass manufacturers.

21. (a) 15th September, 1772. *London Gazette.*

"Fugitive debtor, surrendered to Wood St. Compter, London, Henry Levy, formerly of Stourbridge, late of Shoemaker Row, London, glass-flowerer."

(b) 12th July, 1774. *Ibid.*

"Insolvent and a prisoner in Stafford Goal, William Rider, late of Wordsley, glassmaker."

22. (a) 3rd July, 1780. *Birmingham Gazette.*

"Gorman sheet and crown glass. Honeybourne and Ensell, having established a manufactory of German sheet and crown glass near Stourbridge, beg leave to inform the public that they may be supplied with any quantity on the shortest notice and upon the most reasonable terms."

(b) 3rd September, 1781. *Ibid.*

"Mr. Robert Honeyborne near Stourbridge," is mentioned.

(c) 1789. Tunnicliffe, *Survey*, etc.

---

[*] Edward Westwood was at Brierley Hill, 1818 Directory.

"Stourbridge, George Ensell, glass manufacturer."
(d) 1st April, 1793. *Birmingham Gazette.*
List of Stourbridge traders includes Robert Honeybourne.
(e) 27th May, 1828. *London Gazette.*

"The partnership between Joseph Silvers, James Mills and Joseph Stevens, as flint glass manufacturers, at Moor-Lane in the parish of Kingswinford, was dissolved the 10th May, 182,8, by mutual consent."

23. 23rd July, 1781. *Birmingham Gazette.*

"To be let, a Glass-House near Stourbridge, well situated and in every respect fit for the manufacture of any kind of glass. Enquire of the Printers of this paper."

24. 27th October, 1783. *Birmingham Gazette.*

"To be sold, all that Glass Pot Clay and Coal Work situated at the Lye, near Stourbridge, heretofore the property of John Bourn,* Clay Merchant; a considerable quantity of glass pot clay already got lying in warehouses at Bristol, Stourport, Stourbridge and at the Lye aforesaid. The Clay Works at the Lye are the only works that supply the whole Kingdom with pot clay, without which glass cannot be made; and unless this work is carried on (which is not intended by the present owner) the whole glass pot clay is likely to come into so few hands that the price will be considerably advanced."

25. 16th November, 1789. *Birmingham Gazette.*

"To be disposed of a flint glasshouse, conveniently situated for coal and carriage, and now in full work. Enquire of the printer of this paper,"

---

* Until 1776, J. Bourn was in partnerships with Messrs. Onions and Bache, but after 1776 he carried on the clay business alone. *Birmingham Gazette*, Feb. 19th, 1776.

26. (a) 1789. Tunnicliffe, *Survey*, etc.

"Stourbridge, Sarah Grazebrook, glass manufacturer."

(b) 1st April, 1793. *Birmingham Gazette*.

List of Stourbridge Traders includes T. & M. Grazebrook.

(c) 10th June, 1799. *Ibid*.

"Died at Stourbridge on Friday, aged 80, Mrs. Glazebrook" (sic).

27. (a) 1st April, 1793. *Birmingham Gazette*.

The list of Stourbridge Traders includes: Coltman and Grafton.

(b) 31st December, 1811. *London Gazette*.

"The partnership between Michael Coltman of Wordsley, William Grafton of Brittle-Lane, and William Bacon of Wolverhampton, glass manufacturers, and trading under the firm of 'Coltman and Grafton,' this day expires and is dissolved as far as relates to the said W. Bacon, 30th December, 1811."

28. (a) 1st April, 1793. *Birmingham Gazette*.

The list of Stourbridge Traders includes: Thomas Wheeler.* (sic).

(b) 21st November, 1796. *Ibid*.

The accounting house of Thomas Wheeley and Benjamin Littlewood of Brettell Lane, near Stourbridge, was opened by thieves."

(c) 11th May, 1816. London Gazette.

"The partnership under the firm of 'T. & W. Wheeley,' glass manufacturers, of Stourbridge, and carried on by Susannah Wheeley (one of the executrixes of Thomas Wheeley deceased) and Thomas Wheeley and William Seager Wheeley, so far as respects the said Susannah Wheeley was dissolved the 26th March, 1816. T. & W. S. Wheeley to carry on the business."

29. (a) 1st April, 1793. *Birmingham Gazette*.

---

* Quite possibly a misreading of the signature of Thomas Wheeley.

The list of Stourbridge traders includes: Serjeant Witton.
(b) 30th May, 1801. *F. F. Bristol Journal.*

"Bankrupt, Serjeant Witton of Oldswinford, in the County of Worcester, glass manufacturer."

30. (a) 23rd September, 1805. *Birmingham Gazette.*

"Flint Glass Manufactory. To be disposed of, an established flint glass manufactory, a regular set of men at work, a quantity of orders on hand. Letters post paid, directed left at the Printers, will be attended to. Principals only need apply."

(b) 7th October, 1805. *Ibid.*

A similar notice, adding, "This is such an opportunity for young beginners as seldom occurs, and the premises may be had upon lease at a low rent." Apply "N. I."† &c.

(c) 4th November, 1805. *Ibid.*

A similar notice, adding, "A gentleman having not less than £4,000 at command may be accomodated with a share in the concern." Apply "N. I." &c.

31. (a) 2nd December, 1805. *Birmingham Gazette.*

"To Flint Glass Managers. Wanted, a steady respectable active person, capable of conducting a work of the above description on a large scale. Also wanted at the same Works, a few good foot-blowers; such as understand their trade may earn from 12s. to 18s. a week. Apply to Mr. Grafton, of Longport Glass Works, in the County of Stafford."

(b) 22nd September, 1807. *London Gazette.*

"The partnership lately carried on at Longport in the County of Stafford, between Thomas Kinnersley, John Davenport and Edward Grafton, as manufacturers of and dealers in glass, is dis-

---

† It is presumed that "N. T." is a misprint for " N. I." or vice versa.

solved by mutual consent."

32. 15th September, 1807. *London Gazette*.

"The partnership between James Rooker and William Jackson, glass manufacturers and glass dealers, carrying on trade at Darlaston in the County of Stafford was dissolved the 12th September, 1807.

SHROPSHIRE

33. 30th May, 1732. *London Gazette*.

"Whereas John Barnett, alias Jackus, a pale thin-faced slender youth, a white glass servitor and bottle blower, eloped from his master, Benjamin Batchelor and Company, at Broseley Glasshouse in Shropshire, the 8th May last, where he is a hired servant; this is to require all Masters of that business and others not to employ him, but upon their peril."

34. (a) 29th November, 1814. *London Gazette*.

Richard Mountford, glassmaker, of Donnington-Wood, in the parish of Wrockwardine, Salop, is mentioned.

(b) 20th August, 1816. *Ibid*.

"The partnership between William Cope, John Biddle, Richard Mountford and William Henry Cope, of Wrockwardine-Wood, Salop, glass-manufacturers, carried on under the firm of 'Cope, Biddle, Mountford, & Cope,' was dissolved the 20th December, 1814, so far as respects the said William Cope. The said trade is now carried on under the firm of ' Biddle, Mountford & Co.'"

Universal British, Directory, 1793

Stourbridge. About 10 glasshouses; the output so great, that £20,000 per annum is paid in duty.

Glass manufacturers:
Thomas & Michael Grazebrook.
Richard Bradley.

Hill & Waldron.
Robert Honeyborne (flint).
John Pidcock & Sons.
Serjent Witon,

Stourbridge Directory, 1818

Glassmakers
Bradley, Ensells & Holt, Wordsley Glass Works.
M. Grazebrook & Sons, Stourbridge Glass House.
Hill, Hampton & Co. (bottles), Stourbridge.
Benjamin Littlewood, Holloway End.
Francis Rufford & Sons, Heath Glasshouse.
Westwood, Price & Co. (bottles), Stourbridge.
T. & W. S. Wheeley, Brettle Lane.

TUNSTEAD, GREENFIELD, YORKSHIRE.

The Glasshouses of Dudley and Worcester
By Francis BUCKLEY, F.S.A.

THERE is not very much doubt to-day about the number and character of the old glasshouses near Dudley. There are still short gaps in their history which remain to be filled; but these are comparatively few. The Dudley glass-makers seem to have devoted themselves from first to last almost entirely to the production of flint glass. And when we remember how large a proportion of the glasshouses at Stourbridge and Birmingham also made flint glass, we may get some idea of the vast output of flint glass from the Midland area, commonly called "Stourbridge."

DUDLEY

Dixon's Green Glasshouse[1,3] *

The Dixons seem to have been the pioneers of glass-making in Dudley, and possibly also in Worcester. A member of this enterprising family founded the Whittington glasshouse near Chesterfield in 1704; and it continued in the hands of this same member and his descendants nearly the whole of the 18th century. Possibly the Dixons, glass-workers of Bristol, also came from Worcestershire.

There is no evidence of a glasshouse at Dudley in the 17th century; but, in 1713, Hugh Dixon, of Dudley, glass-maker, became bankrupt; and it may be that he gave the name to Dixon's Green. Jonathan Green seems to have acquired this glasshouse in the middle of the 18th century. He was a somewhat eccentric man, and he called the place "Green's Own Green" or "Green's Green"; although most probably it was identical with Dixon's

---

* The numbers refer to references in the Appendix.

Green. The Dudley Directory of 1781 gives Jonathan Green, glass-maker, at Dixon's Green; this may have been a son of the original Jonathan, who disappeared mysteriously in 1770. In 1793, John and Joseph Green, possibly sons of the second Jonathan Green, seem to have taken over the glasshouse, and they may have continued until the end of the century. Rather later, the following were probably the glass-makers at Dixon's Green:† – 1804, Lee and Large. 1805, William Large. 1806-1808, Large and Hodgetts. The directory of 1829 gives Davies and Hodgetts as glass-makers at Dixon's Green. They continued until 1833; but Bentley's Worcestershire (1841) makes no mention of a glasshouse here. [See Addenda.]

The Holly-Hall Glasshouse[5]

This glasshouse was situated about a mile west of Dudley Market Place.* The first mention of it occurs in 1783, when it was offered on lease in consequence of the death of John Keelinge, Esq., the proprietor. A list of the contents of the glasshouse will be found in the Appendix, No. 5 (b); this is the most complete and instructive list yet discovered. It is not quite certain that Keelinge was the founder of the glasshouse. It may be noted, for instance, for what it is worth, that an apprentice ran away in 1754 from Thomas Griffin (trade not stated) of Holly-Hall and was thought to have gone to Bristol.† After the death of Keelinge, George Ensell took over the glasshouse, but became bankrupt in 1786; and it is thought most probable that at this point Zachariah Parkes, senior, became the glass-master. He appears in lists of Dudley traders (trades not stated) in 1793 and 1800; and at the

---

† See Bradbury, Old Sheffield Plate.
* Bentley, Worcestershire (1841), p. 49. Birmingham Gazette, 11th March, 1754.

latter date James Grainger also appears. Then these two went into partnership with John Roughton, as glass manufacturers, at Holly-Hall, under the firm of "Roughton, Parkes & Co." In 1813, Roughton left the partnership, and the firm became "Parkes, Grainger, and Green." The members of this firm were Zephaniah Parkes, Major Parkes, James Grainger, and George Joseph Green. In 1817, Green left the firm, which became known as "Major Parkes & Co." In 1821, there was a general dissolution of the firm; and at this point, or, perhaps, a little later, Joseph Stevens became glass-master at Holly-Hall; he is recorded as such in 1829, 1833, and 1835, at the latter date the manufacture being given as of "ruby, achromatic, and coloured" glass. Before 1841, "Page and Ensell," Edward Page and Richard Bradley Ensell, took over the business.‡

The Phoenix Glassworks[4]

The Phoenix Glasshouse was situated in Hall Street. Bentley§ states that it was founded about 1780 by William Penn. William Penn was certainly in possession in 1781 (Directory) ; but it may be that he was preceded by Philips Penn of 'Dudley, who lost a servant glass-cutter and an apprentice in 1772.|| William Penn appears in lists of Dudley traders of 1793 and 1800; and he was succeeded (possibly after another proprietor) by John Roughton, who left the Holly-Hall glasshouse in 1813, and probably took over the Phoenix glasshouse at this date. Roughton was in possession in 1818, but had been succeeded by Badger

---

‡ Bentley, *loc. cit.*
§ *Ibid.*
|| It is possible, of course, that Philips Penn was himself only a glass-cutter.

Bros. & Co. some time before 1829. The latter firm (senior partner in 1833 Thomas Badger), remained in possession until 1841, at any rate. At the latter date, the partners were Isaac and Septimus Badger.*

The Dudley Flint Glassworks[6]

Bentley states that these glassworks were situated at the corner of Priory and Stone Streets, and that they were established in 1766. The founder was Abiathar Hawkes, who appears in the 1781 Directory and again in a traders' list of 1800. We do not yet know when he died. A London directory, dated 1816, but based apparently on information at least 4 years earlier, gives Thomas and George Hawkes as glass merchants in Stone Street. These were sons of Abiathar Hawkes. The firm-name was "Thomas Hawkes & Co." in 1818, and so continued until 1841, at any rate. At some date before 1822, Roger Wright Hawkes was taken into the firm, and George Wright Hawkes† died. Thomas Hawkes left the firm in 1827; and about this time Abiathar. Hawkes (the second) joined R. W. Hawkes. In 1841, William Greathead was a partner. [See Addenda.]

The Castle Flint Glassworks[7]

Situated at the end of Tower Street, these were founded before 1818. In 1818, "Cooke, Price & Wood" were the proprietors; namely, Benjamin Cooke, Joseph Price, and James Wood. This firm was dissolved in 1820, and James Wood was apparently left to reconstitute the business. He is mentioned in 1820 and 1823.‡

---

* Bentley, *loc. cit.*
† Presumably the same as George Hawkes mentioned in 1816.
‡ Rollason, Dudley *Non-parochial Registers*.

He was joined by members of the family of Guest; in 1829, the firm was "Guest, Wood & Guest," Joseph Guest being senior partner. In 1841, Joseph Guest and James Wood were still carrying on the business under the same firm-name.

WORCESTER[2]

Of the Worcester glasshouse very little is known. It was at work in 1696, making "flint, green, and ordinary glass." Edward Dixon, glass-maker of Worcester, got into debt and is found in a London debtors' prison in 1727. He was probably at one time the proprietor of this glasshouse. We know nothing further of its history, except that it was standing (not necessarily at work) in 1736.

Acknowledgment

The author wishes to acknowledge with grateful thanks the help of his brother, Dr. G. B. Buckley, M.C. Also that of Mr. T. Duckworth, of the Victoria Institute, Worcester, for having a search made of the Worcester newspapers to the end of 1760.

APPENDIX

1. 7th November, 1713. *London Gazette*.
    "Bankrupt, Hugh Dixon, of Dudley, glassmaker."
2. (a) 3rd June, 1729. *London Gazette*.
    "Insolvent debtor in the Fleet Prison, London, Edward Dixon, late of Worcester, glassmaker."
(b) 5th March, 1736. *Weekly Worcester Journal*.
    "The 26th February last there was taken from the Riverside, out of a meadow near the Glass-house, about mile above Worcester, a fishing rod &c."
3 (a) 4th June, & 2nd July, 1770. *Birmingham Gazette*.
    Jonathan Green, white glass maker, near Dudley, issued a

notice about his wife, signed "J. Green, Green's Own Green" [or "Green's Green"]. His wife replied in a later issue of the same paper, charging him with various offences. To this Green's solicitor issued a reply.

(b) 23rd July, 1770. *Ibid.*

"Mr. Green, who on the 14th day of this month fell into hands, which in defiance of law and reason, as he enjoys a clear exercise of his understanding and prosecutes his business with industry, have under a pretence of lunacy dragged him into an unknown confinement. Reward offered. (signed) JAMES SHAW."

(c) 20th May, 1782. *Ibid.*

"Sale of Coal Mine … situate near and convenient for the sale of the coal at Dixon's-Green Glass-house* at Dudley."

(d) 1st April, 1793. *Ibid.*

List of Dudley traders includes:- John and Joseph Green.

4. (a) 20th June, 1772. *F. F. Bristol Journal.*

"James Horton (glass cutter) hired servant to Philips Pen of Dudley, absconded his master's service on the 25th May, 1772. At the same time went away Daniel Newton (apprentice)."

(b) 8th April, 1793. *Birmingham Gazette.*

List of Dudley traders includes:- William Penn.

(c) 23rd April, 1798. *Ibid.*

"Contributions to the Defence of the Realm, Dudley area. William Penn £21."

(d) 19th May, 1800. *Ibid.*

Another Dudley subscription list includes:- William Penn.

5. (a) 1st December, 1783. Birmingham Gazette.

"To be let and entered upon immediately, a glass-house, in full work belonging to the late John Keelinge, Esq., situate at

---

* Dudley Directory, 1781-Jonathan Green, Dixon's Green.

Holly-Hall within, mile of Dudley, with all convenient out-houses and several houses for workmen. And to be sold all the stock in trade belonging to the said glass-house. Enquire of Joseph Nicklin, at Holly-Hall, who will shew the premises."

(b) 19th April, 1784. *Ibid.*

"To be sold by auction, the whole of the very valuable manufactures stock of glass-ware, late belonging to John Keelinge Esq. deceased, at his glasshouse at Holly-Hall, consisting of above 140 doz. decanters, barrel and Prussian shaped, cut and plain; 80 doz. goblets, sorted sizes, square and round feet, cut and plain; 800 doz. wines, cut and plain; 1100 doz. pint, half-pint, and quarter-pint Weight and Tale tumblers; 640 doz. punch glasses and tumblers; 40 doz. cut and plain ale glasses; 41 doz. rummers, cyders and carofts; 116 doz. castors and cruets, cut and plain; 262 doz. salts and salt linings, cut and plain; 154 doz. sorted smelling bottles; 206 gross white and green phials, sorted sizes; 43 gross Lavender's, Daffy's, Turlington's and Smith's Bottles;* 216 doz. bird fountains and boxes; 52 street lamps. Together with a large quantity of salvers, butter-boats, trifle dishes, scollop-shells, mustards, patty-pans, candlesticks, compleat apparatus, blue bacons, cream jugs and many other articles.

"Also the furnaces, moulds, machines, and all other the utensils and interiors of the said glasshouse and mill; together with a large quantity of cullet, about 140 pounds of borax, about 3 cwt. of American pearl. ashes, salt-petre, arsenic, emery, antimony, pumice stone, &c., &c."

(c) 10th June, 1786. *London Gazette.*

"Bankrupt, George Encell, of the parish of Dudley, glassmaker."

---

* These were shapes used by famous medicine-sellers, who thus gave their names to the different shapes.

(d) 3rd July, 1786. *Birmingham Gazette*.

"To be let and entered upon immediately a glass-house, situate at Holly-Hall in the parish of Dudley, together with all necessary buildings for carrying on the flint glass trade. The manufactory is now in full work by the assignee under a commission of bankruptcy against George Encell.

(e) 8th April, 1793. *Ibid*.

List of Dudley traders includes:-
Zachariah Parkes, sen., and Zachariah Parkes.

(f) 19th May, 1800. *Ibid*.

A Dudley subscription list includes:-
Zachariah Parkes. James Grainger.

(g) 31st August, 1813. *London Gazette*.

"The partnership lately subsisting between John Roughton, Zachariah Parkes the Elder and James Grainger, glass manufacturers at Holly-Hall near Dudley, under the firm of 'Roughton, Parkes & Co.,' was dissolved the 28th August, 1813. J. Roughton to collect debts, &c."

(h) 9th August, 1817. *Ibid*.

"The partnership carried on by Zepheniah Parkes, Major Parkes, James Grainger and George Joseph Green, of Holly-Hall in the parish of Dudley, glass manufacturers, under the firm of 'Parkes, Grainger and Green,' was dissolved the 19th July, 1817, so far as relates to the said G. J. Green."

(i) 14th August, 1821. *Ibid*.

"The partnership between Zepheniah Parkes, Major Parkes and James Grainger, as glass manufacturers at Holly Hall, Dudley, under the firm of 'Major Parkes & Co.' was dissolved the 1st March, 1821."

6. (a) 8th April, 1793. *Birmingham Gazette*.

List of Dudley traders includes:-
Abiathar Hawkes.

(b) 19th May, 1800. *Ibid*.

A Dudley subscription list includes:-
Abiathar Hawkes.

(c) 28th January, 1816. *London Gazette*.

Messrs. Hawkes & Co., of Dudley, glass manufacturers are mentioned.

(d) 31st August, 1822. *Ibid*.

"The partnership between Thomas Hawkes, Roger Wright Hawkes, and the executors of the late George Wright Hawkes, deceased, as glass manufacturers at Dudley, under the firm of 'Thomas Hawkes & Co.,' was as regards the executors of the said G. W. Hawkes dissolved on the lot July, 1822."

(e) 20th March, 1827. *Ibid*.

"The partnership between Thomas Hawkes and Roger Wright Hawkes, as glass manufacturers at Dudley, was dissolved by mutual consent on the 31st December, 1826."

7. 19th September, 1820. *London Gazette*.

"The partnership between Benjamin Cooke, Joseph Price and James Wood of Dudley, glass manufacturers, was dissolved the 11th September, 1820. All debts due to the said firm of 'Cooke, Price and Wood,' are to be received by the said James Wood."

DUDLEY DIRECTORIES
(1) 1781

Glassmakers
  Jonathan Green, Dixon's Green.
  Abiathar Hawkes, High St.
  William Penn, Hall St.

(2) 1818

Glass Manufacturers
  Thomas Hawkes & Co., Stone St.

Major Parkes & Co., Holly-Hall. John Rowton (sic), Phoenix Glass Works.
Cooke, Price & Wood, Castle St.

(3) 1829

Glassmakers
Badger Bros. & Co., Phoenix Glass Works.
Davies & Hodgetts, Dixon's Green.
Guest, Wood & Guest, Tower St.
Roger Wright Hawkes and Abiathar Hawkes, Stone St.
Joseph Stevens, Holly-Hall.

ADDENDA

6th March, 1829. *London Gazette*.
"The partnership between Roger Wright Hawkes and Abiathar Hawkes, as glass manufacturers, under the firm of 'Roger Wright and Abiathar Hawkes' is this day dissolved by mutual consent. 24th December, 1828."

21st August, 1832. *London Gazette*.
"The partnership between Thomas Davies, William Edward Davies and William Hodgetts, carrying on the business of glass manufacturers at Dixon's Green in the parish of Dudley, under the firm of 'Davies and Hodgetts,' was dissolved the 1st June last. All accounts will be settled by the present firm, William Hodgetts and William Edward Davies."

TUNSTEAD, GREENFIELD,
YORKSHIRE.

The Birmingham Glass Trade: 1740–1833
By Francis BUCKLEY, F.S.A.

THE early history of glass-making at Birmingham is still buried in obscurity. There is just enough to show that ordinary glass-making was carried on there before 1750. Birmingham had also taken up the "small glass" trade, the making of glass buttons, beads, and toys, and "glass pinching," which appears to have been of the same character. And for this the town became as famous as any district in the country. When glass-cutting came into fashion in the Midlands, it was taken up with enthusiasm by the people of Birmingham. They supplied the Sheffield plate-makers with a considerable amount of cut glass from 1784 onwards, and in 1800 and 1805 a celebrated firm of cut glass manufacturers from London advertised in Birmingham for glass cutters.*

Several, of the owners of large glasshouses about Birmingham first started business in a small way, as fabricators of glass toys or as glass cutters.

The Snow Hill Glasshouse[1,3] †

Mr. Hammond, proprietor of a great glasshouse near Birmingham, who died in 1743, was perhaps the founder. But this is by no means certain, because there were several glasshouses in Birmingham in the middle of the eighteenth century.‡ Mayer Oppenheim, or Opnaim, has long been famous far obtaining a patent in respect of red and ruby flint glass; this happened in

---

* Appendix, 22.
† The numbers refer to references in the Appendix.
‡ Hartshorne, p. 102.

1756.§ We now know that he worked at the Snow Hill glasshouse. And although he tried to dispose of the glass business in 1762, it is probable that he continued work there until 1775, when he became bankrupt. After that, he languished for several years, an insolvent debtor, in a London debtors' prison, making repeated attempts to obtain release under the Insolvent Debtors Relief Acts. Eventually he became free and went abroad to retrieve his fortunes. In France he made two unsuccessful attempts to establish the manufacture of English flint glass; first at Petit-Quévilly, in 1783, and later near Rouen, in 1784.‖

After Oppenheim left Birmingham a relation, Nathaniel Oppenheim, remained on Snow Hill, and is heard of in connection with an attempt to start a new glasshouse. But nothing further is known of him or of the Snow Hill glasshouse. Glass toy-making, etc., was carried on at 87 Snow Hill until 1795.¶

The Park Glasshouse, Birmingham Heath[6]

Isaac Hawker, the founder of this glasshouse, started as a glass-cutter in Spiceal Street, Birmingham. In 1772 he removed to 14 Edgbaston Street, where eventually a small furnace for making glass was established. It is called a "glasshouse" in 1778. About this time Hawker was joined for a very short period by John Hodgson as partner. Isaac Hawker left the premises in Edgbaston Street in 1788; this was, therefore, probably the date of the opening of the Park Glasshouse. Isaac Hawker took his son John into partnership, and the latter continued the glass business, both as glass-maker and glass-cutter, after his father's death in 1792. John Hawker still worked the glasshouse in 1803; but before 1808 it

---

§ Ibid., p. 461.
‖ M. le Vaillant, "Les Verreries do la Normandie," pp. 300, 521.
¶ Appendix, 9 (b).

passed into the hands of Biddle and Lloyd. This firm probably consisted of John Biddle and David Lloyd, who were until 1815 also partners with Thomas Fearon as glass-cutters. Biddle and Lloyd retained the Park Glasshouse until 1822, at any rate, and John Biddle appears in 1833.

Glass Factory, 4 Bartholomew Street[7]

This seems to have been a short-lived affair, and it is an incident only in the career of a successful glass-cutter, Daniel Hughes. He was one of the earliest glass-cutters in Birmingham, carrying on business at first in Brick-kiln Lane. In 1779 he removed to New Market Row, and later on took a partner, Barrett, who appears with him in 1797 at the cut glass factory in Bull Street. Shortly afterwards Barrett left the partnership, which became by 1799 "Hughes and Harris" (D. Hughes and Thomas Harris). It would seem that the factory for making glass had already been commenced in Bartholomew Street, and a list of articles "manufactured" is given in 1799. A directory of 1803 shows that the glass-cutting business still continued in Bull Street, whilst the making of glass took place in Bartholomew Street. Next year Daniel Hughes and Thomas Harris dissolved partnership, the former taking over the glass-cutting business, the latter the glass-making business; and this closes the connection of Hughes with glass-making. In 1805 he became partner as glass-cutter with Thomas Fearon, and the partnership continued until 1810. Daniel Hughes only lived a few months after this, during which period he was partner with William Lowe, as "Daniel Hughes & Co."

Belmont Glass Works[16]

We now continue the career of Thomas Harris, who left the partnership firm "Hughes and Harris" in 1804 in order to take up the glass-making business. It would seem that two glass-making establishments were founded a smaller one in Fazeley Street, "Thomas Harris & Co." (T. Harris and Thomas Lakin Hawkes, which is mentioned in the Directory of 1808 and came to an end in 1810; and a larger affair at Ashted, in the parish of Aston, the Belmont Glass Works, carried on under the firm of "Harris, Smart and Co." The partners here were Thomas Harris, T. L. Hawkes, Thomas Smart, and Rice Harris. In 1810 Hawkes and Smart left the firm, and Thomas Harris and Rice Harris continued the business until 1814. Then Rice Harris left and was replaced by John Harris. John Harris retired in 1819, and the firm became "Harris, Gammon & Co." (probably Thomas Harris, William Gammon and Thomas Lowe. T. Harris eventually died or retired, and the firm became "William Gammon & Co." T. Lowe retiring in 1832, William Gammon appears under the same firm name in 1833.

Aston Glass Works

These were situated on Aston Hill, and may have been founded as early as 1794, when James Smart began to supply the platemakers of Sheffield with cut glass.* The manufactory here is mentioned in 1799. At this time a partnership was formed between George Jones, James Smart, Charles Glover, and Francis Bird, and they carried on the glassworks under the firm of "Jones, Smart & Co." The firm was dissolved in 1810. In the Directory of 1816 Brueton Gibbons & Williams appear at the Aston Glassworks. The former was supplying cut glass to Sheffield between 1806 and 1812.† It is not possible at present to trace these glassworks later than 1816, and they may have been abandoned be-

---

* Bradbury, Sheffield Plate.
† Bradbury, loc. cit.

fore 1822. Brueton Gibbons is mentioned as "Merchant and Manufacturer" in 1831.‡

The New Town Glasshouse, Walmer Lane[9,12]

Up to the year 1790 William Avery and Richard Hudson had carried on the business of glass button- and toy-makers at 87, Snow Hill. In that year Avery left the business, and Hudson was joined by William Shakespear. The partnership firm of "Hudson and Shakespear" continued to carry on business at the same premises until 1795, when Hudson left and Shakespear continued the business on his own account. Shortly after this Owen Johnson (a glass toy-maker) and William Fisher joined William Shakespear, and they set up a glasshouse in Walmer Lane, called the New Town Glasshouse. In 1799 Fisher left the firm, which continued as "Shakespear and Johnson," being mentioned in 1803. But within the next two years a new partnership was formed and the business of making glass was transferred to the Islington Glass-works on Birmingham Heath. Nothing further is heard of the New Town Glasshouse.

The Islington Glassworks[12]

Owen Johnson had a glass toy manufactory of his own in Birmingham, which was destroyed by fire in 1799. Shortly after this he seems to have set up glassworks at Islington on his own account, and he appears here alone in the Directory of 1803. On the abandonment of the New Town Glasshouse, however, the partners there, W. Shakespear and O. Johnson, were joined by John Berry, and these three carried on business as glass manufacturers at Johnson's Glassworks at Islington until 1816, when

---

‡ London Gazette, Jan. 4th, 1831.

the partnership was dissolved. Shakespear founded or went to the neighbouring Soho Glassworks, and Johnson and Berry took a now partner, Rice Harris. The same firm, "Johnson, Berry & Co. is mentioned in 1822. In 1829 Owen Johnson retired, and in 1832 John Berry did the same. Thus, in 1833 we find "Rice Harris & Co." in the parliamentary list of Birmingham glassmakers; and presumably he still worked at the Islington Glassworks.

The Soho Glassworks[12]

William Shakespear left the Islington Glassworks in 1816 and, took into partnership Thomas Fletcher. They are described in the Directory of 1816 as of the Soho Glassworks, and in 1822 as of Birmingham Heath. So it would appear that these glassworks were situated on Birmingham Heath. In 1822 Fletcher left the firm, and in 1833 we find the name "Hannah Shakespear & Co." in the parliamentary list.

The Union Glassworks

Between 1816 and 1818 Messrs. Bacchus, Greer, and Green appear to have set up these glassworks. The firm is mentioned again in 1822 as "Bacchus and Green," and in 1833 as George Bacchus & Co.

The Greatbrook Street Factory[15]

John Hodgson left the firm of Hawker and Hodgson in 1778, and at once advertised for a partner in the glass trade. The name Hodgson occurs again, first as William Hodson (sic) in two notices of 1807, but in 1808 as William Hodgson. "Madeley, Hodson & Co." made both china and glass, the partners being G. Madeley, W. Hodson, W. Haywood, P. F. Muntz, and J. Roberts.

In 1807 Madeley took over the china business, and the other partners (as "Haywood, Hodson & Co.") the glass business. But later in the same year the glass partnership was also dissolved, and W. Hodson was left to carry on the business on his own account. He appears in the Directory of 1808 as "William Hodgson, glass manufacturer, Greatbrook Street." Nothing further is known of the business.

The Span Lane Glassworks[17,20]

These glassworks were founded in 1815 by Thomas Shutt, of Smethwick, for making crown window glass. He appears alone in the Directory of 1816. He was joined later by Philip Palmer. Together they carried on the business as "The British Crown Glass Works Company" until October 17, 1822, when Thomas Shutt died. In 1824 Messrs. Chance bought these works, and thus became associated with the business, which they have made famous all over the world. It is interesting to note that R. L. Chance had from 1816 onwards a London glass warehouse at Dowgate Wharf, Thames Street, possibly in connection with the Nailsea glasshouse, near Bristol; also that Messrs., Chance and Co. had a business as "factors" in Birmingham, at least as early as 1809.

Osler's Broad Street Glassworks

This famous firm was founded in the early years of the nineteenth century. Mr. Thomas Osler came to Birmingham in 1807, and started business as a glass toy-maker in partnership with Mr. Shakespear. The business was at first carried on in Great Charles Street ;and at this time they acquired a reputation for making "glass-drops" and spangles. Thomas Osler was succeeded about 1831 by Messrs. A. F. Osler and T. C. Osler, who in 1832 removed to premises in Broad Street. It was under the direction of these two gentlemen that the firm rose to eminence, at first chiefly as makers of glass chandeliers, but later on in many other departments of the out glass trade.

Miscellaneous

The following local items may be noticed:-
- 1755 Richard Rose, glass button-maker.[2]
- 1765 Jonas Peploe, glass toy-maker.[4]
- 1772 John Barr, glass pincher.[5]
- 1772 Benjamin Bridgman, glass pincher.[5]
- 1790 Abner Wheeler and Richard Barber, glass toy-makers.[8]
- 1793 Mr. John Price, glass manufacturer.[10]
- 1796 Mr. Shaw, Glass Manufactory, High Street.[11]
- 1799 William Darby and John Phillips, glass toy-makers.[13]

The following glass-cutters are referred to in the Appendix:
- 1815 Fearon, Collins & Co. 1824. Fearon & Parkes.[18]
- 1820 J. and J. Allen & Co.[19]
- 1825 Cox and Johnson.[21]

Also Thomas Henley, glass-cutter, of Birmingham, was bankrupt in 1832. [*London Gazette*, 10th August, 1832.]

Two isolated notices of glass-makers in Warwickshire also appear,[23, 24] namely, John Bench, a wandering glassmaker, from Warwick, and George Roberts of Emscote,* in the parish of Milverton, who came to grief in 1763. There appears also to have been some glass-making carried on at Wolverhampton in the early nineteenth century.[25]

Acknowledgment

The author wishes to acknowledge the help of his brother, Dr. G. B. Buckley, M.C., in undertaking part of the research work.

---

* Half-way between Leamington and Warwick.

Also the courtesy and assistance of the officials at the Birmingham and Manchester Public Libraries.

It is well to insist once again that the object of these articles on the Glasshouses of England is to stimulate further local research, and that they are limited in scope by the newspaper record. Thus famous firms may not appear in this record, just because they prospered from the start and made no partnership change. The author is accordingly much indebted to Prof. W. E. S. Turner for procuring the materials for a short note on the famous firm of Osler, who commenced business within the period covered by this article.

APPENDIX
1. BIRMINGHAM

1. 8th October, 1743. *Craftsman*.

"Dead, Mr. Hammond, proprietor of a great Glasshouse near Birmingham."

2. 10th May, 1755. *London Gazette*.

"Insolvent debtor, Richard Rose, late of Birmingham, glass button maker."

3. (a) 22nd February, 1762. *Birmingham Gazette*.

"Mayer Opnaim, at his Glass-House on Snow-Hill, Birmingham, being willing to leave off the foreign hard ware trade, or the inland Glass Manufactory, any person that is disposed to carry on either of the above trades, may by allowing him a reasonable premium (with a capital of £1,000) be put in such a way as to clear £500 a year, or with a less sum, in proportion."

"The above Glasshouse, and the Dealing House, or Part of the said Building, to be let for a time, as can be agreed upon. Enquire of the said Mayer Opnaim, who has to sell a large parcel of Lynn sand and fine white arsenick. N.B. The Red Transparent Glass is to be had at the above Glasshouse, either in a light rose or deep ruby colour."

(b) 1st January, 1770. *Ibid*.

"Wanted immediately, different Hands, men and boys, glassmakers and tisseurs, either to work at Birmingham or at London, in the said business. Any person being out of employment may apply to Mr. Mayer Opnaim at his glasshouse on Snow Hill, Birmingham. N.B. Good wages will be allowed to good workmen."

(c) 13th February, 1775. *Ibid*.

Mayer Oppenheim issues a notice.

(d) 13th May, 1777. *London Gazette*.

"Bankrupt, Mayer Oppenheim, otherwise Opnaim, late of Birmingham, Glassmaker."

(e) 4th July, 1778 to 26th February, 1780. *Ibid*.

"Prisoner for debt in King's Bench Prison, London, Mayer Oppenheim, otherwise Opnaim, late of Birmingham, glassmaker."

(f) 7th December, 1778. *Birmingham Gazette*.

"Glass-house. Any person willing to be concerned in erecting a glass-house, for the purpose of carrying on the glass trade in the Cane and Ware way, may be acquainted with particulars respecting the same, by applying to Mr. Nathaniel Oppenheim, on Snow-Hill, who intends to join in carrying on the same."

4. 25th. November, 1765. *Birmingham Gazette*.

"William Hall, apprentice to Jonas Peploe, Glass Toy-maker in Birmingham, eloped his master's service."

5. (a) 25th April, 1772. *London Gazette*.

"Insolvent, John Barr, formerly of Sleaney St., Birmingham, glass-pincher."

(b) 19th May, 1772. *Ibid*.

"Insolvent, Benjamin Bridgman, formerly of Birmingham, glass-pincher."

6. (a) 27th July, 1772. *Birmingham Gazette*.

"Isaac Hawker, Glass cutter, is removed out of Spiceal Street to No. 14 Edgbaston Street, Birmingham, where he has laid in a fresh assortment of cut and plain glass, and a great variety of smelling bottles, which are sold much cheaper than anywhere else in Town.

"N.B. Wanted, a boy about 14 years of age, as an apprentice to the above trade. A premium will be expected."

(b) 14th September, 1772. *Ibid*.

[Adds to the above notice.] "Ran away from the above Isaac Hawker, Timothy Heseltone, hired servant, and took with him Thomas Wharton, an apprentice to the above Isaac Hawker."

(c) 2nd June, 1777. *Ibid*.

"Samuel Grange, an apprentice to Isaac Hawker, glass-cutter, left his master's service."

(d) 16th November, 1778. *Ibid*.

"At Hawker and Hodgson's Glasshouse in Edgbaston Street, Birmingham, are made all kinds of plain and cut glasses. The best price for broken glass."

(e) 21st December, 1778. *Ibid*.

"John Hodgson, who has lately been connected with Mr. Isaac Hawker, which partnership being now dissolved, would be glad to engage with a person already concerned in the glass trade as partner, or in erecting a house suitable for that business in Birmingham or any of the adjacent towns."

(f) 27th March, 1786. *Ibid*.

"James Nutt, glass-cutter, apprentice to Isaac Hawker, glass manufacturer and cutter, absconded."

(g) 29th September, 1788. *Ibid*.

"Isaac Hawker, glass manufacturer and cutter, is removed from No. 14 Edgbaston Street to No. 14 New Street, where he continues to sell, wholesale and retail, a great variety of cut and plain glass. All sorts of smelling bottles, cut, mounted in gold, silver, &c., &c."

(h) 16th April, 1792. *Ibid.*

"John Hawker, since the decease of his Father, Isaac Hawker, continues to manufacture all kinds of cut and plain glass on his own account. Park Glasshouse, Birmingham Heath."

7. (a) 18th October, 1779. *Birmingham Gazette.*

"D. Hughes, glass cutter, is removed from Brickiln Lane to New Market Row, where he continues to sell all sorts of plain and cut glass."

(b) 11th December, 1797. *Ibid.*

"Glass cutters wanted. Good workmen may obtain employment by applying to Hughes and Barrett at the Manufactory, Bull Street, Birmingham."

(c) 26th August, 1799. *Ibid.*

"Hughes and Harris, Bull St., Birmingham, manufacture and sell Glass Chandeliers, Girandoles, Candlesticks and Brackets, Epergnes, Sallad Bowls, Salts, Liquor Squares, Decanters, Smelling Bottles mounted in gold, silver or other metals; with a variety of other articles in glass."

(d) 18th November, 1799. *Ibid.*

"Two or three under-hand Glass-cutters may meet with constant employ by applying to Hughes and Harris, Bull St., Birmingham."

(e) 5th May, 1804. *London Gazette.*

"The partnership lately subsisting between Daniel Hughes and Thomas Harris of Birmingham, glass manufacturers and glass cutters, was dissolved on the 21st April by mutual consent. The branch of the business which consists of glassmaking will in future be carried on by Thomas Harris; and that branch of it, which consists of glass cutting, by the said Daniel Hughes."

(f) 20th January, 1810. *Ibid.*

Birmingham, Jan. 17th, 1810: "The partnership which hath subsisted between Daniel Hughes and Thomas Fearon, glass manufacturers, trading under the firm of Hughes and Fearon, was this day dissolved by mutual consent."
(g) 20th October, 1810. *Ibid.*
"The partnership, which subsisted between Daniel Hughes and William Lowe, of Birmingham, Glass cutters and Glass grinders, under the firm of 'Daniel Hughes and Co.,' was this day dissolved by the death of the said Daniel Hughes, 18th October, 1810."
8. 10th May, 1790. *Birmingham Gazette.*
"The partnership lately subsisting between Abner Wheeler and Richard Barber, of Birmingham, seal-stone engravers and glass toy makers, was dissolved the 1st May, 1790."
9. (a) 24th July, 1790. *London Gazette.*
"The partnership lately subsisting between William Avery and Richard Hudson, under the form of Avery and Hudson, Glass Button and Toymakers, in Birmingham, was dissolved the 1st Instant by mutual consent." [W. Avery to collect debts, &c.]
(b) 23rd May, 1795. *Ibid.*
Birmingham, 19th May: "The partnership hitherto subsisting between Richard Hudson and William Shakespear, of Birmingham, Glass Button, Bead and Toymakers, carried on under the firm of Hudson and Shakespear, was on the 19th May dissolved by mutual consent. The trade in all its branches will be continued by Richard Hudson at No. 30 Great Charles Street, and by William Shakespear at their late Manufactory No. 87 Snow Hill."
10. 18th. April, 1793. *Bristol Gazette.*
"Last week was married, at Aston, near Birmingham, Mr. John Price, glass manufacturer of Birmingham."
11. 13th June, 1796. *Birmingham Gazette.*

Mr. Shaw's Glass Manufactory, High Street, Birmingham, is mentioned.

12. (a) 4th February, 1799. *Birmingham Gazette*.

"The partnership lately subsisting between Owen Johnson, William Shakespear and William Fisher, of Birmingham, glassmakers, trading as Shakespear and Co., was the 1st February, 1799, dissolved by mutual consent. The trade will in future be carried on by Owen Johnson and William Shakespear."

(b) 4th February, 1799. *Ibid*.

"To Glassmakers. Wanted immediately a good Caster-hole Workman, and a good Bye-place ditto. None but such need, apply. Liberal wages will be given by applying to Messrs. Shakespear and Johnson, New Town Glasshouse, Walmer Lane, Birmingham."

(c) 5th September, 1799. *Bristol Gazette*.

"Sunday evening last, an alarming fire broke out in the glass toy manufactory of Mr. Johnson of Birmingham, and burnt with such rapidity that the whole was destroyed."

(d) 19th November, 1814. *London Gazette*.

Messrs. Shakespear, Johnson and Barry (sic), of Birmingham, glass manufacturers, are mentioned.

(e) 2nd February, 1816. *Ibid*.

"The partnership between William Shakespear, Owen Johnson and John Berry of Birmingham, flint glass manufacturers, under the firm of 'Shakespear, Johnson & Berry,' was dissolved the 20th December, 1815."

(f) 2nd July, 1822. *Ibid*.

"The partnership between William Shakespear and Thomas Fletcher of Birmingham Heath, glassmakers, was dissolved the 29th June, 1822."

(g) 8th May, 1829. *Ibid*.

"The partnership between Owen Johnson, John Berry, and

Rice Harris of Birmingham, glass manufacturers, was dissolved the 4th May, 1829, so far as respects the said Owen Johnson. In future the trade will be carried on by Messrs. J. Berry and R. Harris."

(h) 14th August, 1832. *Ibid.*

"The partnership between John Berry and Rice Harris of Birmingham, glass manufacturers, was dissolved the 9th August, 1832, by mutual consent. The trade will in future be carried on by Rice Harris."

13. 1st July, 1799. *Birmingham Gazette.*

"Dissolution of partnership between William Darby and John Phillips of Birmingham, glass toy-makers. Each to carry on business on his own separate account.

"To glass-bead and glass-toy makers; wanted several hands. Apply to John, Phillips, Bartholomew Row."

14. (a) 7th October, 1799. *Birmingham Gazette.*

"Glass cutters. Wanted two or three over-hand cutters. Good workmen will meet with constant work and good wages, by applying at Jones, Smart & Co.'s Glass Manufactory, Aston Hill, Birmingham."

(b) 2nd January, 1810. *London Gazette.*

"The partnership, which subsisted between George Jones, James Smart, Charles Glover, and Francis Bird, of the parish of Aston nigh Birmingham, glassmakers, under the firm of Jones, Smart and Co., was dissolved on the 27th February, 1806, by mutual consent."

15. (a) 7th April, 1807. *London Gazette.*

"G. Madeley retires from the Partnership between George Madeley, William Hodson, William Haywood, Philip Frederick Muntz, and Joseph Roberts, of Birmingham, 'Glass and China Manufacturers,' trading under the firm of 'Madeley, Hodson & Co.' The other partners continue to carry on the glass trade un-

der the firm of 'Haywood, Hodson & Co.'"
(b) 19th September, 1807. *Ibid.*

"The above glass partnership was dissolved, William Hodson to carry on the business on his own separate account."

16. (a) 10th April, 1810. *London Gazette.*

"Dissolution of partnership between Thomas Harris, Thomas Lakin Hawkes, Thomas Small,* and Rice Harris, of Birmingham, glass manufacturers, under the firm of 'Harris, Smart & Co.'

"Dissolution also of partnership between Thomas Harris and Thomas Lakin Hawkes of Birmingham, glass manufacturers, under the firm of 'Thomas Harris and Co.'"

(b) 8th November, 1814. *Ibid.*

"Dissolution of partnership between Thomas Harris and Rice Harris, of Ashted nigh Birmingham, glass manufacturers. Thomas Harris to continue the business on his own account."

(c) 7th September, 1819. *Ibid.*

"The partnership between Thomas and John Harris, of Birmingham, glass manufacturers, was dissolved the 10th July last by mutual consent."

(d) 9th November, 1832. *Ibid.*

"The partnership between William Gammon and Thomas Lowe of Ashted juxta Birmingham, Flint Glass Manufacturers was dissolved the 6th November, 1832, by mutual consent. The business will be carried on by the said William Gammon."

17. (a) 10th April, 1810. *London Gazette.*

"The partnership lately subsisting between William Chance, Edward Homer and Robert Lucas Chance, of Birmingham, factors, under the firm of 'Chance, Homer and Chance,' was dis-

---

* Possibly an error for "Smart."

solved the 29th August, 1809."

(b) 1st November, 1823. *Ibid.*

"The partnership between William Chance the Elder, Robert Lucas Chance, William Chance the Younger, George Chance, Edward Chance and George Crane, of Birmingham, factors, was dissolved the 31st December, 1814."

18. (a) 21st January, 1815. *London Gazette.*

"The partnership between John Biddle, David Lloyd, Thomas Fearon and George Collins, Birmingham, Glass cutters, under the firm of 'Fearon, Collins & Co.,' was dissolved the 13th January, 1815."

(b) 9th March, 1824. *Ibid.*

"The partnership between Thomas Fearon and Jeremiah Parkes, of Birmingham, glass-cutters, was dissolved by mutual consent the 1st November, 1823."

19. (a) 12th August, 1805. *Birmingham Gazette.*

"To glass-cutters. Wanted immediately several Hands in the above line. Either under-hand or over-hand workmen may hear of constant employ. Enquire of Mr. W. Allen, druggist, Bull Ring, Birmingham."

(b) 30th September, 1820. *London Gazette.*

"The partnership between John Smart Allen, James Smart Allen and Benjamin Smart Allen, of Birmingham, glass-cutters, carried on under the firm of 'J. and J. Allen & Co.,' was dissolved the 14th August, 1820, by mutual consent. The trade will in future be carried on by the said John S. Allen."

20. 13th November, 1824. *London Gazette.*

"The partnership between Philip Palmer and Thomas Shutt of Smethwick, in the County of Stafford, glass manufacturers, carried on under the firm of the 'British Crown Glass Works Company,' was dissolved the 17th October, 1822, by the death of the said Thomas Shutt."

21. 8th January, 1825. *London Gazette*.

"Dissolution of partnership between Isaac Cox and Henry Johnson, of Canal Street, Birmingham, glass-cutters, on the 12th October, 1824. Isaac Cox to continue the business."

22. (a) 6th October, 1800. *Birmingham Gazette*.

"Glass-cutters. Wanted in a respectable Glass Manufactory in London, one overhand Cutter and one underhand Cutter. Messrs. Handcock and Shepherd, Glass Manufacturers, Charing Cross, London."

(b) 15th April, 1805. *Ibid*.

"Wanted at Messrs. Hancock, Shepherd & Co.'s Glass Manufactory, Cockspur Street, London, a number of under-hand cutters."

II. WARWICKSHIRE

23. 6th December, 1760. *Ipswich Journal*.

20th July, 1761. *Salisbury Journal*.

"Mr. John Bench, from Warwick, glass toy-maker and glass blower. He has likewise a wheel for spinning glass, and also blows hollow glass men, called 'Merry Merrills,' to show the public the pressure of air in a decanter of water."

24. 25th January, 1763. *London Gazette*.

"Bankrupt, George Roberts of Edmondscott in the parish of Milverton, in the County of Warwick, glassmaker."

III. WOLVERHAMPTON

25 (a) 24th August, 1811. *Bristol Journal*.

"Bankrupt, W. Glaye of Wolverhampton, glass manufacturer."

(b) 4th January, 1812. *London Gazette*.

"William Bacon of Wolverhampton retired from the firm of 'Coltman and Grafton,' glass manufacturers, on the 30th December, 1811." [Note.- This was a Stourbridge firm, but there may have been a business also at Wolverhampton.]

BIRMINGHAM DIRECTORIES–GLASS-MAKERS

1801

John Hawker, Birmingham Heath. Owen Johnson, Islington. Shakespear & Johnson, New Town Row.

1808

Biddle & Lloyd, Park Glasshouse, B. Heath.

1816

Biddle & Lloyd, Park Glasshouse.
Brueton, Gibbons & Williams, Aston Glass Works.
Thomas & John Harris, Belmont Glass Works.
Johnson, Berry & Harris, Islington Glass Works.
Shakespear & Fletcher, Soho Glass Works.
Thomas Shutt (crown window), Spon Lane.

TUNSTEAD, GREENFIELD,
   YORKSHIRE.

Old London Glasshouses. I. Southwark
By Francis BUCKLEY, F.S.A.

THE earlier fragmentary accounts of the old glasshouses of Southwark may be found collected in the Victoria County History of Surrey. Mr. W. H. Bowles mentions some of them incidentally in his privately printed " History of the Vauxhall Glasshouses," etc. (1926). The present writer gave a more detailed account of them, based chiefly on old newspaper advertisements, in a small privately-printed book, "Old London Glasshouses," issued in haste in 1915. Since then further systematic research amongst the newspapers and the discovery of several old billheads of glassmakers have added considerably to our knowledge. So that it has become desirable to make a public record of the present information collected about the Southwark glasshouses.

1. St. Mary Overies Glasshouses[1-8]

"The great old glasshouse next St. Mary Overies Church" (i.e. St. Saviour's) stood between the Church and the Dock Head. It was probably the oldest glasshouse in South London at the end of the seventeenth century; it may indeed have been one of the sites of window glass making about 1550. We get a more satisfying glance at the history of this glasshouse between 1672 and 1676, when it was being worked as a bottle and green glasshouse by Capt. Thomas Morris. There is no evidence whatever that this particular glass-house ever came directly under the control of John Bowles. But before the end of the century, probably by 1690 it was in the hands of a syndicate or "Stock-jobbing" company, of whom Peter De Lanoy and Richard Richmond were the

---

* The numbers refer to the Appendix.

figure heads. The glass-house survived till 1702 or 1703; and we know that during its last few years as a glasshouse it was occupied by Mr: Jackson, perhaps one of the working members of the syndicate. After an abortive attempt to re-let the place as a glasshouse, it was in the year 1703 converted into warehouses; and apparently the old foundation was dug up in 1772.

This was not the only bottle-house near St. Saviour's, Southwark. There was another, described in 1742 as "behind St. Mary Overys." It was probably one of the glasshouses owned by the De Lanoy syndicate about 1696, and seems to have passed into the hands of Joshua Jackson, who died in 1742, a member of a well-known family of Southwark glassmakers. This glasshouse was taken over, sooner or later, by Gerard Vanhorn and worked by him as a bottle-house. He is mentioned here in 1751, but came to grief financially in 1760.

2. The Tooley Street Glasshouse[9 & 10]

There appears to have been a glasshouse in Tooley Street, not far away from St. Saviour's. It is described as being "at the corner of Tooley Street," and the warehouse "opposite St. Olave's Church." Here, apparently, in 1758 Mr. Thomas Bradford was in possession; and in 1795 Mr. Page is recorded as being at the glasshouse. It is not known what kind of glass was made, or when the concern was given up; and there is no record of it in the Parliamentary list of glasshouses in 1833.

3. The Stony Street Glassworks[11-18]

Glassworks, of considerable celebrity in the eighteenth century, stood not far away from St. Saviour's Church, but to the southwest. They were situated at the corner where Deadman's Place crossed Stony Street. These works, consisting of a flint glasshouse and a bottle house, were erected by John Bowles (with William

Lillington as partner), shortly before 1678; and from first to last they remained, so far as we know, in possession of members of the family of Bowles. The factory was famous for its excellent flint glass, including curious glasses for ornament. Later on, it is recorded as the principal factory in England for the production of enamel glass, used in the making of clock dials and for decorating the stems of wineglasses, etc. (1774–1777). There is no record amongst the Bowles family papers of these two glasshouses after 1738; but they are mentioned by Dossie as being in their possession in 1764. Probably the business was given up about the same time that the Vauxhall and Ratcliff factories came to an end, if not before. It now appears to be certain that the two glasshouses at Stony Street are referred to in the Foreigner's Guide to London, 1729 to 1763, as worthy of a visit of inspection. The wealth of the Bowles family enabled them to hire and employ the ablest glassworkers in the country, and no doubt some of the, finest English table glass was made here in the eighteenth century.

4. The Bankside Glasshouses[15,19-36]

The earliest glasshouse at the Bankside, Southwark, known as the "Bear Garden Glasshouse," was also an early venture of John Bowles, who established bottle glassmaking here before 1684. But this glasshouse was destined for more meritorious and profitable work. Shortly after 1684 John Bowles commenced those experiments in making fine window glass, which resulted in the invention of "Crown Glass," as he called it. This was an improvement on Normandy glass, and also on the earliest English varieties of Normandy glass, first made by John Bellingham at Lambeth under Patents of 1679 and 1685. On the completion of his invention, in 1691 Bowles removed the Crown glass manufactory to a glasshouse in Ratcliff, and the Bear Garden glasshouse came into other hands. It is thought that the syndicate of glassmakers who took it over included Robert Hookes and Christopher Dodsworth, who on June 12th, 1691, obtained a patent for 14 years for making fine window glass and "casting glass and particularly looking glass plates, much larger than ever was blown in England or any foreign parts." Crown glass was also made here in 1699. By 1702 blown plate glass was being made, and for some years was the main production. The work was now in the hands of a syndicate or company, eight in number, of whom Henry Richards was one, and probably Mr. Clyatt another. There is ample evidence that the making of plate glass at the Bear Garden was successful, and that it continued to be made there for many years, being overshadowed eventually by the celebrated Plate Glass Works at Vauxhall. In 1717 the syndicate of eight seems to have concluded operations at the Bear Garden, and a new Company took over the works, making both plate glass and crown glass. The glassworks in Southwark, "towards Vauxhall," mentioned in the Foreigner's Guide to London, 1729 to 1763, as making the finest pier and coach glasses, were undoubtedly the Bear Garden glasshouses. It is possible that the Vauxhall Plate Glass Company acquired the Bear Garden glasshouse in 1717. In 1775 we do find a notice of a looking glass manufactory on the Rankside, in the hands of Messrs. Webb & Philips, but hardly the Bear Garden. The "Bear Garden" glasshouse was situated in Bear Alley near Bear Garden Square. It is therefore quite distinct from another Bankside glasshouse, once a pot-house, which was situate at the Bear Garden Stairs, and is mentioned in 1710 and 1712. This building was used for a short time as a glasshouse and closed down before March 1710. A third glasshouse was set up on the Bankside in 1770, for the purpose of making fine flint glass; the actual site being on Pike Green. For three years it was worked by Robert Armistead and

Francis Philpot, until they became bankrupt. Richard Russell, Junr., another flint glassmaker, from the Salt Petre Bank glasshouse, came into possession; but he also came to grief, in 1782. Thomas Stocks, a bottle maker, then took the works and is found there or in the neighbourhood until 1797.

5. *The Falcon Glasshouses*[37-48]

The "Falcon Glassworks" is a name still famous in English glass history. Originally the name was given to a glasshouse near the Falcon Stairs, situate at the south end of what is now Blackfriars Bridge. When the original glasshouse site was abandoned, at the beginning of the nineteenth century, the name was carried to a new site in the same neighbourhood. In 1877 the "Falcon Glassworks" were removed to a spot near the Old Kent Road and finally, in 1895, to Stourbridge.

The original glasshouses near the Falcon Stairs were founded, it is thought, by Francis Jackson, who was here in partnership with John Straw in 1693, making "the best and finest drinking glasses, and curious glasses for ornament, and likewise all sorts of glass bottles." Francis Jackson is famous for organising a strong and successful opposition to the War Tax on Glass during the period 1695 to 1699. This alone is an indication of his energy and capacity as a business man. But it brought him into acrimonious conflict with John Bowles, who was a Commissioner of Glass Duties and favoured the tax. It is interesting to note that Jackson was accused by the Commissioners of trying to engross the flint glass trade of the country. And he appears to have been widely engaged in floating joint-stock glass companies. Later on, the breach between "Jackson" and "Bowles" was healed, for we find these two families in partnership at the Vauxhall Plate Glass Works. Probably Francis Jackson died shortly after 1700; he was succeeded by William Jackson (probably his son), who carried on business at the Falcon Stairs Glasshouses as "William Jackson & Co.," until 1752. In 1751 he had offered the two glasshouses known as the "Falcon" bottle-house and the "Cockpit" flint glasshouse, for sale or on lease. It is not quite certain what happened to these two glasshouses after 1752. One of them was taken by a firm of flint glassmakers, Hughes & Winch, in 1752; this presumably was the Cockpit " glasshouse. Their successors were Hughes, Hall & Co. (17(30), and Stephen Hall & Co. (1765-1780). Stephen Hall then left the Falcon Stairs and went to the Whitefriars Glasshouse. At this point the "Cockpit" glasshouse probably was abandoned. The connection of Jerom Johnson, a well-known London glass-cutter, with this glasshouse in 1757, is interesting; perhaps he became a partner for a time. The "Falcon" Glasshouse, formerly the bottle house, is not mentioned between 1752 and 1768; but it may have been taken over by William Barnes & Co. at the former date. The directories give William Barnes & Co. (1768); Cox and Farquharson (1774); Daniel Cox and his sons (1781-1803); Green & Pellatt (1803-1814). This glasshouse was known as the "Falcon Glass-house" (1802 and 1803) and can probably be identified safely with the old "Falcon" bottle-house, although flint glass was made there at least from 1774. In 1814 the old Falcon glasshouse was abandoned, and Green & Pellatt removed their works to a site in Holland Street near the Blackfriars Road. In 1831 Apsley Pellatt & Co. succeeded to the business, and this is the present firm's name. Besides especially beautiful cut glass, this firm produced (about 1820-1840) a special kind of "crystallo-ceramic," or cameos in glass, much prized to-day.

6. The Gravel Lane Glasshouse[49-56]

The original Falcon Stairs Glasshouses were situate to the east of Gravel Lane; on the west side of the Lane, not very far away, another glasshouse stood at least as early as 1720. For a time there are only slight indications of the owners, it is still a matter for conjecture. Thus Charles Lowdin, bottle-maker, in this Parish (Christ Church, Surrey) became insolvent in 1730; whilst Francis Dixon, presumably his partner, fled abroad to escape his creditors. Four years later, John Hunt and William Warden of Southwark, glass-makers, are listed as bankrupts. They may have worked here or at the Tooley Street glasshouse. A little later the history of the glasshouse becomes more certain. Joseph Hughes and John Brettel, makers of enamel glass, are mentioned here in 1748. Clearly they also had been in some financial difficulty, but they were able to continue the business. Later on, in 1762, Thomas Flower and John Barras were using the glasshouse as a bottle factory. The partnership changed before 1774, when Robert Vigne & Co. were the glass-makers; Barras, however, remained with the firm until he became insolvent in 1776. Robert Vigne & Co. continued until 1778, but after that they disappear from the Directories and probably the glasshouse came to an end.

7. The Old Barge Stairs Glasshouse[57-60]

In February 1730 a new glasshouse was completed on the Surrey shore, opposite the Temple. John Matthews & Co., makers of bottles and green glass, were the first in possession. Sooner or later, the business was taken over by Messrs. Brent and Lowe, who in 1748 and 1752 advertised their "double-annealed" bottles at this glasshouse. Samuel Lowe, the junior partner, acquired the business before 1760 and continued it until 1776, when his name disappears from the Directories. Shortly after 1776 therefore it is probable that the glasshouse was closed down. The Glass Excise Act of 1777, imposing further heavy duties on glass, may have been very discouraging to the Southwark glassmakers; several firms disappear from view just about this time.

Acknowledgment

The author is much indebted to Mr. Ambrose Heal for valuable information from his Collection of Bill Heads, and to his brother Dr. G. B. Buckley, M.C., for a few very helpful references.

TUNSTEAD, GREENFIELD,
   YORKSHIRE.

APPENDIX

   1. The St. Mary Overies Glasshouses.

1. 1550. *Aliens in London* (Hug. Sec.) Vol. I.
p. 202. "Augustyn Imbreck of Antwerp, with Willem Thomas, een glassmaker."
p. 203. "Baldwin Bunckenson, a glaesmaker, with Rober."
p. 204. "Jacob Nannes of Lyfherden, glassmaker, at Southwark."
2. 1672-76. *Clayton Collection of M.S.S.* [Ambrose Heal Collection of Bill Heads.]

A bill directed to Sir Robert Clayton and endorsed "Capt. Morris receipt for Bottell."

"At the Green Glasse house in Southwark.

			£	s.	d.
1672 Nov. 11.	30 doz. quart Bottles		6	0	0
„ 12.	17 doz. quar. mar.		4	5	0
	10 doz. qua. pla.		2	0	0
„ 14.	6 doz. qua. mar.		1	10	0
1673 Apr. 17.	10 doz. qua. pla.		2	0	0
1674 June 15.	2 gross qua. pl.		4	4	0
Sept. 4.	12 doz. qua. mar.		2	14	0
1675 Apr. 27.	24 doz. quarts mar.		5	3	0
May 5.	12 doz. „ „		2	14	0
Nov. 30.	24 doz. „ „		4	16	0
1676 Apr. 1.	12 doz. „ „		2	3	0

Received for the use of Mr. Thomas Morris, (signed) Wm. Wilson."

Note.– A higher price was charged for bottles "marked" with the owners crest or monogram.

3. 15th January, 1696. *Journals House of Commons*, xi. 391.

"A Petition of the Masters, Workmen and Servants of the Glass-houses in Southwark was presented to the House and read, setting forth reasons against the War Tax on Glass."

17th February, 1697. *Ibidem*. xi. 707-710.

"Mr. Jones said that at St. Mary Overs Glass-house, he has had but 15 weeks work since the duty; and that the Glass-house is offered to Sale."

4. c. 1695-99. *Treasury Papers*, xlii. 29.

"To the Right Hon. the Lords Commissioners of the Treasury. The humble petition of Peter De Laney, Esq., and Richard Richmond, Gentleman, and others, the owners of the Green Glass Houses near St. Saviour's, Southwark."

Another petition against the War Tax on Glass (1695-99.)

5 (a) 10th January, 1702. *The Flying Post/ The Post Man*.

"In Southwark, near St. Mary Overies Dock and Church, is a convenient Glass-Bottle-House, Warehouses, Store-yard for Coals, and Tenement for Clerk, and other Conveniences, and for Carriage and Recarriage of the Goods, is to be lett. Inquire at Mr. Peters near the Monument."

(b) 25th April, 1702. *The Flying Post*.

"Near St. Mary Overies Church and the Dock head there is the convenienst Glass-House about London, with Ware-houses and several Counting-Houses, Dwelling-houses and Store-yard, and other Conveniences, to be let, late in the Occupation of one Mr. Jackson. Enquire at Mr. Peters," &c.

(c) 9th March, 1703. *Ibidem*.

"The great Old Glass-House, next St. Mary Overies Church,

is now converted into fins Ware-Houses, and a large square yard in the middle, and a Dwelling-House, fit for any trade that requires room, is to be lett. Inquire at Mr. Peters's," &c.
(d) 15th August, 1772. *F. F. Bristol Journal*.

"London. Some workmen … were employed to dig up the old Foundation of the Glass-House in the Borough Market."
6. 23rd March, 1731. *Daily Post*.

"Between St. Margaret's Hill and the Glass-House at St. Mary Overy's."
7 (a) 8th October, 1742. *Rayner's London Morning Advertiser*.

"Friday. On Thursday last died at his House in Goodman's Fields, Mr. Jackson, Master of the Bottle Glass House behind St. Mary Overy's Church in Southwark."
(b) 6th September, 1743. *London Gazette*.

"All persons that have any demands on the estate and effects of Joshua Jackson, Glassmaker, late of St. Saviour's, Southwark, deceased, are to bring in the same to Messrs. Smith and Horne, his Executors."
8 (a) 12th June, 1751. *Daily Advertiser*.

"John Simpson, late servant in the Glasshouse of Mr. Gerrard Vanhorn in the Borough of Southwark, on the 15th March last left the service of his said Master."
(b) 15th April, 1760. *London Gazette*.

Gerard Vanhorn, of the Parish of St. Saviour's Southwark, Glass Bottle-Maker, bankrupt. (Certificate granted 31st May.)

2. The Tooley Street Glasshouse

9. 16th March, 1758. *Public Advertiser*.

"The Glass Warehouse of Mr. Thomas Bradford, opposite St. Olave's Church, Southwark, was broke open."
10. 1795. *London and its Suburbs*. (Concanen & Morgan), p. 157.

"Jackson's Gift. Mr. Page at the glasshouse, the corner of Tooley Street, pays yearly Mrs. Jackson's gift." (Gift founded in 1660, by the will of Henry Jackson.)

3. The Stony Street Glasshouses

11 (a) 1st January, 1678. *History of the Glass Sellers' Company*, S. Young, p. 69.

By Indenture of this date it is recited that John Bowles and two others "are Masters of several Glasshouses and works for making green glass near to the City of London."

(b) 1st April, 1678. *Ibidem*, p. 70.

By Indenture of this date it is recited that "John Bowles and William Lillington do in partnership keep and are Masters of a Glasshouse and works for making white and green glasses in Southwark."

12. 19th September, 1710. *London Gazette*.

"Deadman's Place, near the Glasshouse, in Southwark."

13. 1720. J. Strype's 1st edition *Stow's Survey*, p. 28.

"Stony Street begins at Counter Street end and runs to St. Mary Overies Stairs, a pretty long street ... with a Glass House in it."

"Glass House Yard, a mean place, goes to the Glass house, and thence with a turning passage into Rochester Yard."

14. 11th June, 1723. *London Gazette*.

"George Hickson, late of Stone Street, St. Saviour's Southwark, Labourer to the Glasshouse," insolvent debtor.

16. 1729-1763. *Foreigner's Guide to London*, p. 140.

"There is a very considerable Market in the Borough of Southwark; and particularly two very fine Glass-Houses, in one of which Glass Bottles and Drinking Glasses and several pretty Curiosities in Glass worthy of sight are made; but in the other, towards Vauxhall, are made large Pier-Glasses, also Glasses for Coaches, and others of the finest work."

16. 25th April, 1744. *Penny London Morning Advertiser*.

A man was committed to prison, "for stealing a large quantity of Composition Glass, value £3, out of the Warehouse of Benjamin Bowles, Esq., of Stony Street, Southwark."

17. 1st January, 1747. *London Courant*.

"To be disposed of for ready money. At the White Glass House, near St. Mary Overies Church, in Southwark. A quantity of Glass Cane for making Beads, of various colours, and of very good temper, which as the Warehouse is to be cleared in a little time, will be sold greatly under the present price. Also about 56 lb. of White Enamel, and a few Half-Pint and Quarter-Pint green Bottles for Elixirs, to be had cheap in proportion. The Clerk attends every Day, Thursday Excepted."

18. 1758-1764. Dossie, *Handmaid to the Arts*.

(N.B.-Written about 1758 and published 1764).

"White opake glass has been made at a considerable work in London in great quantities, not only manufactured into a variety of vessels, but used as a white ground for enamel in dial plates, &c."

"The white glass made at Mr. Bowles's glasshouse in Southwark is frequently used for the grounds of enamel dial plates."

4. The Bankside Glasshouses

19. 1st September, 1684. *History of Glass Seller's Company*, p. 72.

By Indenture of the above date it was recited that "John Bowles is Master of several Glasshouses at St. Mary Overye's and the Bear Garden in Southwark, for making of Green glass."

20. 4th June, 1691. *London Gazette*.

"There is now made at the Bear-Garden Glass-house on the Bank-side Crown Window-Glass, much exceeding French Glass in all its Qualifications; which may be squared into all sizes for

Windows, and other uses."

21. 6th June, 1692. *Ibidem*.

"Whereas the Patentees and Undertakers for the Improvement of the Glass Manufacture in England did think fit till things Were settled, to close their Books, And whereas all Makers are now agreed, they do give Notice, that the Books are now opened, and that all sorts of exquisite Looking-Glass Plates, Coach-Glasses, Sash and other lustrous Glass for Windows and other uses (far exceeding Normandy) may be had at their several Workhouses as formerly."

22. 23rd January, 1699. *Ibidem*.

"The best sort of Window-Glass for Sashes or Pictures, commonly called Crown or Normandy Glass, is made in greater Perfection than formerly at the Bear-Garden Glass-house in Southwark and sold at reasonable rates."

23. 15th January, 1702. *Ibidem*.

"At the Bear-Garden Glass-house in Southwark, are Looking-Glass Plates, blown from the smallest Size upwards to 90 inches, with proportionable Breadths, of lively Colour, free from Bladders, Veins, and Foulness, incident to the large Plates hitherto sold."

24. 1703-1726. Neve's *Builder's Dictionary* (1st & 2nd editions).

"Crown-glass … Was at first made at the Bear-garden on the Bankside. … But now at the Bear-garden Looking-glass-plates are made."

[N.B.-In the 3rd edition, 1736, the last sentence is omitted.]

25. 7th October, 1703. *Post Man*.

"Stolen out of the Glass-house Field at Vauxhall in Lambeth, Surry, a mare. Notice to … Henry Richards at the Bear Garden Glasshouse."

26. 5th January, 1706. *Ibidem*.

"Isaac Colonet, alias Gurney, Glass-maker, being under articles for some years to come, and having absented himself from his service above two years, to the great damage of the Concerned. Whoever will discover the said Isaac Colonet to the Proprietors of the Plate Glasshouse on the Bank Side, Southwark, so that he may be taken into custody, shall be well rewarded."

27 (a) 20th February, 1706. *Journals H.C.*, xv. 163.

A Bill for preventing the setting up of any new Glasshouse, &c., within a mile of Whitehall Palace.

(b) 7th December, 1706. *Ibidem*, 207.

A Bill for the suppression of all new Glasshouses, &c., erected since the beginning of this Parliament within a mile of Whitehall Palace, &c.

(c) 16th January, 1707. *Ibidem*, 239.

The latter Bill was defeated.

(d) Case of John Gurnley. *Guildhall Tracts*, Z.Z. 110.

Petitioning Parliament against the above Bills, John Gurnley stated,

For several years last past the Proprietors of a Glass-House at the Bear-Garden, eight in number, had "endeavoured to engross to themselves the making of Looking-Glass-Plates"; … and "came at last to have the sole trade of Glass-Plates" … "Therefore Mr. Gurnley and his partners, about two years ago, did purchase several tenements and a large piece of Ground in Lambeth, over against Hungerford Market, on which they built a Glass-House at the expense of about £7,000," &c., &c.

28. 25th May, 1717. *Daily Courant*.

"The Glass-houses, &c., commonly called the Bear-Garden, near the Bank Side in the Parish of St. Saviour, Southwark, to be let, from Michaelmas next. Enquire of Mr. Clyatt in New Thames Street, near the said Glass houses."

29. 1st June, 1720. *Ibidem*.

"The Company at the Bear Garden Glass-House in Southwark, do hereby give Notice, That they have made, and do continue to make the finest of Crown Glass."

30. 1775. *Directory*.

"Webb and Philips, looking glass manufactory. Bankside, Southwark."

31 (a) 7th March, 1710. *Post Man*.

"To be let, several warehouses, and other large buildings, yards and conveniences, formerly a Pot-house,' lately a Glasshouse, fit for a Brew-house or to build upon, near the Bankside at the Bear-Garden Stairs in Southwark."

(b) 27th November, 1712. *Daily Courant*.

"To be let, several warehouses and other large buildings, lately a Glasshouse, near the Bank Side at the Bear Garden Stairs."

32 (a) 29th May, 1773. *London Gazette*.

"Bankrupt, Robert Armistead and Francis Philpot, of the Bankside, Southwark, Glassmakers and copartners."

(b) 7th April & 2nd June, 1778. *Ibidem*.

"The Commission of Bankruptcy against Robert Armistead and Francis Philpot formerly of the Bankside, Southwark glassmakers, was superceded."

33. 26th July, 1773. *Morning Post*.

"By order of the assignees of Messrs. Armistead and Philpot, glass-makers, bankrupts, at their Manufactory, situate on the Pike Green, facing Mason Stairs, Bankside, Southwark. To be sold, all their elegant valuable and extensive stock and implements in trade, consisting of a great variety of rich cut, wrought and plain glass of every denomination, colour, &c., a large parcel of fine unworked metal, cullet and other articles. Also the unexpired term of 38 years from Christmas next of their large Glasshouse, &c., now in good repair, having been built but little

more than 3 years, subject to a small annual ground rent of £10."
34. 12th February, 1774. *F. F. Bristol Journal.*

London … "near the glass-House, Bankside, Southwark."
35. 24th December, 1782. *London Gazette.*

"Bankrupt, Richard Russell; the Younger, of Bankside, Southwark, Glassmaker."
36. 1785-1790. *Directories.*

"Thomas Stocks, bottle glasshouse, Bankside, Southwark."

[1797. Thomas Stock. Glass Manufacturer, Falcon Stairs, Southwark.]

5. The Falcon Glasshouses

37. 27th February, 1693. *London Gazette.*

"To be sold all sorts of the best and finest Drinking-Glasses, and curious Glasses for Ornament, and likewise all sorts of Glass Bottles, by Francis Jackson, and John Straw, Glassmakers, at their Glass-Houses near the Faulkon in Southwark, and at Lynn in Norfolk."
38. 17th February, 1697/1st April, 1699. *Journals House of Commons*, xi. 707, xii. 627.

Francis Jackson gave evidence before the House of Commons relating to the hardship of the War Tax on Glass.
39. 7th June, 1718. *The Post Man.*

"The Faulcon Glass House in the Upper Grounds, Southwark," is mentioned.
40. 1720. J. Strype's 1st edition *Stow's Survey*, IV. 27.

"Cockpit Yard, with narrow passages falls into Gravel Lane, having in it only two Glass Houses." Cockpit Yard is marked on the Map, and lies to the east of Gravel Lane, in the angle formed by Gravel Lane and Upper Ground (Willow St.).
41. 7th September, 1728. *London Gazette.*

"Whereas William Sherry, Michael Lasher, John Matthews and

John Skinner, all covenant servants by Articles, and Daniel Matthews, an apprentice, to Mr. William Jackson and Company, Glassmakers in South-wark, have lately deserted their service, and are supposed to be gone to a Glass-House near Yarmouth," – notice against employing them. William Jackson.

42. 25th May, 1751. *Ibidem*/21st February, 1752. *Daily Advertiser*.

"To be lett, two well-accustomed Glass-Houses, situated in Gravel. Lane, near the Falcon, Southwark, known by the names of the Falcon and Cock-pit Glass-Houses; one a Flint-Glass house, with an eight-pot Furnace, almost new, with tools and all other necessaries for immediate working; the other a Bottle-Glass House, with a very good Furnace, and all manner of materials, fit for immediate use. If not let to the same business, the materials will be disposed of. Enquire of Mr. William Jackson, of the same place."

43 (a) 20th October, 1757. *London Evening Post*.

"Glass Shop the corner of St. Martin's Lane, Strand. All the glass and stock in trade to be sold off cheap, &c. After all are sold, shall remove to the Cockpit White Flint Glasshouse near the Falcon Stairs, Southwark. Jerom Johnson."

(b) 19th November, 1757. *Whitehall Evening Post*.

"Before I remove to the Cockpit White Flint Glass-house, &c., some month's notice will be given by Jerom John Johnson."

44. 1752-1780. *Directories*.

Glasshouse near Faulkon Stairs, Gravel Lane, Southwark.
    1752   Hughes and Winch.
    1760   Hughes, Hall & Co.
    1765-1780   Stephen Hall & Co.

45. 1768-1814. *Directories*.

Glasshouse near Falcon Stairs, Southwark.
    1768   William Barnes & Co.
    1774   Cox & Farquharson.

1781	Daniel Cox.
1790.	Daniel Cox & Son.
1792	Alexander Thomas Cox & Co.
1793-1803	A. T. & J. Cox.

46. 27th February, 1802. *London Gazette*.

"7th Jan., 1802. All persons indebted to the estate of John Chapman late of the Falcon Glasshouse, Blackfriars Bridge, gentleman, deceased, are to pay the same to Messrs. Alexander Thomas Cox and James Cox of the Falcon Glasshouse."

47. 21st May, 1803. *Ibidem*.

"The partnership lately subsisting between Alexander Thomas Cox and James Cox, late of the Falcon Glasshouse, Gravel Lane, Southwark, Glass Manufacturers, was dissolved by mutual consent on the 20th February, 1802."

48. 1803-1814. *Directories*.

Glasshouse near Falcon Stairs, Southwark: Green & Pellatt.

6. The Gravel-Lane Glass-House

49. 1720. J. Strype's 1st edition *Stow's Survey*, Appendix, p. 83.

A map of the Gravel-Lane area is shown, with a glasshouse marked a little to the west of the Lane, in the Upper Ground, near Paris Gardens.

50 (a) 7th March, 1730. *London Gazette*.

"Insolvent debtor, Charles Lowdin, late of the parish of Christ-Church, Surrey, Glass Bottle-maker."

(b) 2nd March, 1731. *Ibidem*.

Francis Dixon, late of the parish of Christ-Church, Surrey, glassmaker, being a fugitive for debt, returns and surrenders himself, with a view to taking advantage of the Act for Relief of Insolvent Debtors.

51. 2nd April, 1734. *London Gazette*.

"Bankrupt, John Hunt and William Warden, late of Southwark, glass-makers and partners."

52. 16th November, 1748. *Daily Advertiser*.

"All persons indebted unto Joseph Hughes and John Brettel, of the Parish of Christ-Church, Surrey, Glassmakers and partners, are to pay their debts to E. Shallett, Southwark, Coal-merchant." … Thus notice "refers to only such debts as were due to them before the 5th November last, and the work is carried on by the said Joseph Hughes and John Brettell as before, who hope to have the continuance of the favours of their former customers. Note, at their Glasshouse in Gravel Lane, Southwark, may be had all sorts of colour'd Cane at 10d. per pound, black at 5d. per pound, likewise all sorts of composition and enamels."

53. 25th August, 1761. *London Gazette*.

Insolvent, Timothy Verren, glass-blower, Christ Church, Surrey.

54 (a) 8th January, 1762. *Public Advertiser*.

"At the Glass House in Gravel Lane, Southwark, are made best Mould Wine Bottles of all sizes, best champagne Bottles, Mould Pottle Bottles, commonly called Scotch Pints; Gallon Squares for Sea service; Pottle and Quart Squares for Oil, Olives, Anchovies and Pickles; Pints and Half-Pint Squares for Snuffs and Mustard; Pint, Quart and Pottle Fruit Bottles for Pastry Cooks; Variety of Chemical Ware, as Retorts, Receivers, Bolt heads; large Bottles from one to eight, ten to twelve gallons; Globes of all sizes, from 20 to 30 Gallons for Aquafortis; from 100 to 160 gallons for oil and spirit of vitriol; Imparting Glasses for Refiners; large Mellon glasses for gardeners; and all other, goods in the Bottle-Glass way, at the lowest price. All orders will be diligently observed by Thomas Flower, John Barrass. All the above goods are doubly anneal'd."

(b) 2nd October, 1762. *Ibidem*.

The above notice is repeated, adding, "N.B. Bottles mark'd with Coats of Arms or Names."

55. 1774—1778. *Directories*.

Robert Vigne and Co. Glasshouse, Gravel-Lane, Southwark.

56. 25th June, 1776. *London Gazette*.

"John Barras, formerly and late of Gravel-lane, St. Saviours (sic) Southwark, glassmaker, insolvent debtor."

Further notices of his insolvency appear on the 12th, July, 1777 and 9th June, 1778. *London Gazette*.

7. Old Barge-House Glasshouse

57. 3rd February, 1730. *London Gazette*.

"At the new Glass House by the King's Old Barge-House, over-against the Temple, in Southwark, are made all sorts of Glass Bottles, Chymical Glasses, Mellon Glasses, &c., and sold at reasonable rates by John Matthews and Company."

58 (a) 1st April, 1748. *Clayton M.S.S., Ambrose Heal Collection of Bill Heads*.

"Messrs. Brent and Lowe, at ye New Glass-house at ye Old Barge House, opposite ye Temple, in the County of Surrey.

" All glass made at this House is double annealed; no other has convenience for that purpose, though the most effectual way to make it durable and fit for exportation."

Sir Kenrick Clayton	£	s.	d.
36 Mellon glasses	3	12	0

(b) 28th February, 1752. *Ibidem*.

"Messrs. Brent and Lowe, at ye New Glass-house," &c., &c.

(c) 6th May, 1760. *Ibidem*.

"Samuel Lowe at the New Glasshouse at ye Old Barge-House, opposite ye Temple, in the County of Surrey."

58. 25th March, 1769. London Gazette.

Mentioned in a list of London merchants, Samuel Lowe.

60. 1763-1776. *Directories*.

Samuel Lowe, glasshouse, Old Barge Stairs, Southwark.

Notes on Various Old Glasshouses
By Francis BUCKLEY, F.S.A.

The author has already, in a series of papers, been able to give some account of the early history of the glasshouses in the more important glass-making centres, basing his information on contemporary newspaper records. A continuation of the investigation of these records has brought to light references to a number of scattered glasshouses, references which are not capable of being welded into a continuous story. Yet the following notices of such glasshouses and glass makers may be useful to those who are working out the trade history of the localities concerned. It happens not infrequently that only a single notice is found in the old newspapers, showing that glass-making was once carried on at a certain place, but giving no other details.

The history of the Norfolk glasshouses is now known in outline. Probably the glasshouse at Lynn did not survive long after 1747. The glasshouse at Yarmouth is believed to have been continued until nearly the end of the eighteenth century. It is likely that the John Matthews mentioned in 1728 is identical with the well-known "glass-seller" of Norwich. He probably had an interest in the Yarmouth glasshouse, which justified his description as "glass-maker" in his epitaph.

The Attercliffe glasshouse near Sheffield, and the Masborough glasshouses near Rotherham came in for more or less continuous notices, which give their earlier history in outline. The facts relating to glass-making in Scotland are like pieces in a jigsaw puzzle, few of which can at present be fitted together. In other hands these notices may afford a clue or fill a gap in a connected history of the glass industry in Scotland.

The author is indebted to his brother, Dr. G. B. Buckley, for

Bristol references; and to Mr. A. J. B. Kiddell for two references from the *Daily Post Boy*.

APPENDIX

List of References

LYNN REGIS, NORFOLK

27th February, 1693. *London Gazette*.

"To be sold all sorts of the best and finest Drinking-Glasses, and curious Glasses for Ornament, and likewise all sorts of Glass Bottles, by Francis Jackson and John Straw, Glass-makers, at their Warehouse in Worcester Court near the Fountain Tavern in the Strand, or at their Glass-Houses near the Faulkon in Southwark, and at Lynn in Norfolk; where all Persons may be furnished at reasonable rates."

12th December, 1696. *Journals H.C.* xi. 624.

"A petition of the Masters and Servants belonging to the Glass-works in Lynn Regis, in the County of Norfolk, was presented to the House and read, setting forth, That the Petitioners formerly supported themselves and families by making and vending Glass-bottles; but since a Duty has been laid upon Glass-wares, the Consumption of Glass-bottles is so lessened, that the Petitioners have not been employed since, nor are like to be so, if the said duty be not taken off."

17th February, 1697. *Journals H.C.* xi. 707-710.

"Francis Jackson gave evidence before the Parliamentary Committee, to whom the Petitions of the glassmakers were referred. He said (amongst other things) as follows:- That the Duty on Glass Wares has so lessened the Consumption thereof, that himself and Partners were forced to lay aside their Flint and Bottle-works at Lynn in Norfolk where the Trade was become so considerable that they consumed 600 Chaldrons of Coals yearly therein; and paid £30 per Week Wages to the poor people there,

employed in and about the said Works; who are now become burden to the Parishes wherein they dwell."
21st March, 1698. *Journals H.C.* xii. 282.

"In evidence, taken before a further Committee to consider the Glass Duties, Mr. Jackson said. That at Lynn there were two Workhouses before the Duty; but that they neither of them worked since the Duty commenced; but that he has sent down 5,000 or 6,000 Dozen of Bottles thither, for a Market, and had as many in stock there, when he left off working."
10th March, 1699. *Journals H.C.* xii. 558.

"A petition of the Proprietors, workmen and artificers, in the glass manufacture of Lynn Regis, was presented to the House and read. Setting forth, That the Duty Bath lessened the Consumption and made the Petitioners unable to carry on their Trade as formerly, they not having six months work since the commencement of the duty."
1st April, 1699. *Journals H.C.* xii. 627.

"Mr. Francis Jackson gave the following further evidence:- That he was forced to lay down his Glass-Works at Lynn-Regis, so soon as the Duty was at first laid; and since the Half-Duty was off, has only set his Flint-house to work, only for working up his present stock; but must be forced to leave it off again, if the remaining Duty be not taken off."
3rd June, 1729. *London Gazette*.

"Insolvent and prisoners for debt in the Fleet, London, Gilbert Dixon, late of Lyn Regis in Norfolk, Glassmaker, Gillians Dixon, late of the same place, glassmaker."
17th January, 1746. *Ipswich Journal*.

"The Proprietors of the glass-house at Lynn are selling, at their. Ware-house in Common Strath-Yard, the best White Flint Glass at 10d. per pound retail and 9d. per pound wholesale, also Vials of all sorts and bottles at lowest prices."

7th June, 1746. *Cambridge Journal*.

"At the Glass House in Lynn, Ready Money is given for any quantity of broken Bottles or Flint Glass."

28th November, 1747. *Ipswich Journal*.

"To be sold by the glass-house in Lynn, a large quantity of fine Flint-Glass both figured and plain, well sorted, the stock consisting of a great Variety of the most Valuable sorts of drinking Glasses, Decanters, Salvers and other glassware."

YARMOUTH

3rd September, 1728. *London Gazette*.

"William Sherry, Michael Lasher, John Matthews and John Skinner, all covenant servants by Articles, and Daniel Matthews, an apprentice, to Mr. William Jackson and Company, Glassmakers in Southwark, have lately deserted their Service, and are supposed to be gone to a Glasshouse near Yarmouth."

7th September, 1728. *Norwich Mercury*.

"The Glass-House by Yarmouth has been at Work for some time. Where persons may be furnished with the best Goods of all sorts at reasonable prices."

18th October, 1729. *Norwich Mercury*.

"At the Glass-House near Yarmouth are to be sold, Quart Bottles at 16d. per dozen, Pint ditto at 1s. 2d. per doz. and 1s. 0d. a Hundred is given for broken Glass Bottles."

MALTON, YORKSHIRE

29th October, 1822. *London Gazette*.

Insolvent debtor, "George Hudson, late of Malton, in the North Riding, glass manufacturer."

WOOLWICH

1703. *Neve, Builder's Dictionary*.

"Woolwich. This also was one kind of our English (window) glass, which did receive its name from the place of its make; but by reason they met with some discouragement in their proceedings there, they have laid it down there for some time, and do not now make there."

19th June, 1701. *London Gazette.*

"At Woolwich in Kent, is a good wharf, Crane, Glass-house, Warehouse, Cole-yard, and several Out-houses thereto belonging, all in good Repair, to be let. Enquire of Mr. Taynton at Woolwich aforesaid, or of Mr. Portman, Scrivener, Southwark."

CHESTER

5th August, 1774. *Adams's Weekly Courant.*

"The Glass house near Chester" is mentioned in the news column. It is conceivable, however, that this is a satirical reference to a building that did not exist.

HERTFORDSHIRE

23rd April, 1745. *Daily Advertiser.*

"The Bottle-House in Whaddon Chace" is mentioned.

WALES

30th July, 1737. *London Gazette.*

"Roger Anderson, late of Flint, North Wales, Chemist and Glais-maker (sic:), now a prisoner in custody of the Warden of the Fleet."

4th December, 1824. *Felix Farley's Bristol Journal.*

"A gentleman … has entered into the establishment of a Black Bottle Glass Manufactory at Cardiff, from which of course lie means to freight his American vessels from that port and to save the local charges of Bristol."

8th July, 1826. *Ibidem.*

"Wanted, a person as agent to conduct a Bottle Warehouse in Bristol. Apply to the Cardiff Glass Bottle Company, Cardiff."
19th August, 1826. *Ibidem*.

John Dix of Bristol appointed agent in Bristol, warehouse in Baldwin St., of the Cardiff Glass Bottle Works.
6th February, 1827. *London Gazette*.

"The partnership between Josiah John Guest, of Dowlais-house in the County of Glamorgan, Thomas Revell Guest and William Jones, both of the town of Cardiff, carried on at Cardiff, as glass manufacturers, under the firm of the Cardiff Glass Company, was dissolved the 26th January, 1827, by mutual consent."
9th April, 1830. *Ibidem*.

"The partnership between Adam Stodart, James Bowden and William Henry Land of Cardiff, Glass bottle manufacturers, carried on under the firm of The Cardiff Glass Company, was dissolved the 3rd April 1830, by mutual consent."

SHEFFIELD AREA

7th May, 1773. *York Chronicle*.
"Glasshouse at Attercliffe, near Sheffield."
"Gentlemen, merchants, chemists, druggists, apothecaries, glaziers and other in the Glass Trade, may be served with Bottles, Phials, Crown Glass, &c. upon the best terms and with great expedition, by Joseph Allwood & Co."
7th December, 1793. *Newcastle Chronicle*.
"To be let, a Conic Glass-House, conveniently situated at Attercliffe, on the Turnpike Road 2 miles from Sheffield, near a large colliery and the navigable River Dunn. There is no other Glass House within 6 miles of Sheffield, and only one Flint House within 60 miles. Apply to Nathaniel Cosins of Wheat-Hill near Rotherham."
6th May, 1769. *Newcastle Chronicle*.

To be sold, ten sixteenths of a glasshouse, lately erected at Rotherham, with the utensils and materials for the trade, belonging to the said shares. Any person well qualified to conduct the works may apply to Mr. John Wright & Co. of Rotherham, the owners. N.B. The said house is contiguous to the River Don, and well supplied with coals.
14th May, 1781. *Birmingham Gazette*.

"The owners of the Glass-houses situated at Rotherham are desirous of taking a Partner, who can superintend the Works, and who can advance a sum of money. Particulars may be had of Mr. Foljambe or Mr. Boomer in Rotherham."
10th May, 1783. *Newcastle Chronicle*.

"Glasshouses to be let, either from year to year or by term. Two glass-houses at Rotherham, The one is a Crown House, and the other a Bottle and Flint House. There is only one other Crown House within 70 miles. A considerable quantity of all sorts of materials, ready for beginning the business, will be disposed of, together with every implement of the trade. Particulars may be had of Messrs. Foljambe and Boomer, Rotherham."
7th June, 1803/8th January, 1806. *London Gazette*.

Notices relating to "William Beatson the Elder, Robert Beatson, John Beatson and William Beatson the Younger, all now or late of Masbrough near Rotherham, Chymists, Common Brewers and Glassmen."
20th September, 1814. *Ibidem*.

"The partnership heretofore subsisting between Joseph Bargh and William Bargh, as glass manufacturers and carried on at Rotherham, under the firm of Messrs. Joseph & William Bargh, was dissolved the 18th September, 1814."
6th December, 1817. *Ibidem*.

"The partnership between Henry Close and William Close of Masbrough in the parish of Rotherham, as Glass and Bottle

Manufacturers, trading under the firm of Henry Close was dissolved the 27th November, 1817, by mutual consent. William Beatson of Masbrough, Glass Manufacturer, and the said William Close will in future carry on the business."
12th January, 1822. *Ibidem*.

"The partnership between William Beatson and William Close, of Masbrough, glass and bottle manufacturers and potters, under the firm of Beatson and Close, was dissolved the 8th January. The said William Beatson will in future carry on the business on his own account."
20th June, 1828. *Ibidem*.

"The partnership between Martha Beatson, William Close and John Graves Clark, all of Masbrough, as glass manufacturers, under the firm of Close & Clark, was dissolved the 21st May 1828. W. Close and J. G. Clark will in future carry on the business."

SCOTLAND

LEITH
Bremner *Industries of Scotland* (1869), p. 376.
"Operations at Leith were begun in 1682, bottles being the principal articles produced." A price list is given, including wine and "beir" glasses.
12th January, 1751. *Bristol Weekly Intelligencer*.
15th January, 1751. *Manchester Magazine*.
"Leith, Dec. 28 (1760). A globular bottle has been lately blown here by Mr. Thomas Symmer, principal Director of the Glass-Work of South Leith, at the desire of several gentlemen, undertakers of a private work at Preston-Pans, containing two hogsheads, and being measured the dimensions are 40 inches by 42. This piece of curiosity is not yet removed from Mr. Symmer's House, and is reckoned by all who have seen it, to be completely

done and to exceed anything ever done in any glass-work in Britain."

PORT SEATON, &C.

6th January, 1730. *Daily Post Boy*.

"Edinburgh, Dec. 29, 1729. Last week ten Horse Loads of Drinking Glasses came here from the New Manufactory at Port Seaton, and we are informed that their Mirrors and other Pieces of Work exceed any that come from abroad. They have made a Monteith with the Crown and Arms of Great Britain, which is esteemed a Masterpiece."

29th June, 1731. *Daily Post Boy*.

"Edinburgh, June 22. We hear from Cockney, that some of the Houses belonging to the Glass-Work there suddenly sank down, and the Water rushing up, several of the servants perished and others narrowly escaped. The Ground below is all wrought coal."

GLASGOW

25th April, 1752. *Newcastle Journal*.
2nd May, 1752. *London Advertiser*.

"At Glasgow they have begun a new branch of manufacture, the making of the best Crown Window Glass, which is already brought to great perfection, and is found preferable when compared with that of the same kind and price made at Bristol; so that it is not doubted that the proprietors of this work will meet with all encouragement from those who wish to see our own home manufactures flourish."

1st February, 1779. *Bristol Journal*.

"The Glasgow Bottle Work Company, carried on under the firm of Robert Scott Junior and Company, being now dissolved, their whole heritable subject at the foot of Jamaica Street, with

all the utensils &c. are to be exposed to public sale in Glasgow on the 24th February. The situation of this work and its vicinity to the harbour of Broomielaw and to that of the City of Glasgow renders it exceedingly convenient for carrying on the manufacture of glass."
16th November, 1785. *London Gazette.*

"The Copartnery of the Glasgow Bottlework Company, carried on there under the firm of William Henderson and Company was dissolved by mutual consent the 3rd September last.

William Henderson.   Rob. Cowan.
Peter Murdoch.   Robert Rogle.
James Gordon.   Rob. Dunmore.
James Hopkirk.   Peter Blackburn.
James Warroch.   James McDowall.
Richard Marshall.   John Baird."
Charles Bell.

26th May, 1793. *Ibidem.*

"Glasgow, Feb. 14, 1793. The business, carried on here under the firm of the Glasgow Glasswork Company, was dissolved by mutual consent 31st December last."
4th June, 1822. London Gazette.

"The trustees of the late Alexander Houstoun, Esq., of Clerkington and Jacob Dixon, Esq. (surviving partners of the Dumbarton Glass Work Company) do hereby intimate that the said Alexander Houstoun ceased to be a partner of that Company and the various concerns connected therewith."

West-Country Glasshouses
By Francis BUCKLEY, F.S.A.

In the Transactions of the Society for 1925 an account was given of the rise and progress of the early glasshouses of Bristol. This triumphant progress of the Bristol glass-makers must be borne in mind in order to understand the reason for the melancholy fate of other glass concerns in the neighbourhood of Bristol. The hand of Bristol lay heavy on its minor competitors in the West. And in some cases small factories may have been bought and closed down by Bristol glass-makers; this, we know, was a procedure not unknown; to the glass-makers of Stourbridge.

Newnham

Newnham has probably the distinction of being the first town in the West Country to own a proper glasshouse. Rudder, writing in the "New History of Gloucestershire" (1779), states as follows "Sir Edward (*sic*, but, of course, Sir Robert) Mansell, in the reign of Charles I, erected here the first glasshouse in England which was worked with stone-coal, the foundation of which still remains. The glass manufacture has been discontinued a long time." For a time, however, the glass business at Newnham seems to have flourished. In 1696 there were two bottle factories here, mentioned by Houghton. They were represented several times in the petitions to Parliament against the unpopular glass tax, 1695-1699.[1] The repeal of the glass duty does not seem to have been in time to save these two factories. We hear indeed of one in 1706, which was then offered on lease.[2] But this is probably the obituary notice of glass-making in Newnham.

Gloucester

In 1696 there were three bottle factories in Gloucester, which had sprung up to meet the demand for bottles for the cyder trade. They were hard hit by the glass tax, as many as 100 families being affected, when the bottle works temporarily closed down. Messrs. Baldwyn, John Ellis, and John Morris seem to have been the proprietors of the business, Baldwyn being the leading figure, with an interest in all the glasshouses, and chosen as spokesman in the Parliamentary inquiry into the effect of the glass tax. On the repeal of the tax in 1699, Gloucester seems to have recovered its bottle trade. We hear of a new-built glasshouse in 1712, of which John Ellis was probably the owner or tenant. After this, it is quite clear that two at least of the earlier glasshouses had disappeared; and probably the newer glasshouse came sooner or later into the hands of John Platt and Company.[4] They advertised fine bottles in 1741, stamped if necessary with the purchaser's initials or coat of arms. But three years later the company had the misfortune to lose its guiding spirit. The manager, who was also a partner, died, and the rest of the company felt unable to carry on.[5] It is quite uncertain whether the business ever recovered from this disaster. When we next hear of the glasshouse, in 1762, it is merely "the Building called the Glasshouses," and in the occupation of a grocer and two others.[6] After a further notice in 1764,[7] when the building was offered for practically any kind of business, we hear nothing more of glass-making or of "the Glasshouse" in Gloucester. The *Gloucester Journal* is well preserved in the Gloucester Library, but no subsequent reference to the place has been discovered. On the whole it is probable that glass-making came to an end about 1744.

Topsham

Exeter at first supplied its need for bottles at a glasshouse two miles away from the city. The Topsham Bottle House is heard of first in 1696, when Houghton mentions it in his list of glasshouses. We know very little of its history. It was probably in the hands of a man named Renell, who died, it is thought, in the early part of 1702. His widow or daughter Elizabeth offered the glasshouse on lease in June 1702.[8] Quite possibly it was let to Joseph Hodder for 14 years. Something brought the glasshouse rather prematurely into the market in 1713.[9] Between that date and 1764 the business of glass-marking came to an end. In the latter year the glasshouse had degenerated into "the premises called the Glasshouse," showing that it then survived only in name.[10] Exeter was too accessible by water to the great glass-making centres of London, Bristol and Newcastle. In 1770 Topsham was still supplying Exeter with bottles, but they were Newcastle bottles.*

Odd Down

There was, many years ago, a glasshouse at Odd Down, in the parish of Widcombe, then near to, and now actually part of, Bath. "Glasshouse farm,"[13] a well-known stage for the Bath electric trams, probably marks approximately the site. It is little wonder that the record of this glasshouse is now almost lost, for it is more than 160 years since it collapsed, after years of disuse. It is mentioned as a bottle-house by Houghton in 1696, and there is nothing to show that the manufacture changed. Probably it provided the local need for cyder bottles until the Bristol factories

---

* *Exeter Evening Post*, Feb. 16th, 1770, "Samuel Hill in Topsham has constantly by him the best Newcastle … glass bottles."

overwhelmed it. The glasshouse was advertised for sale or lease, in a London newspaper, in 1710.[11] Up to this point its survival as a working glasshouse may be assumed. In 1740 it was still a landmark at Odd Down, even if no glass-making was carried on.[12-14] In 1764, the building fell in, after it had long been used merely as a barn for storing carts and wagons.[15]

Bridgwater

A single notice in 1728 tells us that a bottle factory was set up in Bridgwater and carried on by John and Charles Prowse.[16] Probably it was erected during the first quarter of the 18th century. But the bankruptcy notice of the Prowses in 1728 probably also marks the end of this business venture, and no further trace has yet been discovered of glass-making at this town.

Stanton Drew

During the greater part of the 18th century there was a glasshouse at Stanton Wick or Stanton Drew, probably always employed for the manufacture of bottles. Apparently it was owned by a group of Bristol merchants or glass-makers, and it was therefore in safe hands. It is likely that it was erected ill 1726 and let out on a 99 years' lease., Clearly it was at work before 1739, when two glass-makers of Stanton Drew polled at the Bristol election as "out-voters," that is, freemen of Bristol resident outside the City.[17] Charles Hodges and Henry Smith were probably practical glass-makers, working at the factory. But they were, if not employees, only members of a Bristol syndicate with ten shares.[19] One of these shares was owned until 1745, by Lionel Lyde, an Alderman of Bristol.[18-19] Eventually John Robert Lucas, famous in the history of the Nailsea glasshouses, acquired the Stanton Drew bottle house,[21] and it became one of the business premises of the firm of Lucas, Pater, and Coathupe.[20] The latter firm in the year 1821 became Lucas, Coathupe, and Homer.* Probably glass-making at Stanton Drew came to an end in 1825, on the termination of the "long lease," for the freeholders then offered the premises for any kind of trade.[22]

The author owes a considerable debt of gratitude to his brother, Dr. G. B. Buckley, M.C., for much kind help with the West Country newspapers. Also to Mr. Roland Austin, Curator of the Gloucester Library, for supplying a reference to the Gloucester glasshouses and for giving every facility for a search at that Library.

APPENDIX

List of References
Gloucester and Newnham

1. *House of Commons Journals.*
(a) 16th December, 1696. XI. 628.

"A Petition of John Ely [? Ellis] and John Morris and divers glass-masters in behalf of themselves and many families in and near the City of Gloucester and Town of Newnham was presented to the House. Setting forth, that since the Duty upon glass wares no glass hath been made in Gloucestershire, the glasshouses being converted to other uses, to the utter ruin of the petitioners."

(b) 17th February, 1697.

"Mr. Baldwyn gave evidence on the above petition. He said that there are 5 glasshouses in Gloucester and Newnham and not one of them have worked a fortnight since the duty commenced."

(c) 10th February, 1698. XII. 93.

"A Petition of John Ellis and John Morris and divers other glassmakers in Gloucester and Newnham was presented to the House."

---

* *London Gazette*, Sept. 18th, 1821.

(d) 21st May, 1698. XII. 282.

"Mr. Baldwyn, owner of a glasshouse, said in evidence, that he is concerned in three glasshouses at or near Gloucester; and that he has not worked 10 days since the duty upon bottles; whereas before, there were above 100 families that depended upon the said houses, who now for the most part want bread. That his customers, among whom he chiefly dealt for Cyder, do now put the same into Cask instead of bottles, the duty raises the price of bottles so high."

(e) 4th March, 1699. XII. 547.

"A Petition of poor working glass-makers of Gloucester and Newnham was presented to the House."

2. 18th March, 1708. *London Gazette.*

"A good glasshouse, well situate, at Newnham on the River Severn, very, convenient for making of Broad Glass or Bottles, is to be let or sold. Enquire at Mr. William Wilcocks at the Sugar House, Old Market, Bristol, or of Mr. Job Dowle in Gloucester."

3. 17th June, 1712. *Post Boy.*

"A new built Glasshouse, with convenient Warehouses, lying upon the River Severn, in the City of Gloucester, together with several pots and all manner of tools, to be let or sold. Enquire of Benjamin Burroughs in London, or John Ellis at the said Glasshouse in Gloucester."

4. 30th June, 1741. *Gloucester Journal.*

"The Glasshouse in the City of Gloucester is now at work. Where Glass Bottles are made with as fine and good metal as any in England, and of all sorts and shapes. And any gentlemen may have their Coats of Arms or any other Mark on them as they please. Likewise Pickling Pots, Melon Glasses & Butter Pots. John Platt and Company,"

5. 1st May, 1744. *Gloucester Journal.*

"Whereas by the decease of some of the partners belonging

to the Glasshouse in the City of Gloucester (one of whom was the manager of the works), it is a difficult matter to carry on the work by the rest of the partners. The said Glasshouse and Warehouses are to be let immediately. The stock of bottles will be sold separately. John Porter, Clerk."

6. 26th July, 1762. *Ibidem*.

"To be sold one third share of the Building called the Glasshouses in Gloucester, situate on the banks of the Severn, consisting of a very large Glasshouse, a dwellinghouse, warehouses, now in the possession of Mr. Elton."

7. 3rd December, 1764. *Ibidem*.

"To be let at Christmas next, the Glasshouse with its appurtenances, fit either for a glasshouse or any other kind of business that requires room, consisting of two tenements, the Glasshouse, &c. situate on the River bank and adjoining to the Quay. Enquire of Mr. Elton, grocer, Gloucester."

Topsham

8. 22nd June, 1702. *London Gazette*.

"A round Bottle Glasshouse, 94 foot high and 60 foot broad, with all conveniences, in Ware, between Topson and Exon, near the River. It is to be let at 7, 14 or 21 years. Enquire of Eliz. Renell at the Glass-house near Exon, or of Isaac Barnard in Milk St., London."

9. 1st October, 1713. *Post Bay*.

"Near the River, between Exon and Topsham, is a large round Glasshouse, fit for making Bottles, Broad Glass or Flint, with all convenient out-houses &c. to be let from 7 to 21 years. Enquire further at Mr. William Jones in Exon; Mr. Joseph Hodder in Topsham; Mr. Ben Steed at the Custom-house in Minehead."

10. 2nd June 1764. *London Chronicle*.

"To be sold, a messuage and premises called the Glass House

and about 11 acres of land. All which premises are situate within the parishes of Topsham and Exminster, about 2 miles from the City of Exeter."

Odd Down near Bath

11. 14th October, 1710. *Post Man*.
"A Glasshouse at Odd Downe, near Bath, is to be let or sold."
12. 29th April, 1740. *General Advertiser*.
"Bristol: Last Saturday a fire broke out at Old Downe (sic) in the Parish of Whitcombe near the Glasshouse, which burnt down two tenements adjoining thereto."
13. 3rd June, 1745/17th March, 1746. *Bath Journal*.
"To be let, a Farm called Glasshouse Farm in the Parish of Widcombe, near the City of Bath."
14. 11th July, 1748. *Ibidem*.
"Lost, 12 sheep, lately seen about the Glasshouse on Odd Down."
15. 19th January, 1764. *Bath Chronicle*.
"Last week the Glasshouse on Odd Down near this City (and which has long been in a ruinous condition) fell in, and damaged several waggons and carts, which were kept there by people belonging to the neighbouring houses."

Bridgwater

16. 16th March, 1728. *London Gazette*.
"Bankrupt, John Prowse and Charles Prowse, late of Bridgwater in the County of Somerset, Glass Bottle-makers and Partners."

Stanton Drew

17. 1739. *Bristol Poll Book*.
The outvoters in the Poll list include:

  Charles Hodges, glassmaker, Stanton Drew.
  Henry Smith, do.   do.
18. 23rd July, 1745. *General Advertiser*.
  "Lionel Lyde Esq., Alderman of Bristol, lately deceased."
19. 15th January, 1754. *London Gazette*.
  "To be sold by order of the Court of Chancery, one tenth part of a Glasshouse in Stanton Drew, Somerset, together with one tenth of the utensils, stock, &c. belonging to the said glasshouse, late part of the estate of Lionel Lyde, of Bristol, Esq."
20. 21st August, 1790. *Bonner and Middleton's Bristol Journal*.
  "Joseph Dully, Robert Warren and Nathaniel Warren, apprentices to John Robert Lucas of Bristol, have absconded from the Glass bottle Manufactory of Lucas, Pater & Coathupe at Stanton Wick, in the County of Somerset."
21. 12th August, 1815. *Felix Farleys Bristol Journal*.
  "To be resold, the 5th October next, pursuant to a decree of the High Court of Chancery. ... A farm at Stanton wick and Stanton drew Somerset. A Glasshouse containing Pot-rooms, Stabling &c. freehold. The glasshouse is held on an old lease by – Lucas Esq. at £8 per annum, of which 10 years are unexpired."
22. 10th December, 1825. *Ibidem*.
  The Stantondrew Glasshouse is offered on lease. "But there would be no objection to convert the Glasshouse Cone &c. to any other buildings required for a different manufactory."

TUNSTEAD, GREENFIELD,
  YORKSHIRE.

Old Lancashire Glasshouses
By Francis BUCKLEY, F.S.A.

During the eighteenth century glass-making in Lancashire was centred at Liverpool, Prescot, and Warrington. Manchester also became a centre of glass-making, but permanence as such did not occur until nearly 1530. Until the foundation of the celebrated Plate Glass Works at St. Helens, it is doubtful whether the glass industry in Lancashire was designed to supply much more than the local market. This market extended all over Lancashire and Cheshire and into the northern parts of Wales. The great glass works about Stourbridge were rather inaccessible before canals were made; the Yorkshire glass works were hedged off by the barrier of the Pennine Chain. It was natural, therefore, for the Lancashire folk to undertake their own ordinary glass supply. A greater opening for overseas trade was, however, presented later on, when the Bristol glassworks were closed down through lack of dock accommodation, and after the Glass Excise Acts lead been extended to Ireland. These events, besides the general flow of trade from south to north, may account for the greater prosperity of the Lancashire glass trade in the nineteenth century.

Liverpool* [1,6 & 20]

In Liverpool itself the glassworks were hardly as successful in the eighteenth century as the potteries. Frequent changes in the partnerships and periodic bankruptcies indicate that glass-making had a long struggle to survive. Warrington and Prescot were adjacent and better situated for the trade; these two districts sent

---

* The numbers refer to the Appendix.

their glass to Liverpool, and until about 1760 there was also occasional competition from Bristol and Whitehaven.†

Houghton, writing in 1696, states that there was one glasshouse, making flint, green, and ordinary glass, "near Liverpool." Under the circumstances, this glasshouse was probably in, or near Prescot. In 1715 Josiah Poole founded, a glasshouse in Liverpool,‡ which became known after 1756 as the "Old Glasshouse," in Hanover Street. A bankruptcy "issued some time ago" against one "Josia Poole, late of Liverpoole, merchant," mentioned in 1730, probably refers to the same man. The next glassmaker of Liverpool of whom we have any record was equally unfortunate. William Stringfellow, who can also be placed at the Old Glasshouse, was imprisoned for debt in 1743. Probably at this point the Old Glasshouse was taken over by Samuel Woods, mentioned 1754, 1759, 1761, and 1762.§ From the Poll Books we learn that the following glassmen worked at the Old Glasshouse between 1754 and 1761: William Atherton (Sen. and Jun.), Isaac Houghton, John Manchester, and Daniel Parr. Woods also had as partner or manager Josiah Perrin, who shortly afterwards went to the Bank Quay glassworks in Warrington. On the death of Samuel Woods in 1762, Crosbie, Bostock and Co. took over the Old Glasshouse; and the same firm, with rather rapid changes in the partners, continued in possession till 1778. The later firm names were as follows: 1769 Crosbies, Heywood and Co., 1771, Heywood, Staniforth and Co., with Thomas Holt either as manager or junior partner. John and William Crosbie, "merchants," became bankrupt in 1772; and this may account for their disap-

---

† *Liverpool Advertiser*, 22 Oct., 1756; *Liverpool Chronicle*, 6 May, 1757.
‡ *Victoria County History* (Lancashire), Vol. 11. ,
§ *Liverpool Poll Books*, 1754-1761.

pearance from the glass firm. For a short time after 1778 Thomas Skidmore appears to have been in possession of the Old Glasshouse; he is subsequently recorded as a glass engraver. In 1781. Thomas Holt and Co. acquired a glasshouse in Hanover Street, but it is not quite certain that it was actually the Old Glasshouse, which may have been dismantled about this time. The firm of Holt and Co. flourished both as glass-makers and as glass dealers in Liverpool. John Holt and Co. appear in 1800, Thomas Holt in 1814, James Holt and Co. in 1833. The actual glasswares made at the Old Glasshouse are not recorded; but from the association of Perrin and Skidmore with the business it is evident that they made flint glass as well as bottles.

A second glasshouse, called "the New Glasshouse," was set up in Liverpool shortly after 1750, probably by William Knight, mentioned in the Poll Books 1754 and 1761. In 1763 the firm was John Knight & Co. The site of the glasshouse was near South Dock, At first flint glass, crown glass and bottles were made; the making of flint glass may, however, have been abandoned for a short period, when the firm was Knight, Doran & Co. In 1769 Peter Morris and Sons, formerly glass dealers, took over the New Glasshouse, where they made flint glass and bottles. In January 1779 another firm, Leigh, Hesketh, Wicksted, and Kirkby, took over the glasshouse for use as a bottle factory. Two years before that, William Kirkby had had a glass factory at Wapping, Liverpool.* After 1779, no further trace can be found of the New Glasshouse.

A short-lived glass factory, of which much was said at the time, was started rather before 1758 by two brothers, William and John Penkett. It was an ambitious concern, consisting of two glasshouses in Dale Street, where they made all kinds of fine

---

* Directory, 1777.

flint glass. Misfortune soon overtook the business, caused in all probability by trade rivalry and jealousy. John Penkett died and William Penkett became bankrupt in 1759. And although the two glasshouses were frequently advertised for sale, we know that the business was not revived here; because in 1769 there were only two glasshouses in Liverpool.† The following advertisement of glasswares probably relates to the products of Penkett's glasshouses. "To be sold by auction in the Town's Hall, Liverpool, a quantity of glass salvers, salts, cruets, sweetmeat glasses, jelly glasses, glass baskets, comfit glasses, flower bottles, glass plates, glass basins, posset glasses."‡

Gregory Knight, probably a relation of John Knight of the New Glasshouse, had a glass manufactory on the North Shore, Liverpool, in 1796. By 1800 he had moved to the Vauxhall Road glassworks. He became bankrupt in 1801, and sooner or late Thomas and George Hawkes of Dudley acquired the promises, where no doubt they made flint glass. They are mentioned here in 1805, but they, do not appear to have continued this venture very long. They were succeeded by "the Vauxhall Glass Bottle Co." (Thomas Moore, William L. Taylor, and John Manby). In 1811 Taylor dropped out of the firm, but Moore and Manby continued till 1821. Another bottle factory had started in the Vauxhall Road before 1818, known as Orford and Foster's glassworks; and William Foster and Co. appear here in 1833.

Queen Street, Liverpool, was the site of another glass-making establishment. John Knight is found here in 1781, and in 1800 John Rycroft, "joiner and glass-maker." * In the latter year, Peter Sowerby, John Rycroft, and Samuel Prescot [Sowerby,

---

† *Tour in North England* (A. Young).
‡ Liverpool Chronicle, 24 March, 1758.
* Directory.

Rycroft and Co.] started a more ambitious business, for making flint glass, "at the bottom of Queen Street." They could not agree, apparently, and the business came to an end in two months' time. It was taken over, however, by Hargreaves, Graham & Co., with Rycroft as a partner until the end of 1801. Graham and Hargreaves continued the business in 1803 at any rate.

Crown glassworks, erected about 1827 near the Old Swan, three miles from Liverpool, seem to have passed into the hands of Thomas Choll & Co. before 1833.

The Prescot Area[7-11]

It is probable that the glasshouse "near Liverpool" in 1696, already mentioned, was either in Prescot or Sutton ["Sutton-in-Prescot"]. Soon after 1700 Prescot became famous for good window glass of the ordinary kind. A careful survey of the trade in 1703 by Richard Neve does not mention Prescot or Lancashire window glass.† But in 1734 we learn that Prescot was "noted for the best, of that sort in England." This result was probably brought about by the appearance in the district before 1725 of Joseph Henzey and possibly other members of this well-known Huguenot family of broad-glass makers. Although Henzey's own affairs became involved, his instructions seem to have borne immediate fruit. He worked apparently in Prescot itself. There is evidence of one glasshouse here, which was eventually bought by glass-makers of Stourbridge, in order to close it down. This occurred about 1750.‡

During the first half of the eighteenth century there were also two glassworks in Sutton, probably both making window

---

† *The Builder's Dictionary.*
‡ Pocock, *Travels through England.*

glass. One of these, founded by Peter Wilcox, who died in 1721,§ is heard of in 1747 under the name of "Wilcox's Glasshouse." The other was held in 1747 under an old lease by John Woods; 'probably the "glassman" who polled at the Liverpool Election in 1761. John Woods, probably a son, appears in the Poll Book of 1784. Edward Tarbuck, glass-maker of Sutton, died in 1756; he was perhaps the successor of Peter Wilcox. Andrew Stannistreet, a glass-maker of Sutton, polled at the elections of 1754 and 1761. Two glass-makers, members of this family (Henry and Andrew) appear in the Poll Books in 1754 and 1796, and at the latter date they were located at the neighbouring site of Thatto Heath. It would seem, therefore, that the Sutton glasshouses were abandoned before 1800. But the fame of the Prescot area was soon to be revived by the success of the Plate Glassworks at Ravenhead, St. Helens.

For many years a glasshouse existed at Eccleston, probably used at first for the manufacture of bottles. Thomas Fenney, member of a well-known Stourbridge family, was perhaps the first glass maker here; he died in 1752. He was probably succeeded by the John Highton, "glass bottle founder," of Eccleston, who died in 1775. In 1792 Mackay, West and Company advertised their Crown glass at the Eccleston glassworks. The business continued under the same firm till 1818 at any rate; it was eventually acquired by the Pilkingtons of St. Helens.*

Another bottle manufactory was started at Thatto Heath near Prescot, probably before 1750. It is first heard of in 1755, in connection with David Booth, glass-maker, who had already left the place and gone to Bristol, where he came to grief. Soon afterwards the manufactory came into the hands of Orell, Fosters & Co., who in 1767 announced the continuance of the partner-

---

§ and * *Victoria County History.*

ship business. They were succeeded in 1785 by Thomas West & Co. W. A. A. West & Co. are still found here in 1833.

In the latter year there was a second glasshouse at Thatto Heath in possession of Thomas Cockburn & Co. Its previous history is obscure; but it may be noted in the Poll Book that Thomas McCully and John and Andrew Stannistreet were glassmakers at Thatto Heath in 1796. Unless they were servants at West's glasshouse, they were probably interested in a second glasshouse at the same place.

The most famous glass concern in the Prescot area was undoubtedly the Plate Glass Works at St. Helens. On the 25th January, 1773, a society calling themselves "The British Cast Plate Glass Manufacturers" petitioned Parliament for incorporation.† The members of the original society were Hon. Charles Fitroy, Hon. Robert Digby, Peregrine Cust, Thomas Dundas, John Mackay, Phillip Affleck, Henry Bagge, James Bourdieu, James Mowbray, Angus Mackay, Henry Hastings, Ranald Macdonald and Samuel Chollet. They appear also to have secured the services of at least two Frenchmen, Philip Besnard and Jean B. Bruyere, skilled in the art of casting plates after the French fashion. The cost of setting up the manufactory was estimated at £75,000 "before any return of money can be made from the Manufactory." The Company was duly incorporated in 1773 and commenced to advertise their plates (up to 12 feet long and proportionately wide) in 1778. But the original company was not successful, as is shown clearly enough by a despairing notice to shareholders issued in 1794. In 1795 the company was reconstituted as the "British Plate Glass Company," with Mr. Foster in charge of the St. Helens Works. The new venture was eminently successful, and until 1813 the company had a practical

---

† *Journals, House of Commons*, XXXIV, p. 64.

monopoly in England of making cast plate glass. About 1813, however, Messrs. Cookson & Cuthbert of Newcastle commenced to make cast plate glass in addition to their other manufactures.*

The great plate glass works at St. Helens were not the only, glass concern there. Other manufacturers were attracted to the same site. A large company, known at first as "The St. Helens Crown Glass Company," was established in 1826. This company was continued by Peter Greenall and W. Pilkington, jun., alone in 1829, and appears in 1833 under the style of Peter Greenall & Co. The name of Pilkington has of course had a long and honourable association with the glassworks at St. Helens.

Warrington[12-14]

Houghton, writing in 1696, records a glasshouse in Warrington making window glass; and it is probable that there was no break in the continuity of glass-making here, although there are gaps in the story. Shortly before 1757 a company erected a glasshouse at Warrington for making flint glass and bottles. The leading spirit was Peter Seaman, who was apparently a local inn-holder in 1745, and perhaps the capitalist in the glass business. The firm of "Peter Seaman & Co" is' mentioned in 1787, and Peter Seaman died the following year. This glass concern may be identical with the Orford Lane Glasshouse. The first notice of this glasshouse under its place name occurs in 1814. In 1802, however, the firm of "Davies, Glazebrook & Co" was dissolved and succeeded by "T. K. Glazebrook & Co." (of Orford Lane). The names, "Glazebrook" and "Brettel," in the original partnership suggest that it was composed of Stourbridge Glass-makers. But the later notice of the Orford Lane firm, in 1829, shows that the

---

* *Parliamentary Papers* (1835), XXXI, p. 40.

local glass-makers Mackay, West and Holt had then acquired a large interest in the business.

The Bank Quay Glassworks at Warrington were for a long time in the hands of a family named Perrin. Josiah Perrin has already been mentioned in connection with the Old Glasshouse at Liverpool, where he was either manager or partner in 1761. The name strongly suggests that this family came from Bristol, where the Perrins appear often enough as glass-makers in the Bristol Poll Lists. This suggestion is considerably strengthened by the fact that Josiah Perrin advertised in 1767 types of glass peculiarly associated with Bristol glass works, viz. "blue, green, white, and painted enamil." Perrin was sufficiently enterprising to open a warehouse for his glass-wares in Liverpool, which was handed over to John Kirk in 1791 after about 30 years of business. The glass business at Warrington was continued by Josiah Perrin and Co., who appear as "Perrin, Geddes & Co" in 1827. In this year there was a dissolution of partnership and the company became known as the "Bank Quay Company."

In the Parliamentary return of glasshouses in 1833 there are recorded five glasshouses at Warrington, including the Orford Lane and Bank Quay glasshouses. The names of the owners or principal proprietors are given as John Clare, John B. Falkner & Co. (two), John Alderson & Co., and Thomas Robinson & Co.

Manchester[15-20]

Manchester has had a flourishing glass business for about 100 years.

The first notices of glass-making in Lancashire relate to the Manchester area. A "glassman" near Haughton (between Stockport and Hyde) is mentioned in 1605; and "the glasshouse at Haughton" is mentioned in 1636 and 1644.* It is, however, prac-

---

* *Victoria County History.*

tically certain that this glasshouse was closed before 1696, when Houghton compiled his list of English glasshouses. But it is interesting to note the appearance in the Registers of Thomas Longworth, glass-maker, of Stockport, who was married in the year 1765. This record may indicate yet another of the sporadic and unsuccessful attempts to revive the business of glass-making during the 18th century, in the Manchester area. The record of glass-making here in the 18th century is indeed a melancholy one. One after another, glasshouses sprang up and disappeared, leaving scarcely any trace behind them. An attempt was made, or at least considered, to erect a glasshouse at Miles Platting in 1741; but apparently nothing came of it. In 1754 a glasshouse for making flint glass and bottles was erected at Atherton near Leigh, which continued to work for nearly three years, but then closed down, apparently for good. In March 1759 a bottle glasshouse in Salford was completed and set to work; but here there seems to have been trouble from the start. By July 1760 the proprietors had changed their "clerk of the works" and all the hands originally employed. And nothing further can be learnt of this concern after November 1760. It did not survive until the "Directory Period," which in the case of Manchester started in 1772. In 1785 Messrs. Imison and King started a glass factory in Newton Lane; but they too failed to find their way into the Manchester Directories. John Imison seems to have been an ingenious man with many interests, but probably more of a scholar and inventor than of a business man. After this it has been impossible to trace any certain reference to glass-making in Manchester until 1830, when Maginnis Molineaux & Co appear in the Directory. Between 1830 and 1833 the members of this firm parted company and seem to have set up three separate glass-works of their own, viz. Maginnis & Co., Thomas Molineaux and William Robinson. The second of these gave rise later on to

Molineaux, Webb & Co., Ltd., and as this firm celebrated its centenary in 1927, the parent firm must have been in existence in 1827. Meanwhile before 1833 two further glass factories appeared in Manchester in the hands of Daniel Watson & Co. and Frederick Fareham, respectively. Thus in 1833 Manchester appears rather suddenly and unexpectedly in the Parliamentary List as one of the more important glass-making areas in England.

Acknowledgment

The author is much indebted to the officials in charge of the Liverpool and Manchester Libraries for their courtesy and assistance. Also to his brother, Dr. C. B. Buckley, M.C., for several Bristol references and for kind help with the Liverpool Directories.
TUNSTEAD, GREENFIELD, YORKS.

APPENDIX

Liverpool

1 (a) 15th September, 1730. *London Gazette*.

"Josia Poole, late of Liverpoole, Merchant," asks to compound with creditors, after "a commission of Bankrupt issued some time ago against the said Josia Poole."
(b) 17th, May, 1743. *Ibidem*.

"William Stringfellow, late of Liverpoole, glassmaker and dealer, insolvent debtor."
(c) 12th June, 1759. *Williamson's Liverpool Advertiser*.

"To be let ... a good house. Enquire of Samuel Woods, opposite the glasshouse in Hanover Street, who is now selling off all sorts of glass house ware at prime cost or under."
(d) 7th August, 1761. *Ibidem*.

"Stolen out of the Compting-house at the Old Glasshouse

---

* Hereafter called "*W. Liverpool Advertiser*."

in Liverpool a silver caster. Reward offered by Josiah Perrin at the Old Glasshouse."

(e) 1762. Chester Wills. [Lancs. and Chesh. Record Sec.]

Probate granted of the will of Samuel Woods, Liverpool, glassmaker.

(f) *Gore's Liverpool Directories*.

1763 Crosbie, Bostock & Co., glasshouse, Hanover St.

1769 Crosbies, Heywood & Co., Old glasshouse, do.

(g) 6th October, 1769. *Liverpool General Advertiser*.

"To be disposed of, a share in the Old Glass House in Hanover Street. For particulars enquire of Mr. Thomas Holt at the said Glasshouse."

(h) 29th March, 1771. *Ibidem*.

"Liverpool Old Glasshouse, Hanover St, The partnership in the glass manufactory carried on by Crosbies, Heywood & Co., being dissolved, all persons indebted are to pay their debts to Thomas Holt, who is authorised to receive the same. The work will in future be carried on by the firm of Heywood, Staniforth & Co,"

(i) 19th December, 1772. *London Gazette*.

"John Crosbie, William Crosbie and others, merchants and partners of Liverpool, bankrupt."

(j) 21st August, 1778. *W. Liverpool Advertiser*.

Liverpool. "The partnership in the Old Glasshouse Manufactory, lately carried on in the firm of Heywood, Staniforth & Co., being dissolved, persons indebted are to pay the same to Mr. Thomas Holt. As they have a stock of flint glass on hand, all wholesale dealers may be supplied on very advantageous terms. A quantity of ashes and other materials to dispose of."

(k) 1778. *Liverpool Directory*.

Thomas Skidmore, Old Glasshouse, 78 Hanover St.

(l) 19th February, 1779. *W. Liverpool Advertiser*.

"The partnership in the Old Glasshouse, being dissolved and Mr. Christopher Bennett appointed to collect the debts," notice to pay debts to him.

(m) 1781. *Liverpool Directory*.

Thomas Holt & Co., glass manufactory, 75 Hanover St.

2. (a) 27th August, 1756. *W. Liverpool Advertiser*.

"The new Glass-house near Tythe Barn Street in Liverpool," is mentioned.

(b) 19th October, 1759. Ibidem.

"There is manufactured at the New Glass House at the S.E. corner of the Salt House Dock in Liverpool all kinds of the best flint and crown glass, made in the neatest manner. Also bottles, cardevin bottles, & c., of all sorts and sizes. By Messrs. Knight and Co."

(c) 1763 & 1766. *Liverpool Directory*.

John Knight & Co., glassmakers, N.E. side South Dock.

(d) 24th March, 1769. *W. Liverpool Advertiser*.

"Knight, Doran and Co. at the New Glasshouse, manufacture all kinds of window glass, bells for gardens, &c. all sorts of gardevine squares and bottles."

(e) 13th October, 1769. *Liverpool General Advertiser*.

"There will be manufactured and sold at the Now Glasshouse near the Salt House Dock (formerly occupied by Knight, Doran and Co.) but now carried on by Peter Morris and Sons, all sorts of flint glass made in the neatest manner; also common and champagne bottles, cardevines, squares, &c."

(f) 1774. *Liverpool Directory*.

Peter Morris & Sons, glasshouse N.E. side South Dock.

(g) 22nd January, 1779. *W. Liverpool Advertiser*.

"Messrs. Hugh Hindley Leigh, Robert Hesketh, Richard Wicksted and William Kirkby have begun a Bottle Work at the New Glasshouse in Liverpool, where all persons may be supplied with every sort of bottles, squares, &c."

3. (a) 27th April, 1759. *W. Liverpool Advertiser*.

"To be sold the Glasshouse in Dale St., Liverpool, together with all materials of stock in hand, consisting of variety of the best Flint Glass &c. and everything compleat for carrying on the work in all its branches. Apply to Mr. James Bere, clerk of the works. As good a set of Hands as most in England are engaged for a term of years by articles."

[Note. – A MS. note against this advertisement runs, "William Penkett.";

(b) 25th May, 1759. *Ibidem*.

The creditors of William Penkett late of Liverpool, merchant, are to meet to consider the state of his affairs.

(c) 29th June, 1759. *Ibidem*.

"Whereas the value of the estate of the late John Penkett has by some malicious persons in Liverpool been greatly lessened, to the great prejudice of William Penkett, his solo heir and executor, who looks on the false reports as the cause of his name appearing in this day's Gazette.

[An account of debts is given]. … The under mentioned bond debts, which Mr. John Penkett became bond with his brother William Penkett (amounting to £1,650) was wholly employed for the use, of the Glasshouse."

(d) 7th September, 1759. *Ibidem*.

"To be sold by auction the estate of the late Mr. William Penkett, a bankrupt. …"

"Lot 3. All those two new erected Glasshouses near Dale Street in Liverpool, now held by lease from Richard Gildart Esq. for three lives and 21 years."

N.B. Similar notices appear in the *Advertiser*, 12th Dec., 1760, and 26th June, 1761, and in the Public Ledger, 6th July, 1761.]

4. (a) *Liverpool Directory*.

1781 John Knight, glassmaker, 44 Queen St.

1796 Gregory Knight, glass manufactory, 17 Bath St., North Shore.

1800 Gregory Knight, glass manufactory, Vauxhall Road.

(b) 24th March, 1801. *London Gazette*.

Gregory Knight, late of Liverpool, glass manufacturer, bankrupt.

(c) 1805. *Liverpool Directory*.

Thomas and George Hawkes, glass manufactory, Vauxhall Road, and Dudley, Worcestershire.

(d) 5th October, 1811. *London Gazette*.

"The partnership between Thomas Moore, William Leechman Taylor and John Manby, all of Liverpool, as common Glass Bottle-makers, under the firm of 'the Vauxhall Glass Bottle Company' was dissolved the 28th September, 1811. Moore and Manby to collect debts, &c."

(e) 11th September, 1821. *Ibidem*.

"The partnership between Thomas Moore and John Manby, as glass bottle manufacturers in Liverpool, is dissolved the 8th September; 1821."

5. (a) 20th October, 1800. *Billinge's Liverpool Advertiser*.

"Sowerby, Rycroft and Co., Liverpool, Flint Glass Manufactory, bottom of Queen St., have established the above business, where orders will be received."

(b) 16th June, 1801. *London Gazette*.

"Liverpool, Dec. 6, 1800. The partnership lately carried on between Peter Sowerby, John Rycroft and Samuel Proscot, glass manufacturers under the firm of 'Sowerby, Rycroft and Co.', was dissolved by mutual consent on the 26th December, 1800."

(c) 23rd February, 1802. *London Gazette*.

"The partnership lately subsisting between Henry Hargreaves the Elder, Henry Hargreaves the Younger, Walter Graham and

John Rycroft as glass manufacturers at Liverpool under the firm of 'Hargreaves, Graham and Co.' was dissolved on the 5th November last."

(d) 1803. *Liverpool Directory*.

Graham and Hargreaves, glass manufacturers, Queen St.

6. 15th December, 1827. *Bristol Journal*.

"Valuable Crown Glass Works to be sold, by order of the assignees of a bankrupt, newly erected, situate at the top of Edge Lane, West Derby, only 3 miles from Liverpool. The Cone 120 foot high and 60 feet in diameter, containing a furnace for 4 pots, 4 annealing arches, 2 pot arches, &c."

Prescot

7. (a) 31st August, 1725. *London Gazette*.

Joseph Henzey, late of Proscot, Broad-glass maker, prisoner for debt in Lancaster Gaol.

(b) 22nd June, 1734. *Craftsman*.

"Window Glass, to be sold by auction at the Ship Tavern., Wapping Dock (London). 500 half-cases of common broad glass, made at Prescot, being noted for the best of that sort in England."

(c) 31st March, 1747. *Manchester Magazine*.

"To be sold in Prescot, a messuage and tenement and the lands thereunto belonging, containing 14 acres, and a Glass-House standing upon the said premises, situate at Sutton, about 2 miles from Prescot and 5 from Warrington, all late the inheritance of Daniel Lawton of Prescot, deceased."

(d) 16th June, 1747. *Ibidem*.

"To be sold by auction, a messuage and about 9 acres of land, with a Glass-house standing thereon, in Sutton, in possession of James Woods, held by lease for two old lives. Also the reversion in fee of tenements in Sutton aforesaid, near Wilcock's

Glasshouse."

(e) 1756. *Chester Wills* (Record Society).

Administration to the estate of Edward Tarbuck of Sutton in Prescot, glassmaker (personality under £40).

8. (a) 5th July, 1755. *London Gazette*.

Insolvent debtor, David Booth, formerly of Thatto-Heath, Lancashire, late of Bristol, glassmaker.

(b) 4th September, 1767. *W. Liverpool Advertiser*.

"The Glass Bottle Manufactory at Hatto-Heath Glasshouse, near Prescot, is now carried on by Orrell, Fosters and Co. Where all sorts of the best Wine, Beer, Cardevine and other Bottles are made and sold. And as all the late workmen and partners at the said house are engaged, they humbly hope for the continuance of their former favours."

(c) 24th February, 1785. *Ibidem*.

"Thatto Heath Bottle Work. Thomas West and Co. have entered upon the above premises and will have a constant supply of all sorts of bottles and cardevine squares of the very best quality. Orders direct to Thomas West and Co., at St. Helens."

9. (a) 1752. *Chester Wills*.

Administration granted to the estate of Thomas Fenney of Eccleston near Knowsley, glassmaker.

(b) 1775. *Chester Wills*.

Probate of will of John Highton, of Eccleston, glass bottle-founder.

(c) 30th April, 1792. *W. Liverpool Advertiser*.

"Eccleston Glass Works, near Prescot. Mackay, West and Co. manufacture Crown Glass at the above works."

(d) 14th May, 1792. *Ibidem*.

"Crown glass, in crates and squares, of all sizes, sold by Thomas Holt and Co. at their Glass Warehouse, Liverpool, agents to Messrs. Mackay, West and Co., crown glass manufacturers in

Eccleston."

(e) 18th April, 1796. *Billinge's Liverpool Advertiser*.

"Last week, being St. Helens Fair, a shocking accident happened there to a man, Davies, who worked as a glassmaker with Messrs. Mackay and West."

(f) 1818. *Pigott's Northern Directory*.

"Near St. Helens, Mackay, West and Co. crown glass manufactory."

10. (a) *London Gazette*.

"29th May, 1773. British Cast Plate Glass Manufacturers. At a general meeting of the Proprietors held 27th May, resolved that a second call be made of £10 % upon each share. George Mackay, clerk."

12th November, 1774. Fifth call of £10 %.

1st February, 1777. Ninth call on shares.

(b) 20th October, 1778. *General Advertiser*.

"Plate Glass. The public are hereby informed that Cast Plate Glass of all dimensions from 6 inches to 12 feet long, and proportionately wide, is sold at the Warehouse of the British Cast Plate Glass Manufactory in Albion Place, near Blackfriars Bridge. George Mackay."

(c) 1788. *Chester Wills*.

Dead, Jean B. Bruyere, of Ravenhead, plate glass manufacture.

(d) 28th January, 1794. *London Gazette*.

"British Cast Plate Glass Manufactory. To enable the Company to discharge their debts and continue the Manufactory, the proprietors shall be called upon to advance by way of loan a sum equal to their present shares; or if they shall decline such advance, the Company shall be dissolved, the property sold, and the amount after payment of debts divided amongst the proprietors."

(e) 17th October, 1795. *Bristol Journal*.

"Plate Glass Company. The Public may be supplied with Plate Glass in any quantity and of any size from 1 foot to 11 feet long, either in a rough or polished state, by applying to Mr. Foster, Ravenhead, Prescot, where their Plate Glass Manufactory is established, or to Mr. Alexander Black, at their Warehouse, Albion Place, London."

11. (a) 22nd April, 1828. *London Gazette*.

"The partnership at St. Helens between John William Bell, Peter Greenall, James Bromilow, John Barnes, Thomas Bell and W. Pilkington, Junior, under the firm of 'The St. Helens Crown Glass Company,' was dissolved the 15th April, as regards J. W. Bell and T. Bell, who retire from the business. The rest will continue the business."

(b) 23rd January, 1829. *Ibidem*.

"Messrs. J. Bromilow and J. Barnes retire from 'The St. Helens Crown Glass Co.', which is continued by Messrs. P. Greenall and W. Pilkington, Junior."

Warrington

12. (a) 11th March, 1745. *London Gazette*.

Peter Seaman of Warrington holds the "Eagle and Child" Inn.

(b) 2nd September, 1757. *W. Liverpool Advertiser*.

"The proprietors of the Glasshouse lately erected at Warrington have now begun to work Bottles and Flint Glass. Peter Seaman and Co."

(c) 1787. *Tunnicliffe's Survey*.

Warrington, Peter Seaman and Co., glass manufacturers.

13. (a) 3rd April., 1767. *Liverpool General Advertiser*.

"Just opened in the Old Church Alley, Liverpool, The Warrington wholesale and retail Warehouse. Where are sold all kinds of Blue, Green, White and Painted Enamil, double and single Chrystal Flint; Cut, Flowered and Plain Glasses of all sorts; and Apothecaries' phials, as cheap as at the Manufactory. Also Bottles and Cardevine Squares. Broken glass taken in exchange or for ready money. Josiah Perrin and Co."

(b) 19th May, 1791. *Ibidem*.

Josiah Perrin, Bottle and Flint Glass Warehouse, No. 9 Water St., Liverpool, acquaints the public that Mr. John Kirk (who having had the sole management of his business upwards of 3 years) has purchased his stock and means to carry on the same as usual, having laid in a fresh assortment of Cut and Fashionable glasses, which he will sell at the manufacturer's price. J. Perrin returns thanks for favours experienced during 30 years business. All demands against Josiah Perrin by sending to him at Warrington will be attended to."

(c) 25th May, 1827. *London Gazette*.

"The partnership in the Glass Manufactory at the Bank Quay Glass Works in Warrington, and at Liverpool, under the firm of 'Perrin, Geddes and Co.', was dissolved the 30th June, 1824. (Signed) Hannah Evans, Exors. of the late Edward Falkner, Exors: of the late William Geddes, Josiah Perrin, personal representatives of Amy Seaman dec., P. Nicholson, Peter Vawdray, Joseph Flintoft, Maria Flintoft."

(d) 1828-1848. *Warrington Directory*.

Bank Quay Company, flint and bottles, Bank Quay.

14. (a) 2nd October, 1802. *London Gazette*.

"The partnership of Davies, Glazebrook and Co. of Warrington, glass manufacturers, is dissolved, 7th August, 1802. John Davies, T. K. Glazebrook, Samuel Brettel, Thomas England, John Alderson."

(b) 1814-1828. *Warrington Directories*.

T. K. Glazebrook & Co., glass manufacturers, Orford Lane.

(c) 25th December, 1829. *London Gazette*.

"The partnership between the undersigned as glass manufacturers at Warrington, under the firm of 'Thomas Kirkland Glazebrook and Co.', was dissolved the 30th September last. Thomas Kirkland Glazebrook, J. Mackay as exor. of George Mackay dec., James V. West and W. A. A. West as oxors. of Thomas West dec., Thomas Holt."

Manchester

15. 15th September, 1741. *London Evening Post*.

"Whoever is willing to undertake the building of a Glasshouse and Fire Engine to work a Pump, may send their proposals to Mr. Thomas Brown at Miles Platting near Manchester. N.B. It is intended one fire to do both works."

16. (a) 7th May, 1754. *Manchester Magazine*.

"The Glass-House at Leigh is now begun to work; where persons by sending their orders to the Clerk at the said Work will be well served with good bottles and flint glass at reasonable prices."

(b) 28th January, 1757. *W. Liverpool Advertiser*.

"To be sold at Atherton Glass-House, near Leigh, all the stock in hand, consisting of a choice parcel of flint and other glass wares with sundry materials and utensils for making glass. Apply to Mr. William Farnworth, Clerk of the said Works."

17. (a) 27th March, 1759. *Manchester Advertiser*.

"At the new erected Glass-House in Salford, Manchester, all may be now supplied with bottles of all kinds; likewise vials and white flint-ware, by the Proprietors. All orders sent to Thomas Broxton, Clerk to the said Glass-House, &c."

(b) 1st July, 1760. *Manchester Mercury*.

"May 6, 1760. Salford Glass-House. The Proprietors having engaged an entire new sett of hands, all may now be served with bottles, bell glasses, retorts; vials, &c. of all kinds. Likewise with the neatest and best white flint-ware. Letters to Thomas Gooden, Clerk of the said work."

(c) 4th November, 1760. *Ibidem.*

A similar notice, including "white flint wares, lamps, bell lamps with covers, &c. Bell glasses for gardens, retorts and receivers."

18. 28th May, 1765. *Cheshire Parish Registers.*

Thomas Longworth, glassmaker, of Stockport was married at Prestbury.

19. 25th October, 1785. *Manchester Mercury.*

Glass-house. Imison and King have opened their Works in Newton-lane (Manchester) for the manufacturing all sorts of glass wares. N.B. All sorts of glass toys in miniature; also spectacles. Most money given for old flint glass and green glass. A partner is wanted,"

20. (a) 1830. *Manchester Directory.*

Maginnis, Molineux and Co., glass manufacturers, Kirby St.

(b) 3rd August, 1832. *London Gazette.*

"The partnership between William Robinson, William Maginnis, Senior, Samuel Perrin and John Maginnis, in the business of glass manufacturers, carried on at Manchester, has been dissolved the 30th July, 1832. William Robinson to collect debts, &c."

General

21. *Bristol Oracle.*

Imports at Liverpool between the 23rd July, 1743 and. 9th February, 1745 included 1 Cask of broken glass from the Isle of Man, and 24 casks and 2 hogsheads of broken glass from Ireland, besides kelp and soaper's waste.

22. 17th June, 1828. *London Gazette.*

"The partnership at Bootle, Lancashire, as glass bottle makers, under the firm of 'The Bootle Glass Bottle Co.' is dissolved the 7th April, 1822. Michael Hughes, Joseph Churton, Robert Swift, Elizabeth Percival, Samuel Taylor, Edward Greenall, Edward James Pemberton."

www.ingramcontent.com/pod-product-compliance
Lightning Source LLC
Chambersburg PA
CBHW021824300426
44114CB00009BA/317